Issues in Physical Education

Issues in Physical Education encourages student teachers, NQTs and practising teachers to reflect on issues important to planning, teaching and evaluating in physical education. In school-based initial teacher education there is little time to focus on these issues and their impact on the design, delivery and evaluation of physical education programmes. This book is designed to redress this balance and encourages reflection and debate as an important part of professional development.

The issues discussed include:

* breadth, balance and assessment in the physical education curriculum
* equality and the inclusion of pupils with different needs and from different cultural backgrounds in physical education
* progression and continuity in physical education between primary and secondary schools
* distinctions between sport and physical education and approaches to teaching games
* physical education, health and life-long participation in physical activity.

Issues in Physical Education is written by professionals with a wide experience of teaching physical education in schools and in initial teacher education. It is important reading for all students and teachers of physical education in primary or secondary schools.

Susan Capel is a Professor in the Department of Sport Sciences at Brunel University and Vice President of the Physical Education Association of the United Kingdom. **Susan Piotrowski** is Assistant Principal (Students) at Canterbury Christ Church University College. She was previously a principal lecturer in Sport Science and Education.

Issues in Subject Teaching Series
Edited by Susan Capel, Jon Davison,
James Arthur and John Moss.

Other titles in the series:

Issues in Physical Education

Edited by Susan Capel
and Susan Piotrowski

London and New York

First published 2000
by RoutledgeFalmer
2 Park Square, Milton Park, Abingdon, Oxon, OX14 4RN

Simultaneously published in the USA and Canada
by RoutledgeFalmer
270 Madison Ave, New York NY 10016

RoutledgeFalmer is an imprint of the Taylor & Francis Group

Transferred to Digital Printing 2005

Typeset in Goudy
by Curran Publishing Services Ltd, Norwich

British Library Cataloguing in Publication Data
A catalogue record for this book is available from the British Library.

Library of Congress Cataloging in Publication Data
Issues in physical education / edited by Susan Capel and Susan
Piotrowski.
288 pp. 15.6 x 23.4 cm. (Issues in subject teaching series)
Includes bibliographical references and index.
1. Physical education and training--Study and teaching--Great Britain.
2. Physical education and training--Great Britain--Curricula. I. Capel,
Susan Anne, 1953– II. Piotrowski, Susan, 1958– III. Issues in subject
teaching.
  GV361 .I78 2000
  613.7'071'041—dc21   00-035274
  99–059821

ISBN 0-415-23716-5 (hbk)
ISBN 0-415-18689-7 (pbk.)

Contents

Figures

Tables

Contributors

Tansin Benn is Head of Physical Education, Sports Studies and Dance at the University of Birmingham, Westhill. Her interests are diverse, including all aspects of physical education pedagogy, sociology, sport and dance. She spent over twenty years in the sport of gymnastics, as coach, national administrator and international judge. Dance is another major interest. Tansin recently developed the first customised company degree programme for dancers of Birmingham Royal Ballet.

Susan Capel is a Professor in the Department of Sport Sciences at Brunel University. Susan has taught physical education in schools in the UK and Hong Kong, worked at a university in the USA and in teacher education in the UK. She is currently Vice President of the Physical Education Association of the United Kingdom.

Carolyn Childs trained as a physical education teacher at Bedford College of Physical Education and spent many years working with secondary aged children. She became interested in children with special needs when she worked with Veronica Sherborne in a variety of special school settings, including work with very young children. Carolyn was Head of an Infant School for several years and now works as an Independent Education Consultant and a primary OFSTED Inspector.

Will Katene is a Lecturer in physical education in the School of Education at the University of Exeter. Will has taught physical education in schools in the UK and New Zealand and has lectured on both initial teacher education and sports science courses. His main area of interest is in subject knowledge of physical education student teachers.

Jean Leah taught physical education in secondary schools for fourteen years. She moved on to working in teacher education based at De Montfort University, Bedford and taught there for twelve years. Jean has recently taken up an appointment in the Department of Management at the University of Southampton.

Andrea Lockwood is a Principal Lecturer and Physical Education Subject

Leader at De Montfort University, Bedford. Prior to working at the University Andrea taught physical education in the UK and the Bahamas. Her professional interests include curriculum development and currently she is working on INSET materials focused on the use of Information and Communications Technology in physical education teaching.

Elizabeth Marsden is Senior Lecturer in primary physical education at Canterbury Christ Church University College. She has taught physical education in the UK and abroad through a wide age range, in a variety of situations including special, primary and secondary schools, in a community setting and in a hospital school. Currently, Elizabeth is an International Course Leader for Sherborne Developmental Movement and has led courses in Belgium, Sweden and Japan as well as throughout the British Isles.

Susan Piotrowski is currently Assistant Principal (Students) at Canterbury Christ Church University College. She has a doctorate in Philosophy from the University of London. Susan has taught physical education in both primary and secondary schools. Her lecturing responsibilities have included both primary and secondary physical education initial teacher education and sport science.

Christopher Robertson has had extensive experience in teaching children with physical disabilities and has also worked with pupils with severe learning difficulties and profound and multiple learning difficulties. He has lectured in special education at the London Institute of Education and Canterbury Christ Church University College. Currently, Christopher lectures in inclusive and special education at the University of Birmingham. His research and teaching interests are focused on various aspects of developing inclusive educational practice.

Peter Warburton is the Director of Sport at the University of Durham. In his roles as a teacher, administrator and academic over the last two decades he has made a significant contribution to physical education in the UK. He has published extensively in his main areas of interest: primary physical education, children and physical activity.

Mike Waring is a Senior Lecturer in the School of Education at the University of Durham. He has worked as both a teacher and lecturer in physical education and sport. His main areas of interest are children and young people's involvement in physical activity, pedagogy and teacher education.

Margaret Whitehead is Head of Quality, Faculty of Health and Community Studies at De Montfort University, Bedford. She taught physical education in school, lectured at Homerton College and in 1980 moved to Bedford College of Higher Education. She has devised and taught a range of initial teacher education courses. Margaret is currently President of the Physical Education Association of the United Kingdom.

Acknowledgements

The contributors and publishers are grateful to the following copyright holders for permission to reproduce copyright material:

Extracts from publications of the Department of Education and Science, the Department for Education, the Department for Education and Employment, Her Majesty's Inspectorate, the Office for Standards in Education and the Welsh Office, are Crown copyright and reproduced with the permission of the Controller of Her Majesty's Stationery Office. Figure 10.1 and other copyright material are reproduced from *Sport England Factsheet* (1999) with the permission of Sport England. Figure 5.3 is reproduced with the permission of David Bunker and Rod Thorpe. Figure 14.6, from *How to Write a School Development Plan*, ed. R. Rogers (1994), is reprinted by permission of Heinemann Educational Publishers, a division of Reed Educational and Professional Publishing Ltd. Copyright material and Figures 14.4 and 14.5 are reproduced from M. Fullan, *The New Meaning of Educational Change* (Cassell 1991), by permission of Continuum, Wellington House, 125 Strand, London WC2R 0BB. Copyright material from Open University Course P679: Planning and Managing Change is reproduced by permission of the Open University. Quotations from the *British Journal of Physical Education*, including Figures 5.1, 5.2 and 14.2, are reprinted by permission of the Physical Education Association of the United Kingdom. The poem *Big School*, quoted in Chapter 12, is reproduced by permission of Elizabeth Marsden.

Abbreviations

A level	Advanced Level examinations
A, R & R	assessment, recording and reporting
AOTT	adults other than teachers
ASA	Amateur Swimming Association
BAALPE	British Association of Advisers and Lecturers in Physical Education
BCPE	British Council of Physical Education (disbanded in 1994)
BTEC	Business and Technician Education Council
CCCUC	Canterbury Christ Church University College
CCPR	Central Council for Physical Recreation
CHD	coronary heart disease
CSE	Certificate of Secondary Education (replaced by GCSE)
CSLA	Community Sports Leaders Award
DCD	developmental co-ordination disorder
DCMS	Department of Culture, Media and Sport
DES	Department of Education and Science (became DfE)
DfE	Department for Education (became DfEE)
DfEE	Department for Education and Employment
DNH	Department of National Heritage (now DCMS)
DoH	Department of Health
EKSD	End of Key Stage Descriptions (in 1995 NCPE)
EKSS	End of Key Stage Statements (in 1992 NCPE)
ERA	Education Reform Act (1988)
ESC	English Sports Council (also called Sport England)
FA	The Football Association
GCSE	General Certificate of Secondary Education
GNVQ	General National Vocational Qualification
HEA	Health Education Authority
HEFCE	Higher Education Funding Council for England
HEI	higher education institution
HMI	Her Majesty's Inspectorate
HRE	health related exercise
HRF	health related fitness

ICT	information and communications technology
ILEA	Inner London Education Authority (now disbanded)
ITE	initial teacher education
KS	Key Stage (1–4 in the National Curriculum)
LEA	Local Education Authority
LSA	Learning Support Assistant
MVPA	moderate to vigorous physical activity
NCC	National Curriculum Council (merged in 1993 to form SCAA)
NCF	National Coaching Foundation
NCPE	National Curriculum for Physical Education
NCPEWG	National Curriculum Physical Education Working Group (to develop proposals for the 1992 NCPE)
NGB	National Governing Body (of Sport)
OAA	outdoor and adventurous activities
OFSTED	Office for Standards in Education
OHMCI	Office of Her Majesty's Chief Inspector of Schools
PE	physical education
PEA	The Physical Education Association of Great Britain and Northern Ireland (became PEAUK in 1994)
PEAUK	The Physical Education of the United Kingdom (replaced PEA in 1994)
PGCE	Post Graduate Certificate in Education
PoS	Programme of Study (in the National Curriculum)
QCA	Qualifications and Curriculum Authority
SAT	Standard Assessment Task (in the National Curriculum)
SCAA	School Curriculum and Assessment Authority (merged in 1997 to form QCA)
SCNI	Sports Council for Northern Ireland
SIS	Systems Intervention Strategy
TGFU	teaching games for understanding
TTA	Teacher Training Agency
UK	United Kingdom
UN	United Nations
UNESCO	United Nations Education, Scientific and Cultural Organisation
WHO	World Health Organisation
WO	Welsh Office
YST	Youth Sport Trust

Introduction to the series

This book, *Issues in Physical Education*, is one of a series of books entitled *Issues in Subject Teaching*. The series has been designed to engage with a wide range of issues related to subject teaching. The types of issues vary among the subjects, but may include, for example, issues that:

- impact on Initial Teacher Education in the subject
- are addressed in the classroom through the teaching of the subject
- are related to the content of the subject and its definition
- are related to subject pedagogy
- are connected with the relationship between the subject and broader educational aims and objectives in society, and the philosophy and sociology of education
- are related to the development of the subject and its future in the twenty-first century.

Each book consequently presents key debates that subject teachers will need to understand, reflect on and engage in as part of their professional development. Chapters have been designed to highlight major questions, and to consider the evidence from research and practice in order to find possible answers. Some subject books or chapters offer at least one solution or a view of the ways forward, whereas others provide alternative views and leave readers to identify their own solution or view of the ways forward. The editors expect readers of the series to want to pursue the issues raised, and so chapters include suggestions for further reading, and questions for further debate. The chapters and questions could be used as stimuli for debate in subject seminars or department meetings, or as topics for assignments or classroom research. The books are targeted at all those with a professional interest in the subject, and, in particular: student teachers learning to teach the subject in primary or secondary schools; newly qualified teachers; teachers with a subject co-ordination or leadership role, and those preparing for such responsibility; as well as mentors, tutors, trainers and advisers of the aforementioned groups.

Each book in the series has a cross-phase dimension. This is because the editors believe that it is important for teachers in the primary and secondary phases to look at subject teaching holistically, particularly in order to provide for continuity and progression, but also to increase their understanding of how children learn. The balance of chapters that have a cross-phase relevance, chapters that focus on issues that are of particular concern to primary teachers, and chapters that focus on issues which secondary teachers are more likely to need to address, varies according to the issues relevant to different subjects. However, no matter where the emphasis is, the authors have drawn out the relevance of their topic to the whole of each book's intended audience.

Because of the range of the series, both in terms of the issues covered and its cross-phase concern, each book is an edited collection. Editors have commissioned new writing from experts on particular issues who, collectively, will represent many different perspectives on subject teaching. Readers should not expect a book in this series to cover a full range of issues relevant to the subject, or to offer a completely unified view of subject teaching, or that every issue will be dealt with discretely, or that all aspects of an issue will be covered. Part of what each book in the series offers to readers is the opportunity to explore the interrelationships between positions in debates and, indeed, among the debates themselves, by identifying the overlapping concerns and competing arguments that are woven through the text.

The editors are aware that many initiatives in subject teaching currently originate from the centre, and that teachers have decreasing control of subject content, pedagogy and assessment strategies. The editors strongly believe that for teaching to remain properly a vocation and a profession, teachers must be invited to be part of a creative and critical dialogue about subject teaching, and should be encouraged to reflect, criticise, problem-solve and innovate. This series is intended to provide teachers with a stimulus for democratic involvement in the development of subject teaching.

Susan Capel, Jon Davison, James Arthur and John Moss
July 2000

Introduction

Susan Capel and Susan Piotrowski

The latter part of the twentieth century has witnessed increasing interest by government in educational policy. Perhaps the most obvious manifestation of this in England and Wales has been the Education Reform Act (ERA 1988) which introduced, among other changes, local management of schools and the National Curriculum. Strong government interest in education in general, and in physical education in particular, has led to increased public debate and a high media profile for education and physical education in recent years.

It is important for physical education teachers to be able to join in public debate if they are to help shape physical education in the twenty-first century and to prevent the subject from being determined entirely by external influences. To perform this role effectively physical education teachers need to reflect on issues centrally related to the value of physical education and to the ways in which the subject can be most effectively delivered in schools.

Despite an increasing need for student and in-service physical education teachers to be able to contribute to the public debate, there have been relatively few opportunities for engagement in critical reflection on relevant issues. The approach taken to initial teacher education (ITE) in England and Wales in the 1990s and into the twenty-first century is largely technocratic, with teachers learning how to deliver the National Curriculum. Graham, for example, has referred to teachers as 'artisan deliverers of the authorised curriculum' (Graham 1994b). A large percentage of time is spent in school and emphasis is placed on mastering essential teaching skills, techniques and procedures to achieve the standards to gain qualified teacher status. In higher education institutions (HEIs) emphasis tends to be on developing teaching skills and techniques and on gaining subject knowledge for each of the areas of activity in the curriculum. There is little time in school or the HEI (Evans *et al.* 1997; Carney and Armstrong 1996; Piotrowski and Capel 1996) to reflect on physical education in a wider sense; to consider, for example, different ways of organising the curriculum; the impact of the teachers' values, beliefs and attitudes on, for example, priorities for physical education, content, teaching strategies or style; the implications of teaching boys and girls in mixed-sex and single-sex groups; or the role of sport in physical education.

In order to make a positive contribution to public debate and also to consider the relevance of physical education to the education of all pupils, physical education teachers must move beyond a technocratic approach and consider the subject more widely. Effective physical education teachers are used to reflecting on their teaching, especially when evaluating individual lessons or units of work. This enables teachers to build on lesson successes and to improve where things did not go so well. However, processes of reflection need to be applied more widely; physical education teachers need to reflect on physical education more generally and to consider the broad implications of what is being taught.

In recent years, the focus in physical education has tended to be on activities rather than the broader meaning of the subject. Indeed, Williams (1989a) suggested that physical education is often defined in terms of the activities that make up the programme. The six areas of activity (athletic activities; dance activities; games activities; gymnastic activities; outdoor and adventurous activities; and swimming activities and water safety) are often central to discussions about the National Curriculum for Physical Education (NCPE) in England and Wales. For example, a school physical education programme is often described in terms of the activities that are included, such as football, rugby, cricket, athletics and gymnastics for boys, netball, hockey, athletics, rounders, gymnastics and dance for girls. However, rather than activities being seen to define physical education, the activities should be considered as the means of achieving the aims and objectives of the subject. There is further discussion about aims and objectives of physical education in Chapter 1.

Reflection on relevant issues in physical education helps to place teachers in a stronger position to propose and make rational changes for improvement. Such reflection has been generally neglected in physical education in recent years. Even in professional journals over the last decade or so, emphasis has often been on the implementation of the NCPE rather than reflection on issues more generally. The purpose of this book is to seek to redress the balance of emphasis from a technocratic to a more reflective approach. It is intended that the book should assist physical education teachers to enhance the contribution of physical education in the school curriculum by enabling them to make suggestions for improvement and constructive change. These suggestions for improvement should be grounded in reasoned reflection on aspects of the subject, its delivery in schools, and its role in wider society.

This book focuses on a range of issues designed to prompt reflection on the aims, priorities, content and methods of delivery of physical education in schools. Each issue is presented in a way designed to encourage reflection and debate and is not intended to include exhaustive coverage of the issues raised by each particular topic. Likewise, the issues identified in this book are not intended to provide comprehensive coverage of all the issues a physical education teacher might usefully consider. They are a selection of issues, some of which are long-standing. They have been debated periodically throughout the history of the subject and form part of an ongoing debate requiring reflection for their satisfactory resolution.

Each chapter is designed to engage readers in processes of reflection rather than seeking to generate firm conclusions. The reflective process is further encouraged through the inclusion of a series of questions at the end of each chapter. These can be used to aid individual reflection, or used in debate and discussion in seminars or with other teachers. A list of further reading is also included at the end of most chapters, enabling readers to explore in greater depth aspects of the issues considered in the chapter.

The issues included in the book are divided into five sections:

- aims of physical education
- issues concerned with your pupils
- issues concerned with teaching and learning
- issues concerned with the curriculum
- conclusion.

Each of the first four sections includes chapters which address a range of issues raised by a focus on each of these concerns.

In the first section there is one chapter which highlights the problematic nature of identifying aims of physical education. It examines some different aims in physical education and looks at alternative priorities for the subject, as well as considering the implications of aims for teaching and learning in the subject. The chapter is designed to set the scene for the following chapters as readers are encouraged to reflect on the issues raised. Readers' stance in relation to the alternatives highlighted in this chapter is likely to be related to their stance in relation to many further issues highlighted in Chapters 2 to 13.

The focus of the second section of the book is on equal opportunities for pupils in physical education. Chapter 2 analyses the concept of equal opportunities in physical education, highlighting the complexity of this concept through the use of examples relating to gender equality in physical education. Chapters 3 and 4 focus on aspects of the debates concerning the appropriate inclusion of pupils with special educational needs in physical education and the importance of taking account of the needs of pupils from diverse cultural backgrounds.

In the third section there are two chapters, one of which focuses on approaches to teaching games and the other on assessment in physical education. Both chapters are designed to encourage reflection on specific issues concerned with teaching and learning in physical education. In Chapter 5 the main focus is on looking at two different approaches to teaching games, and some advantages and disadvantages of each of the approaches are identified. Chapter 6 is designed to draw attention to a relatively recent tendency to use more explicit and more formalised methods of assessing pupils' attainments in physical education. Both of these chapters are designed to promote reflection more generally on the relationship between pupils' learning experiences and approaches to teaching and assessment.

There are six chapters in the fourth section of the book, relating to different aspects of the physical education curriculum. Chapter 7 highlights aspects of the debate about breadth and balance in the physical education curriculum, concentrating on what core knowledge is in physical education and the balance of activities offered in physical education in schools. Chapter 8 considers the inter relationship between physical education and sport; it looks at reasons why some people view the two as synonymous, before identifying differences between physical education and sport. Chapter 9 addresses aspects of the debate about competition and/or co-operation in the physical education curriculum. It considers recent influences on the debate, highlighting some of the positive and negative aspects of competition and co-operation, and discussing a few of these in greater depth. It concludes by considering the scope for including both competition and co-operation in the curriculum.

Community initiatives in physical education are considered in Chapter 10, focusing on the political climate in which physical education exists in England and Wales. The chapter identifies recent changes in physical education, particularly the move towards the establishment of partnerships with the community and initiatives taken by Sport England (the English Sports Council). The teaching of health aspects of physical education and the relationship between these and wider issues of health within schools are considered in the next chapter. The final chapter (Chapter 12) in this section looks at progression and continuity in physical education, and in particular considers ways in which to assist an effective transition of pupils from primary to secondary schools. This important stage in the education of pupils has so far received little attention in the physical education literature.

The concluding section has two main purposes: first, to encourage teachers to reflect on their priorities and practices in physical education, both as a basis for improvement and to ensure the relevance of the subject in the twenty-first century; and second, to provide some insight into the process of how to bring about change in physical education. In improving practice it is often important to question values, attitudes and beliefs. Part of Chapter 13 encourages readers to reflect on their values, attitudes and beliefs and how they impact on their priorities for physical education and on their teaching of the subject. The final chapter of the book is based on the premise that through reflecting on the issues in this book and other issues relevant to physical education, it is likely that teachers will want to make changes to their practice. Making change is not easy, therefore some theoretical understanding about making change may be useful in bringing about changes which enhance the contribution of physical education to the education of all pupils.

Part I

Introduction

Aims of physical education

1 Aims as an issue in physical education

Margaret Whitehead

It is perhaps surprising that there should be need for a chapter in this book about the aims of a subject that has been a recognised part of education for almost a century. It is doubtful if there would be call for such a chapter in a book about mathematics or history, for instance. There are perhaps two reasons why the physical education profession needs to confront this issue; one relates to an advantage the subject has in the curriculum and the other to a problem inherent in physical education. To the advantage of the subject there are numerous very worthwhile outcomes of pupils being involved in physical education, for example health benefits, initiation into aspects of the culture of the society and learning to work in groups. (See Capel and Whitehead 1997 for further discussion of a range of outcomes of physical education.) Where there are a number of possible valuable outcomes it is inevitable that there will be debate about where the priority should lie. Working against the subject is the view that physical education is recreation rather than education and therefore does not deserve a place in the school curriculum. From this viewpoint it is held that pupils have plenty of opportu nities for recreation at breaktimes and after school; curriculum time should be used for serious study. Faced with this challenge it is not surprising that the profession has to be both clear about the value of the subject and able to articulate this persuasively.

This chapter begins by addressing what is meant by the terms 'aims' and 'objectives'. It continues by discussing reasons why teachers need aims and objectives. The third part of the chapter aims to clarify some differences between physical education, sport and recreation in order to put the following section about aims in physical education into context. This section looks at intrinsic and extrinsic aims of the subject and interrogates some examples of extrinsic aims, before considering two approaches to presenting physical education in the context of its being intrinsically valuable. The chapter then considers the implications of aims in physical education. This last section looks first at the relationship between aims and planning within the physical education curriculum before considering aims of physical education within the school context.

Aims and objectives

While there is some debate about how these terms are used, there is general agreement that they both refer to intentions underpinning a practice. In this chapter aims and objectives are referred to as planned outcomes that can be articulated and justified. One role for aims and objectives is that they answer the question 'Why?' in relation to a practice. The term 'aim' is used in this chapter to refer to intentions that are generally longer term. Characteristically there are aims for physical education, aims for a physical education department and aims for a scheme or unit of work. The identification of an aim would, for example, answer the question 'Why have you included trampolining in your Year 8 scheme of work?' The term 'objective' is used in this chapter to refer to an intention that is short term, such as the intended outcome of a single lesson or a specific practice in a lesson. The identification of an objective would, therefore, answer the question 'Why are you using a 3 v 2 approach in this football lesson?' Objectives are the building blocks to achieve aims. If the aim is to initiate pupils into a particular game form, they will need to master a whole range of skills, tactical procedures and rules. These specific needs become objectives. Aims, being broader intentions, have to be broken down into smaller steps so that lessons can be planned to work towards a longer term outcome.

The need for clearly specified intentions

Formal education is a social institution designed to be of benefit to a society, especially to the young people of that society. It is a hugely expensive enterprise, usually funded by the government of a country. A government often specifies what purpose education in its society should serve, thus defining the aims that education should achieve. Teachers are expected to work towards this overall purpose and for their part design curricula and lessons to enable this ultimate aim of education to be achieved. This is a fundamental reason why schools, departments and teachers must have clearly specified intentions. However there are also other reasons for teachers needing aims and objectives that relate more closely to actual work with pupils.

First, teachers need aims and objectives because these provide direction for their work. If teachers know what outcomes they want to achieve (where they want to be), they can plan how to get there (what content to use, which methods to employ). Teaching is a planned enterprise designed to achieve a specific outcome. Teaching must have a rationale, a basis from which planning takes place. Having a clear intention therefore is not an option but an essential first step to planning work with pupils. Teaching without a clear intention will result in random activity without coherence or progression.

Second, aims and objectives provide benchmarks to assess success. If teachers know where they want to be, they can judge if they have arrived or how far they have reached. If teachers know what they want to achieve they can identify what they need to assess to judge if they have been successful.

A third reason for having aims and objectives is that they serve to answer the question 'Why?' In other words they justify what the teacher is doing. However, because we are discussing teaching in an educational context, just having an aim or an objective is not enough. The intention has to be worthwhile and supported as such. So, for example, if a teacher were to say in a swimming lesson that his objective was to allow a group of pupils to 'let off steam', or to say in a football lesson that his purpose was to 'keep a class quiet' by playing a full game, it is doubtful if either would be seen as an acceptable educational intention. Aims and objectives advanced by teachers for their work have to be seen as valuable. In fact any stated intention always begs the question 'Why is that valuable?' Because there are those in education who are sceptical about the role of physical education in schools, teachers of this subject have to be able to answer both why questions. 'Why are you doing this activity?' and 'Why is that a worthwhile use of pupils' time in the curriculum?'

Physical education, sport and recreation

In considering the aims and objectives of physical education it is useful to be able to differentiate between this area of the school curriculum and the related practices of sport and recreation. It has to be said that this issue has generated a good deal of literature and could warrant a chapter of its own. Physical education and sport are considered in greater depth in Chapter 8 of this book. All that is proposed here is a working definition to make clear the area of activity which is the focus of this chapter.

Physical education is usually delivered as part of the school timetable and, in England and Wales, is guided by the requirements of the National Curriculum for Physical Education (NCPE). It is normally delivered by personnel in the employ of the school/local education authority (LEA). The NCPE is compulsory in Key Stage (KS) 1 to KS4. Beyond this statutory requirement, schools may make physical education compulsory or offer it as an option within the curriculum. Pupils' ability and progress in physical education are assessed and these judgements are included in reports to parents. Taking part in physical education incurs no additional expenditure in state schools. Some private schools require pupils to provide their own equipment. Characteristically, physical education is child-centred and seen to have value in its own right as well as broad educational benefits.

Extra-curricular (i.e. outside the normal timetable) activities are generally delivered to pupils on school premises, normally by personnel in the employ of the school/LEA. These activities are often seen as part of physical education. Normally, no fee is paid by the participants. They are again child-centred. Pupil progress is monitored and performance may be commented on in reports to parents. The term extra-curricular may also be extended to outdoor adventure trips and other residential excursions organised by the school and run by school staff or other qualified personnel. These may involve such activities as climbing, skiing, camping and sailing and may take place at some distance from the school. Participation in off-site activities usually incurs a cost to pupils involved. Spectators are not involved in curricular work but may be present in some forms of extra-curricular activities.

There is a range of useful definitions of physical education. For example, the Physical Education Association of the United Kingdom (PEAUK) defined physical education as 'those purposeful physical activities and related studies, normally undertaken within an educational context, which develop physical competence, help promote physical development, and enable participants to know about and value the benefits of participation' (PEAUK 1994: 1). The Department of Education and Science (DES) said that 'physical education in schools aims to develop control, co-ordination and mastery of the body. It is primarily concerned with a way of learning through action, sensation and observation' (DES 1989a: 1).

Sport is commonly used to describe a physical activity that has a competitive element. The activity may be carried out by a professional player or by an unpaid enthusiast. Unpaid enthusiasts take part out of choice in their leisure time and very often have a regular commitment so to do. There is usually a cost involved in taking part in sport. Sport characteristically depends on the involvement of other people and in most cases needs some form of organised structure. Participants are often concerned with their level of performance. It is not uncommon for there to be spectators at sports events.

Recreation is a very broad term commonly used to describe activities participants choose to take part in during their leisure time. The motivation to take part may be related to relaxation, health promotion, having fun or mixing socially. These activities include physical activities which are characteristically non-competitive. Individuals can take part on their own, without necessarily needing others, and activities carried out in this context may not need an organisational structure. Participants are not necessarily concerned with their level of performance. They are not paid for their involvement and may take part regularly or irregularly. There may be a modest cost to participate. Rambling, swimming and aerobics are good examples here. Spectators are not involved.

Confusion arises between physical education, sport and physical recreation because many of the same activities are pursued in all three contexts. A description that seeks to differentiate between physical education and sport explains that:

> Sport covers a range of physical activities in which adults and young people may participate. Physical Education on the other hand is a process of learning, the context being mainly physical. The purpose of this process is to develop specific knowledge, skills and understanding and to promote physical competence. Different sporting activities can and do contribute to that learning process, and the learning enables participation in sport. The focus however is on the child and his or her development of physical competence, rather than on the activity
>
> (DES/Welsh Office (WO) 1991: 7)

Confusion arises between sport and recreation as the nature of the involvement depends very much on the personal viewpoint of each participant. For example, in a club tennis match some players may see themselves clearly involved in competitive sport while others may view participation as pure recreation, with the competitive element being incidental.

Aims examined

The discussion of the aims of physical education in this chapter is divided into three sections. The first section looks at aims as intrinsic or extrinsic to the subject while the second interrogates some examples of extrinsic aims. The third section looks at two approaches to presenting physical education in the context of the subject being intrinsically valuable.

Intrinsic/extrinsic aims of physical education or means/ends

One of the long-standing debates in physical education is about whether the subject has value in its own right, or is best seen as a useful vehicle through which desirable attributes can be acquired, for example personal qualities such as perseverance, social skills such as co-operation and cognitive skills such as problem solving. This debate is sometimes referred to as the means/end issue. Is the subject an end in itself or a means to other ends? Whichever option is taken there are further questions to be answered.

If it is advocated that physical education is worthwhile in its own right the case has to be made for the value of pupils participating in and becoming skilful at a range of physical activities. The focus here is on promoting physical development and enhancing physical competence. The recognition of the value of becoming a skilful participant may be easier to promote in respect of some activities than others. Activities that have a high profile nationally and can readily be continued into adult life, such as football, are more often supported than, for example, gymnastics. Activities that relate to personal survival such as swimming are more strongly supported than others such as dance. The more likely the support for some activities than others, however, has a ring of using the subject for extrinsic ends which, in the cases cited above, maybe the production of winning national teams and the prevention of accidental death.

What has to be formulated is a case for the value of becoming physically skilful *per se*. This case will have to take the brave stance of reminding the sceptic that we have physical capacities and potential and that these are fundamental to human existence and integral to human nature. Supporters would need to argue that these attributes are not inferior in the sense that the body/mind split has tended to label the body as of lesser importance. Physical attributes are part of the whole individual and cannot be separated off as a dispensable capacity. They are fundamental to the very being of humankind. Humankind, as far as is known, is characteristically embodied (see, for example, Whitehead 1990). If education is about nurturing all aspects of human potential, the physical has an indisputable place in the enterprise. If challenged to identify outstanding individuals who have achieved at the highest level, most people would include athletes alongside artists, philosophers, politicians and scientists. This in itself indicates that the physical dimension is celebrated alongside other dimensions.

If physical education is advocated as a means to achieving other ends, such as personal and social development, teachers of this subject have to face the challenge that other areas of the curriculum can also realise the same ends. If physical education does not bring anything unique to the curriculum and is only contributing to the broad aims of education, it could be argued that it is not time well spent and should be consigned to an extra-curricular programme.

There are at least two ways to answer this point. One is that the nature of physical education lends itself very clearly to pupils acquiring certain personal and social skills. For example, situations in physical education unequivocally demand team work, challenge pupils to be self-reliant and require pupils to use their imagination. Pupil responses are immediately visible and achievement of any of the above can be easily observed and assessed.

Another way to counteract doubts is to argue that pupils need a range of contexts in which to acquire attributes such as personal and social skills. Some pupils master these skills more readily in one context than in another. It is undeniable that physical education provides a unique context and many cite examples of certain pupils making significant progress as a result of successful engagement in physical education (see, for example, Almond 1989: ch. 8).

Although these arguments may be accepted there may be two further challenges to be faced. First, it could be argued that there is no evidence to prove that the subject makes a significant contribution to such areas as personal and social education. Even if it could be proved that physical education does develop attributes in these areas, doubt has been expressed in some quarters whether learning in physical education is transferable to life in general. Second, it could be argued that nothing is gained from trumpeting the contribution of physical education to the general aims of education, as it is the responsibility of all subjects so to do. If physical educators do not make a worthwhile contribution to general education they would not be worthy of the title of teacher.

It is useful to debate further the two views outlined briefly above. Can physical education be justified purely on intrinsic grounds? Can physical education in its own right claim to be truly part of education? Alternatively, should physical education teachers see themselves very much part of a team, working with other teachers in the interests of the total education and development of young people? (For a useful debate on the role of physical education as educating 'About movement, through movement and in movement' see Arnold 1988: ch. 8. Almond (1989, 1996, 1997) also addresses this issue. There is also further discussion in Chapter 13 of this book.)

Alternative priorities for physical education as a means to other ends

Notwithstanding the cautionary remarks above concerning the problems inherent in advocating the prime role of physical education as a means to achieving other ends, there is a variety of extrinsic ends that are proposed as the *raison d'etre* of the subject. These claims are examined in a little more detail to reveal their implications. The four positions that are considered briefly are physical education as:

• promoting health
• providing education for leisure
• offering vocational preparation
• providing initiation into the culture of the society.

The relationship between physical education and health has long been an area of lively debate and there is much written on this issue. (See, for example, Colquhoun 1990, Evans and Clarke 1988, Harris 1997a, as well as Chapter 11 of this book.)

Some of the discussion has revolved around whether health concerns should permeate all physical education or whether there should be units of work dedicated specifically to this area (see also Chapter 11). Hidden behind this debate are two points of view. Those who advocate dedicated units of work often argue that physical education as commonly taught does little to maintain or enhance health. Much of the lesson time, it would be argued, is spent listening to instructions, waiting for a turn, observing demonstrations and planning sequences or tactics. Furthermore it would be argued that physical education has a vital and unique responsibility to promote physical health and that those teaching the subject should take this aspect of the work seriously. Advocates of this view would remind others that the roots of the subject come from this area, with the early syllabi from the beginning of the last century being designed round such goals as correct breathing and posture. It would also be stressed that the promotion of health is indisputably valuable and that there are no other subjects in the curriculum looking at this area, at least not from a specifically physical perspective.

Those who favour a permeation approach would argue that all physical education lessons should include sufficient practical activity to, for example, raise the heart rate, increase depth of breathing or enhance joint flexibility. They would make the case that the experience of challenging pupils physically in these ways should be inherent in physical education and that pupils should associate physical activity with the satisfactions of feeling thoroughly exercised and in some sense 'fitter'. Supporters of this position would be opposed to a separate group of lessons that resemble 'fitness training', as these would be outside the generally accepted range of activities that, they would argue, constitute physical education. A dedicated series of lessons could well mean that in other lessons the teacher might pay scant attention to the need to be active, judging that this part of the work was being covered elsewhere. There are also views that do not support the body being treated as an object or machine (see, for example, Whitehead 1988). Similarly, others judge fitness training as mindless activity that has little relationship to pupil performance in the activities characteristic of physical education.

Both camps would agree that reference to health should be included in physical education. From this standpoint there are some physical educationists who can see the justification for realigning the whole curriculum to a health focus with activities being used only to achieve this end. It would be true to say that many in the medical profession would support this move. The government might also sign up to this as ultimately saving the National Health Service money.

It could be useful to design a physical education curriculum with the specific aim of promoting health. It may be found that this has a very different nature to a curriculum designed around the requirements of the NCPE.

Education for leisure as the prime aim of physical education is not far away from the health debate and indeed could be seen to be closer to an intrinsic rather than an extrinsic end. Those who advocate that physical education should at all times look ahead to preparing individuals to use their leisure time appropriately would argue that the most important aim of the subject is to ensure that every pupil gains satisfaction from, and self-esteem as a result of, work in the subject. Pupils should carry this positive experience with them outside school and be motivated to continue to take part in physical activity throughout adult life. Taking part in physical activity is beneficial for mental and physical health (Health Education Authority (HEA) 1998a) as well as for the general quality of life. Furthermore, use of leisure time in this way may deter young adults from anti-social activities and, as such, the police force would doubtless be enthusiastic supporters of this aim. (For a discussion on the role of partnerships in achieving the aim of physical education for leisure see DES/WO 1991: Appendix C. Also see Chapter 10 of this book.)

Those who would argue against this aim would fall into two camps. One camp would argue that involvement in physical activity is not everyone's preferred use of their leisure time and that many people are fit, happy and healthy despite living an overridingly sedentary life. The other camp would caution that this is a dangerous aim as education is traditionally seen as a preparation for employment, with leisure needs being catered for outside school. They would argue that the subject must demonstrate the immediate value of physical education to pupils in their development towards adulthood. If physical education were seen to be directed towards appropriate use of leisure time in adult life there would be the danger of the subject being classed as recreation and consigned to the extra-curricular programme. Another problem of valuing physical education in terms of its contribution to leisure is that evidence to prove the success of the subject in this context would be very hard to substantiate.

The aim of physical education as vocational preparation could be seen as opportune in the current climate as it supports the view that education is really just about preparing individuals for employment. Advocates of this view would argue that the subject must demonstrate outcomes that are economically in the interests of society. If the aim of physical education is for vocational preparation, what are the implications of this aim on the totality of the physical education programme? It could be the case that an appreciation of psychological and sociological perspectives would be essential as well as the understanding of principles of management. Those who would oppose this as the prime aim of the subject would argue that if pupils left school with a positive attitude towards physical education, they would have the motivation to develop the skills necessary to work in the industry. Specific focus on vocationalism would not be seen as necessary; rather teachers should ensure that pupils leave school appreciating the benefits that participation in physical activity can have on the quality of life. (For further discussion of this topic see, for example, Hodkinson and Sparkes 1993.)

The aim of seeing physical education as initiation into aspects of the culture of the society has often been used as a justification for the subject. It is certainly the case that much of the school curriculum is based round passing on to young people that which society feels is worthwhile, and much that is seen to be of value is deeply embedded in the culture. In one sense this is uncontroversial in that any education would want its young people readily to take their place in society through an appreciation of its culture and traditions. It would indeed be odd if a whole section of what is seen to be part of everyday life was left out of the education of children. However, just because something is part of the culture of the society it does not necessarily follow that it is always to be valued. To take an extreme example, cock-fighting used to be a common sport, but in time it was seen as cruel and is now illegal. In respect of aspects of contemporary culture the question must be asked at regular intervals as to whether any aspect of the culture is still appropriate and acceptable. To take another extreme example; it is seen as part of becoming an adult in this country to learn to drive a car. A situation could arise that a new strain of bacteria rendered the human race fatally susceptible to all types of fuel used to power cars. The driving of cars could, as a result, be a thing of the past. A real example that currently hits the headlines is the issue over the safety and thus the acceptability of boxing. It is not inconceivable that in the next decade medical evidence will be such that boxing is banned. (For discussion on physical education and culture see, for example, Almond 1996.)

It is useful to consider if the subject can deliver the extrinsic aims outlined above. Would work directed to an extrinsic aim significantly change the nature of the subject? Other extrinsic aims could also be considered, such as cognitive development and aesthetic and artistic awareness. (See, for example, Capel and Whitehead 1997. For discussion of cognitive development as an aim in physical education see, for example, Best 1976. For discussion of artistic and aesthetic aspects of physical education see, for example, DES/WO 1991 and Arnold 1988.)

Approaches to presenting physical education as intrisically valuable

Excellence versus inclusivity

Among those who advocate physical education as of value in its own right, one of two broad aims may be identified as paramount. One aim could be to produce athletes of the highest standard; the other could be to give all pupils the opportunity to improve their movement skills.

Some physical education teachers see their task as enabling those pupils with the most potential in the physical domain to excel. The justification is that every child has particular skills and abilities and it is the responsibility of every teacher to identify and nurture pupils who demonstrate this potential in their subject. Education is about fulfilling potential and physical education teachers should direct their energies towards those pupils for whom physical education is their area of achievement. It is certainly the case that for some young people physical education is the only subject in which they excel and it is through this subject that they develop their self-confidence and self-esteem. An advocate of this view would have to counter the argument that s/he is neglecting a large proportion of the pupils: those not destined to be highly skilful performers. Indeed, it could be claimed that this majority of pupils are those who need the skilled guidance of the teacher more than the naturally gifted pupils. A case could also be made that able athletes can be more than adequately catered for in extra-curricular time and in local or regional clubs and teams. An elitist approach such as this may also result in a curriculum that is comprised predominantly of competitive team games and a situation that allows some pupils to specialise almost exclusively in a limited number of activities. Advocates of this more elitist approach would argue that a focus on high standards and the elite provides inspirational role models for other pupils, and winning school teams can bring prestige to the school and a sense of pride to all in the school community. In addition, this stance would surely be supported by the government and Sport England (the English Sports Council) in its potential to nurture athletes to bring honour to the country in winning Olympic medals and world cups.

Those teachers who advocate entitlement for all would be concerned that every pupil reaches at least a base line level of physical skill through involvement in a wide range of activities. This base line level has been described as 'physical literacy'. Physical literacy endows pupils with a confidence in their ability in physical activity, an understanding of the nature of different physical activities and the knowledge that experience of physical activity is satisfying and rewarding. A physically literate individual is likely to continue to participate in physical activity after leaving school and will not be apprehensive at trying his or her hand at new activities. Critics of this view could argue that physical literacy is too nebulous a concept to serve as an ultimate aim and that the result would be a levelling down of achievement. Furthermore they could point out that many people live fulfilled lives without taking part in any physical activity. They could take the stand that teachers should devote their time and expertise to working with the able and motivated pupils. Those supporting an inclusive approach would argue that their aim is for every pupil to reach his or her potential, not for all to reach a base line level of performance.

Process versus product

The process/product debate cuts across two pairs of competing aims already discussed: means/ends and excellence/inclusivity. The issue is worthy of note as at times in the debate about the physical education curriculum there have been strong advocates for each of these views.

Those who see the principal value of physical education in the process would probably share a number of beliefs with those who support an approach aligned to physical education as a 'means to an end', with the experiences of learning in physical education as being the vehicle to achieve desirable general educational aims. Process advocates could claim that the quality of the product is entirely dependent on the quality of the process and that all learning is crucially about making sense of experience. Through working on challenges set in the subject pupils learn to, for example, co-operate, solve problems, create and persevere. Advocates of the process value of physical education would also favour inclusivity in that the aim would be for all pupils to have equal opportunity to have experiences from which they can learn. This learning would include emphasis on the experience of taking part in physical activities. Time would be taken to reflect on all aspects of the processes of planning movement, performing and replanning in the light of experience. It would also include an appreciation of personal potential and the setting of realistic personal goals.

It is not difficult to anticipate the criticisms that could be levelled at this aim of learning through the process of engagement in physical education. These would include claims that the aims were too vague. Opponents could argue that aims such as these would be impossible to control or measure and that every child would be learning something different through an experience. Opponents could also question the disregard for the quality of the outcome and doubt whether pupils would feel any sense of achievement if no value was placed on the standard of their performance. The importance of process is discussed further by Murdoch (1997: 263).

For the 'product advocates' the aim could be high quality performance. As far as possible the quality would be measurable or clearly judged against predetermined criteria. They would argue that success breeds success and that pupils thrive on the knowledge of how well they are performing. Process advocates could caution against very mechanistic methods of assessment and the demoralising effect of never achieving as well as the most able, particularly if results are made public. A defence for product advocates would be to argue that their approach is one where pupils are competing against themselves, working to improve personal performance, not comparing themselves with others.

These dichotomies are hard to untangle but need careful thought as allegiance to one or the other significantly influences the nature of physical education work in a school. It could be useful to do an analysis of the strengths, weaknesses, opportunities and threats (a SWOT analysis) of each of the two sides of both approaches and then weigh up what could be the best way forward.

Implication of aims

While each of the three needs for aims identified at the start of the chapter are of equal importance, the relationship between aims and planning is fundamental and warrants some consideration before concluding this chapter. This is because aims are not something that are committed to paper and can then be forgotten. As many writers have argued, notably Mosston and Ashworth (1994), aims cannot be achieved unless appropriate planning and teaching are devised (see also Whitehead 1997). To be true to their convictions and to achieve their stated aims teachers must select the curriculum, lesson content and teaching method that enables these aims to be met. So, for example, if health promotion is advocated as the prime aim the teacher needs to plan schemes and units of work that focus on this type of work and all lessons need to be geared to this end. Lesson objectives need to highlight elements of health and the actual movement work covered in lessons must ensure that health objectives are achieved. Feedback to pupils in lessons should highlight health components, and all assessment of pupil progress and lesson success should be based around the achievement of these elements. Similarly, if social development is advocated as a prime aim the teacher needs to design a curriculum that includes substantial opportunity for group work. Lesson objectives should highlight social skills such as leadership, listening skills and tolerance. As above, feedback to pupils and assessment of achievement must be clearly related to the objectives of the lesson. Here it would be mastery of the social skills identified.

Working through the implications of adopting a particular point of view is a valuable exercise and well worth exploring before coming to any firm decision. This exercise could be carried out on all of the aims discussed above. Below are two examples that look at the implications of two different aims, together with resource needs that would be required to achieve them.

Example 1: education for leisure

Curriculum content: A broad range of activities, indoor/outdoor, individual team, competitive/non-competitive are included. Specific attention is given to activity opportunities in the local area available to the pupils when they leave school. There is some opportunity for choice in Years 10 and 11. Involvement in General Certificate of Education (GCSE)/Advanced (A) Level examinations is an option.

Teaching methods: Teaching strategies such as Inclusion, Discovery and Problem Solving (Mosston and Ashworth 1994) are highlighted. Mixed ability teaching is used, with tasks differentiated to cater for all abilities. Teaching is pupil focused. Feedback is linked to personal improvement and effort. There are opportunities for pupils to make decisions, e.g. setting their own goals, evaluating own progress. Ipsative assessment is stressed.

Lesson objectives: These highlight mastery of skills needed to take part in range of activities, as well as social objectives such as working in a team to solve problems. Objectives are differentiated by task and outcome.

Ambience/climate: This is accepting of all, irrespective of ability. It is encouraging and caring. It celebrates progress. Enhancing self-esteem/self confidence are highlighted. It is empowering.

Extra-curricular programme: There is a wide range of open access clubs. The stress is on matches within the school to provide opportunities for all to represent their form/house.

Facilities: A wide variety of facilities would be needed. Appropriate use of local facilities would be an advantage.

Staffing: In years up to Year 9 essential ground work is taught by school staff. In Years 10 and 11 there could be some use of personnel from the local area. These personnel are people whom pupils will meet in out of school contexts, who could be attached to local leisure centres or local clubs. All adults with whom the pupils come into contact should be welcoming of the young people, whatever their level of ability.

Example 2: elite level performance

Curriculum content: Particular focus is on competitive activities, particularly high prestige national sports and some Olympic sports. There is specialisation in fewer rather than more activities. Possibly, examinations are not offered, allowing for staff time to be directed to working to improve quality of pupil performance.

Teaching methods: Teaching strategies such as Command and Practice (Mosston and Ashworth 1994) are highlighted. Classes/years are streamed according to ability in each activity. Staff with particular expertise in an activity teach the most able. There is opportunity for pupils to move up or down groups as their performance changes. Records are kept of levels of success. School records would be displayed and those improving on these records would be rewarded. Assessment would tend to be norm referenced.

Lesson objectives: These identify a key skill, game procedure, compositional technique that was to be practised and mastered.

Ambience/climate: This is performance oriented. Pupils are challenged to work hard, set themselves ambitious goals and beat others. Praise has to be earned through clear improvement.

Extra-curricular programme: Team practices are held in the lunch hour and after school. They are open only to the most able. There is concentration on fewer rather than more activities. The emphasis is on involvement in matches against other schools and in local, regional and national tournaments. There is encouragement for the most able pupils to move on to elite regional squads.

Facilities: Quality facilities are focused on a few activities.

Staffing: School staff are employed to work in specific activities with key teams. There is some involvement of coaches if needed.

The exercise carried out here in respect of education for leisure and elite performance is valuable as it identifies clearly the implications of a particular approach. It would be useful to carry out this same exercise for other aims of physical education.

Aims in the school context

As can be seen from this discussion, there is a complex web of views in respect of the aims of physical education. The NCPE has never offered a definitive answer in that it has made reference to many of the positions outlined in the sections above. There could be a number of reasons for this. The physical education curriculum, along with most other curricula, was designed by a group of people and it is likely that different views were presented and that all points of view were included. It could also be the case that, as certain of the possible aims of physical education appeal to different sections of government, it may have been seen as wise to make reference to more rather than fewer aims, to enlist the widest possible support.

Pragmatically, however, it could be argued that to cater for the range of pupils, both in age and characteristics, who are to be subject to physical education lessons, it is necessary to identify a range of aims or valuable outcomes that can be associated with this area of work. The nature of the pupils and the environment in which they live are certainly features that have to be taken into consideration in, for example, identifying the aims of a school physical education department. Aims have to be realistic and practical. Those for a primary school would, quite legitimately, be different from those in a secondary school. Context is important too, with an inner city school putting certain aims to the fore while a rural school might have different priorities. (For discussion of teachers' views on a wide range of aims see Armour and Jones 1998: chs 10, 11 and 12.)

The situation, therefore, may not be as clear cut as it might be. However, notwithstanding this dilemma about aims, it is still essential for every physical education teacher to have thought through very carefully where his or her priorities lie. This is vital, as mentioned at the start of the chapter, for planning, assessing and justifying work in physical education.

This debate is continued in Chapter 13.

Questions for reflection

1 Is there one prime aim for physical education?
2 Could it be argued that there is no one fundamental aim for the subject? How do you weigh up, out of all the valuable outcomes that the subject can work towards, what the best use of time is with a particular group of pupils?
3 Will a physical education curriculum directed to a particular extrinsic end be a distorted curriculum?
4 Could it be that well taught physical education, approached as a subject with intrinsic value, will have beneficial influences outside its specific remit? Will confidence gained in physical education help individuals to secure a job? Will mastery of skill in a physical activity result in lifelong participation and thus the productive use of leisure time and the maintenance of health?
5 Should physical education teachers believe, without reservation, that there is value in physical activity *per se*?
6 Does the physical education profession have the courage of its own convictions?

Part II

Issues concerned with your pupils

2 The concept of equal opportunities in physical education with reference to gender equality

Susan Piotrowski

Introduction

Article 26 of the United Nations Universal Declaration of Human Rights (1948) recognised that 'everyone has the right to education'. In England and Wales this right is protected through the Education Reform Act (ERA) 1988, which acknowledged that all pupils are entitled to an education which allows access to a broadly based and balanced curriculum. This curriculum should promote the 'spiritual, moral, cultural, mental and physical development of pupils' and prepare 'pupils for the opportunities, responsibilities and experiences of adult life' (Department of Education and Science (DES) 1989b: 2.1). Within this broad and balanced curriculum, physical education was recognised as having a unique role to play in catering for particular aspects of pupils' physical learning and development. Hence, physical education was included as one of the foundation subjects of the National Curriculum, established under the terms of the ERA. The law therefore protects the rights of all children in maintained schools to have access to an education, including physical education, regardless of economic status, gender, race, ethnicity, or ability. But does right of access ensure equality of opportunity?

Reflection on the question of what is meant by equality of opportunity and how this principle might be realised in physical education programmes provides a central focus for this chapter. Such reflection remains an urgent need among both qualified and student teachers, even in a climate which has recently witnessed encouraging signs regarding the commitment of physical education teachers to the principle of equal opportunity in curriculum physical education (Evans *et al.* 1997, Office for Standards in Education (OFSTED) 1995a). Despite this commitment, Evans *et al.* believed the 'heavy demands of National Curriculum implementation' (Evans *et al.* 1997: 43) to have left teachers with too little time to think beyond a realisation of equal opportunities in physical education which goes further than ensuring equal access to the curriculum. While access issues raise difficult and important questions, Evans *et al.* (1997) were concerned to point out that thinking must go beyond issues of access if equity is to be achieved. This matter is considered in depth in this chapter. In the case of student teachers, Flintoff (1993) highlighted concerns regarding the relative lack of attention given to reflection on the issue of equality of opportunity in physical education in initial teacher education (ITE). These concerns remain and Evans *et al.* (1997) identified shortages of time in ITE programmes for both primary and secondary teachers as contributing to a lack of reflection on issues of equality of opportunity.

A possible danger of insufficient reflection on the principle of equality of opportunity by both student and qualified teachers is that this may lead teachers 'to revert back to the methods that they experienced when they were young, relying on practices that were not always "educational" or conducive to the promotion of equity in physical education' (Evans *et al.* 1997: 44). This is likely to result in maintaining the status quo and to lead to what Evans and Davies described as a 'reification of existing hierarchies' (Evans and Davies 1993a: 7). Reflection on the concept of equal opportunities enables the needs of disadvantaged pupils in physical education to be appropriately considered and possible sources of social injustice identified and challenged.

The purpose of this chapter, and the two following chapters which focus more specifically on issues relating to special needs and cultural diversity, is to prompt reflection on the principle of equal opportunities and how this principle might be realised in physical education programmes. Equal opportunities issues relating to gender are not the focus of a separate chapter in this book. Instead, issues relating to sex and gender are a main focus for this chapter in providing illustrative material for discussion of the concept of equality of opportunity in physical education. The examples relating to gender equality in physical education are included in the shaded sections of this chapter.

Literature relating to equality of opportunity in physical education shows many issues of concern. These include the meaning of equality, the impact of individual and group differences on equality of opportunity, and wider issues relating to power relations and equity in society. This chapter focuses on these issues within the context of an overall discussion of what is meant by equality of opportunity in physical education.

By the end of this chapter readers should:

- have a clearer understanding of the meaning of equality of opportunity
- appreciate that equality of access is not the same as equality of opportunity
- recognise that equality of opportunity in physical education is partly a matter of recognising and responding to individual differences
- have greater awareness of the potential role of the subject in challenging those power relations in wider society which affect equality of opportunity in physical education
- appreciate the need for critical reflection on issues relating to gender if equality of opportunity is to be a realistic possibility in physical education.

The meaning of equality of opportunity

Talbot (1990) drew attention to the way in which people attach very different meanings to the word 'equality'. These different interpretations can then significantly influence practice. This chapter attempts to clarify the concept of equality of opportunity by considering the adequacy of some of these differing interpretations.

Is a demand for equality of opportunity a demand to recognise that all people are the same?

In mathematical terms, equality is the condition of being the same. Hence we all recognise the simple truth contained in the following: $2 + 2 = 4$. When we demand equality in physical education is this a plea to acknowledge that all pupils are the same and are entitled to the same treatment?

The proposals for the National Curriculum for Physical Education (NCPE) suggested that equal opportunity should be 'a guiding and leading principle for physical education' (DES/Welsh Office (WO) 1991: 15). To interpret this as meaning that all pupils should have the same physical education because all pupils are the same is unhelpful. All pupils are not the same. They differ in many ways, physically, cognitively and affectively, and do not enter programmes of physical education equally equipped to take advantage of the opportunities available. Gender example 1 is designed to illustrate the futility of looking for an interpretation of equality as meaning that we must acknowledge that all pupils are the same and are therefore entitled to the same treatment.

Gender example 1: boys and girls do not enter physical education as equals

There are both biological differences (sex differences) and culturally created differences (gender differences) between boys and girls which affect attainment and attitudes towards physical education. Sex differences tend to be more influential during the secondary than the primary phase of physical education. Gender differences are significant at both primary and secondary phases of education. Primary aged pupils usually enter the education system with different experiences regarding engagement in physical activities and with strongly formed views regarding gender appropriate behaviour (Williams 1989b, Sports Council for Northern Ireland (SCNI) 1996). Similarly, in the case of secondary aged pupils, Scraton observed that 'by the age of 11, girls on average, do not start from an equal position to boys both in terms of physical skill and hand-eye co-ordination' (Scraton 1993: 144). The following examples focusing on some of the biological and cultural differences between males and females are designed to show that equality of opportunity is unlikely to result if these differences are ignored and all pupils are assumed to be the same.

Biological differences between adolescent males and females

Biological differences between boys and girls from adolescence onwards generally have the effect of making boys taller, faster and physically stronger, on average, than girls. It would be wrong to ignore these biological differences between adolescent boys and girls in secondary school physical education on grounds of assumed 'sameness' between the sexes. To expect girls to compete against boys on equal terms in activities where strength, force and power largely determine success would not only place girls, in general, at a disadvantage to reach equivalent levels of attainment but, in contact sports, could make it unsafe for girls to participate on these terms.

An acknowledgement of general physical differences between men and women led to one of the exemption clauses of the Sex Discrimination Act (1975). The Act generally makes discrimination on the basis of sex illegal. Section 44 is an exemption clause which sanctions banning mixed competitions where the activities require 'strength, speed and physique' such that the 'average' man or woman would be at a disadvantage.

In some cases, Section 44 has perhaps been applied inappropriately, for example, to primary aged children, when differences between strength, speed and physique for 'average' boys and girls are not apparent. If anything, girls are 'frequently bigger and stronger than their male counterparts' at this age (Williams 1989b: 146). Nevertheless, Section 44 was used by the Football Association (FA) (1978) to win an appeal in a court case Theresa Bennett *v.* the Football Association. This ruling continued to prevent girls from playing with boys in local FA leagues. It was not until 1990 that the FA eventually conceded to the pressure to allow mixed football for children under eleven years of age.

The recognition of biologically based differences between 'average' adolescent and post-adolescent boys and girls should also be tempered by an acknowledgement that there are wide differences within the sexes. Women at the upper end of a continuum relating to physical characteristics of size, weight, speed, strength, force etc. are likely to be superior, in these qualities, to many men. Rather than segregating according to sex differences those activities in which strength, speed and physique are likely to determine outcomes, it might be more appropriate to rank sport-related activities according to height/weight/strength etc. Physically powerful women would then have the opportunity to compete safely with men of similar capacities on equal terms, other things being equal (the phrase 'other things being equal' being of particular significance as explained later).

Culturally created differences between boys and girls

The phrase 'other things being equal' is highly significant in drawing attention to the fact that relevant differences between the sexes include culturally determined 'gender differences' as well as the biologically determined sex differences. Men and women are unable to compete on equal terms if either sex has been disadvantaged by their cultural experiences in developing the kind of skills, knowledge and understanding necessary for successful participation in a particular activity. Early socialisation processes can advantage boys and disadvantage girls when they first enter school physical education. This was acknowledged by the SCNI, 'The roots of inequality are laid early in life as boys are provided with more opportunities to develop self confidence and basic motor skills through play' (SCNI 1996: 8).

In addition to differences in opportunities to develop motor skills, differences in upbringing which encourage boys to develop masculine identities and girls to develop feminine identities may disadvantage girls from succeeding in many sports. Sports are sometimes described as 'gendered' because success in those contexts generally requires the display of characteristics, e.g. physical power, speed, strength etc. which are more frequently associated with masculinity than femininity. The upbringing of girls is more likely to develop those characteristics traditionally associated with femininity such as supportiveness, kindness, responsiveness and caring. The upbringing of boys is more likely to develop those characteristics typically associated with masculinity such as aggression, physical power, competitiveness and dominance. This gives boys an advantage in those physical activities which predominantly require the display of qualities associated with masculinity rather than femininity for their success.

The demand for equality of opportunity in physical education is not therefore a demand for recognition that people are all the same in a descriptive sense. There are differences between individuals, including sex and gender differences, which may influence achievement in certain environments.

Is the demand for equality of opportunity in physical education a demand that everyone is given the same treatment?

If the demand for equality of opportunity is not a demand to recognise that all pupils are the same in a descriptive sense, perhaps, as Downey and Kelly suggested, 'it asserts an ideal, a demand for certain kinds of behaviour in our treatment of other people' (Downey and Kelly 1986: 215).

Debates about equality of opportunity date back at least to the time of the ancient Greeks and certainly there were those such as the Greek dramatist Euripedes who considered equality of opportunity to mean impartial treatment for everyone (cited by Downey and Kelly 1986). However, to interpret the term 'equality of opportunity' prescriptively and to see it as carrying a moral requirement to treat everyone the same is clearly inappropriate in many cases. For example, it would be inappropriate to propose that everyone is given the same medical treatment regardless of need. The ancient Greek philosopher Aristotle was among the first to recognise that injustice arises as much from treating unequals equally as from treating equals unequally. This point is illustrated with reference to gender differences in Gender example 2.

Gender example 2: the principle of equality of opportunity is not realised if unequals are treated equally

The injustice that can result when unequals are treated equally is illustrated through the following example adapted from a non-sporting example previously put forward by Williams (1962: 126).

Suppose that in a particular school great prestige is attached to membership of the school cricket team, where players are required to demonstrate considerable physical skill. The team has in the past been recruited from boys only but after some strong campaigning by female pupils and staff they achieve a change in the rules which allows girls to be recruited for the team, on the results of a suitable skills test. The effect of this, however, is that the boys still make up all the team members, because the physical co-ordination and the skill levels of the girls in the school are inferior to those of the boys. The girls and female staff protest that equality of opportunity has not been achieved: the boys reply that in fact it has, and that the girls now have the opportunity of becoming members of the cricket team; it is just bad luck that their skill levels are too low for them to pass the test. 'We are not,' the boys might say, 'excluding anyone for being a girl; we exclude people for being less skilful, and it is unfortunate that the girls are also less skilful.'

It can be assumed from this example that all pupils, male and female, have equal access to the school cricket team in the sense that the rules allow both girls and boys to enter the test for selection of the cricket team. The girls have won the right to play in the cricket team and hence have equal access *de jure*. However, because of gender differences affecting the experiences of girls to acquire the prerequisite skills, the girls were not equally placed to complete the test successfully. Equality of opportunity is more than a matter of having an equal right of access to provision.

The following section explores the problem of equating equality with access and begins with further consideration of the inadequacy of equating equality of opportunity with equality of access *de jure*.

EQUALITY OF OPPORTUNITY IN PHYSICAL EDUCATION IS MORE THAN EQUAL ACCESS *DE JURE*

Gender example 2 illustrates that for equality of opportunity to be realised, in practice there must be more than equal access to provision. Following the change in the rules, all were given equal access *de jure*, in that there were no obstacles or rules preventing access to the test for membership of the cricket team. Having the right to access a desirable social good such as membership of the cricket team is necessary for equality of opportunity but does not guarantee that there is genuine equality of opportunity to succeed in those contexts. See Gender example 3.

Gender example 3: gender equality in physical education requires more than equal access de jure

Boys and girls could be given equal access *de jure* to the physical education curriculum. All pupils could have the right to choose to follow any aspect of the curriculum, such as rugby or triple-jump for girls or netball, dance or synchronised swimming for boys. Even under these circumstances, however, it may not follow that the sexes do in fact have equal opportunities to follow the curriculum of their choice. The stereotypical expectations of the teacher and peer groups and the pupils' own established views as to what is appropriate behaviour for different gender groups can sometimes make it difficult for pupils to take advantage of accessing the opportunities available. Scraton gave an example of the kind of pressure faced by two girls who opted to do a mixed sex football lesson. The female teacher was quoted as saying to the pupils, 'Football, you must be mad, you should have been born a lad.' Hence, Scraton went on to comment, 'even when equal access is available, stereotyping results in pupils having to run the gauntlet of comment from both teachers and pupils' (Scraton 1993: 150).

This example shows that stereotyped expectations of gender appropriate behaviour can make it difficult for boys and girls to access certain opportunities even when the rules allow for their participation. The pupils have equal access *de jure* but this does not result in equality of opportunity to pursue their interests.

Like the example above, relating to membership of the cricket team, this illustrates that realisation of the principle of equality of opportunity in practice requires more than a legal right of access. Account must be taken of differences between pupils which affect their ability to take advantage of those rights of access.

EQUALITY OF OPPORTUNITY IN PHYSICAL EDUCATION IS MORE THAN EQUAL ACCESS *DE FACTO*

In a situation where a pupil not only has the right to participate in a particular activity but does indeed exercise that right through participation, there is equal access *de facto*. Applied to physical education, equal access to the physical education curriculum *de facto* means that all pupils do, as a matter of fact, participate in the same activities. It can still nevertheless fail to achieve a state of affairs in which all pupils genuinely enjoy equal opportunities to develop their learning in physical education. This point is illustrated through Gender example 4 which focuses on inequalities of opportunity that can still arise even in mixed sex groupings where all pupils participate together in the same activities.

Gender example 4: mixed sex (coeducational) grouping in physical education achieves equality of access de facto but may still fail to offer equality of opportunity

One way of ensuring equality of access *de facto* would be to require pupils to be taught the same activities in mixed sex groups. *Prima facie*, mixed sex grouping in physical education seems to offer equality of educational opportunity since it ensures that all pupils are offered the same educational access. However, as Scraton observed, 'the equation of coeducation with equal opportunities is by no means straightforward' (Scraton 1993: 140–1).

Even though girls and boys appear to have the same treatment in terms of access to the same curriculum in mixed sex groupings, this is not sufficient to ensure equality of opportunity. While mixed sex grouping allows girls and boys to have access to the same curriculum, equality of opportunity may nevertheless fail to be realised for the following reasons.

- Sex and gender differences (see Gender example 1) tend to affect the relative abilities of boys and girls in different physical contexts. Hence, boys tend to have more confidence and highly developed skills in many sport-related environments (Hastie 1998). This can affect the confidence and participation levels of girls who may be less involved than boys in mixed sex physical education lessons. Girls are in danger of losing out in mixed sex lessons in terms of teacher attention, use of space and inclusion in activities (Scraton 1993). Scraton remarked that 'girls require both the space and the time to develop their potential in physical education. This will not be achieved by an uncritical move into coeducation' (ibid.: 151).
- There is a danger that mixed sex groups in physical education may intensify forms of sexual harassment and abuse (verbal, physical and emotional) with girls perhaps feeling uncomfortable as their bodies become the object of comment, stares, admiration and/or criticism (Scraton 1993: 145). This may limit girls' enjoyment of physical education and prevent them from participating to their full potential.
- Mixed sex grouping may encourage intensified displays of masculinity and femininity as adolescent boys and girls recognise that judgements as to their attractiveness may be based on these qualities. This can cause girls to disengage from sport as the display of feminine qualities, unlike the display of masculine qualities, are not congruent with sporting prowess and, indeed, are likely to require disassociation from 'tomboyish' behaviour. Girls who do not conform with dominant definitions of femininity may find their female status questioned and find themselves the target of disparaging labels such as 'lesbian'. Similarly, boys who fail to display the qualities associated with

dominant forms of masculinity may find themselves referred to as wimps, cissies or gays. Dance is less associated with masculine traits and is more closely associated with typical feminine qualities such as sensitivity, expression, grace and poise. It is not surprising that OFSTED should have found a good standard of work for girls at Key Stages (KS) 3 and 4 in body management skills in gymnastics and dance, while the work of boys in these activities was frequently found to be 'poor or undeveloped' (OFSTED 1995a: 3). Mixed sex groupings may intensify these differences as adolescent pupils look to gain acceptance through conformity with dominant definitions of masculinity and femininity.

- Mixed sex grouping in physical education may not provide equality of opportunity to pupils of particular ethnic groupings, such as Muslim pupils, who may find their participation in mixed sex contexts in conflict with the requirements of their religion. According to Carrington and Leaman, Muslim parents frequently raise objections to mixed sex grouping in physical education on the grounds that it 'may bring their daughters into direct contact with males in what is regarded as a shameful and potentially compromising situation' (Carrington and Leaman 1986: 222). Mixed sex grouping for certain ethnic groups may therefore lead to feelings of discomfort and may limit the achievements of pupils who feel inhibited by these arrangements (see Chapter 4 of this book).

This illustrates that while it would be easy to assume that mixed sex grouping in physical education satisfies a demand for equal opportunities in providing same treatment (in the sense of access to the same curricular opportunities) for all pupils, inequalities can still remain as a consequence of gender differences which affect opportunities to learn and succeed in physical education.

Gender examples 2 to 4 show that equality of opportunity, as a guiding principle in physical education, fails to be achieved when insufficient attention is given to those differences between individuals and groups of pupils which affect the chances of their succeeding in these contexts. Instead of looking for an interpretation of the meaning of equality of opportunity as implying 'sameness' of provision, the following section considers whether a solution to achieving equality of opportunity lies in differentiated provision.

Equality of opportunity in physical education and differentiation

The view that equality of opportunity is not a 'demand for similarity of treatment but . . . (a demand for) justification for differential treatment' is a development of the view shared by Plato and Aristotle, who considered that the 'the idea of equality is only operative within categories of human being' (cited by Downey and

Kelly 1986: 213). This approach acknowledges that equality of opportunity is not to be achieved through sameness of provision where there are relevant differences. In the search for an adequate interpretation of equality of opportunity in physical education, it is appropriate to consider whether different groups should be given access to a different but equivalent curriculum.

Does access to a different but equivalent curriculum provide equality of opportunity in physical education?

According to this approach equality of opportunity in physical education is not viewed as access to identical provision but access to equivalent provision. The emphasis is on programmes being of equal value without being the same. However, such an approach often fails to offer genuine equality of opportunity if the 'equivalent' curricula offer equivalence in some respects but not others. For example, two curricula could offer access to a range of physical activities but these activities may fall short of equivalence in terms of the level of prestige and status associated with these activities. This point is illustrated through Gender example 5.

Gender example 5: can equality of opportunity be achieved through access to an equivalent physical education curriculum for boys and girls?

Hargreaves (1994) drew attention to the way in which single sex provision in physical education is sometimes justified on the grounds of providing an 'equal but different' curriculum. The provision of an equivalent curriculum provides all pupils with access to a physical education curriculum, but while boys may pursue activities such as football, rugby and cricket, girls may be given access to dance, gymnastics, netball and rounders. It may be considered that such an approach provides access to activities which conform more closely to female and male interests and values. An advantage of this approach may be that girls experience less role conflict between being feminine and being active and therefore may be less inclined to withdraw from involvement in physical activity. However, there are a number of difficulties in achieving equality of opportunity through such an approach.

- Male and female physical activities are often not of an equivalent status. Female activities are generally of lower status and prestige and in their adult forms receive less media coverage. The prestige sports might come to be viewed as exclusively masculine (Carrington and Leaman 1986). Both Williams (1989b) and Talbot (1986) drew attention to differences in prestige accorded to male and female activities. Williams observed, 'netball is not equivalent to football, neither is rounders equivalent to cricket. . . . Girls are being taught games . . . which are rarely if ever pursued in adult life, in sharp contrast to the high profile professional team games being taught to the boys' (Williams 1989b: 150).

- Since female physical activities tend not to exist in the adult world in a form comparable in status and participation opportunities to many male sports, the hidden message to girls is that they can expect to grow up and grow out of playing games 'because they are not seen as having any significance in adult life' (Williams 1989b: 152).
- Boys might be denied opportunities to achieve in those areas of the curriculum considered to be more suitable for females, such as dance and gymnastics.
- Access to a different curriculum for boys and girls can reinforce rather than challenge gender stereotypes and existing patriarchal relations in wider society. These gender stereotypes may limit the opportunities of women (and of some men who do not conform closely to traditional conceptions of masculinity). For example, the inferior status of women's sports may reinforce the idea that women are naturally weaker and inferior to men and may appear to confirm that having fewer women in positions of power in wider society follows the 'natural order' of things. In contrast, in the coeducational adventure environments studied by Humberstone (1990), where boys and girls were often equally inexperienced in the activities, the girls were often found to outshine the boys and in so doing able to challenge the assumption that boys are the stronger sex. The coeducational adventure environments were found to encourage:

  - collaboration between boys and girls
  - greater understanding and respect from boys of not only girls, but of other boys and of themselves
  - behaviours demonstrating collaboration, responsibility and group support rather than aggressive, competitive individualism
  - boys to rethink their views about girls' physical potentials and competencies.

Sex segregation in physical education would seem inappropriate as a long term strategy for equal opportunities since it 'reflects and maintains male hegemony' and 'does little to create greater understanding between the sexes' (Humberstone 1990: 203). However, coeducational grouping for physical education is not an instant solution to the provision of equal opportunities (see Gender example 4) as there are significant sex and gender differences that should not be ignored in the quest for equality of opportunity in physical education.

While it may be appropriate for equal access to a common curriculum in physical education for boys and girls to remain the long term goal, the means of reaching this goal may require short term strategies which enable the 'traditional base of gender imbalance' to be redressed (Scraton 1993: 152). For example, it may be necessary to assess the physical skill levels of all pupils entering schools and to implement programmes for any pupils (male or female, though most likely girls) who exhibit a motor skills deficit. Evans *et al.* referred to such interventions as the equivalent of a 'Headstart' programme (Evans *et al.* 1997: 44).

Gender example 5 illustrates the difficulties that arise if too blunt an instrument is used for assigning pupils to different groups for receiving different provision (e.g. according to sex group). Differential provision should take account of individual needs in accessing the particular provision in question.

Does access to appropriately differentiated provision provide equality of opportunity in physical education?

Figueroa subscribed to an interpretation of equality as differential provision according to need. He defined equality as

> the principle that relevant similarities and relevant differences should be given due recognition – while irrelevant similarities and irrelevant differences should be ignored. . . . [In] physical education – this means giving full recognition to everyone's rights and legitimate needs, and inseparably recognising and taking into account relevant similarities and relevant differences, relevant resources and relevant disadvantages, but disregarding irrelevant ones.
>
> (Figueroa 1993: 91)

This implies eliminating any unfavourable treatment on the basis of the individual's membership to a particular category (e.g. skin colour) which may be irrelevant to accessing particular 'goods' in society. It also implies that where there are relevant differences (such as sex and gender differences) which are affecting an individual's ability to benefit from physical education programmes, these differences are given due consideration in order to allow each individual a maximum chance of achieving his or her potential.

In searching for the meaning of 'equality of opportunity', initial consideration was given to the question of whether this was a matter of treating everyone in the same way. Paradoxically, the view that has been arrived at is that the possibility of equality of opportunity in educational contexts requires that 'the educational diet of every child is different from that of every other' (Downey and Kelly 1986: 241). This raises practical concerns. How can this degree of differentiation be achieved in schools where, on average, there is just one teacher to every thirty pupils? Some allocation to categories and groups is likely to be necessary. The question is, how can the grouping process be handled with accuracy and sensitivity so that the physical learning needs of individuals can be addressed most effectively?

The issue of equality of opportunity in physical education is related to appropriate differentiation of curricular provision. This was acknowledged by Vickerman: 'If you are to respond to the challenge of providing equality of opportunity for all pupils, whilst catering for diversity of need, you have to plan for differentiated teaching and learning' (Vickerman 1997: 139).

Gender example 6 considers ways in which to differentiate provision in physical education.

Gender example 6: differentiating provision for boys and girls in the quest for equality of opportunity in physical education

Differentiated provision in physical education (as noted in Gender example 5) need not imply automatic allocation of boys and girls to separate groups or the automatic allocation of separate tasks for boys and girls. It may be that in some cases it is more appropriate to run separate experienced and beginner curricular and extra-curricular sessions which include opportunities for participation by both boys and girls. Similarly, in the setting of tasks within classes, it may not be appropriate, as Harris recognised, for girls to be asked to perform 'easy' versions of exercises, such as 'girls' press ups' while boys are asked to perform the 'full' or 'real' version. Instead, Harris recommended setting tasks which cater for individual differences and which allow pupils to answer at their own level. This selection of tasks, Harris identified,

> is not a simple gender-related issue; an individual's ability to perform exercises is dependent on many personal factors such as physique, stage of maturation, and appropriate exercise training. Many girls can adequately perform 'harder' exercise alternatives and many boys would benefit from working through exercise progressions rather than being forced to tackle inappropriate exercises.
>
> (Harris 1993: 35)

Vickerman (1997) suggested that in seeking to provide for equal opportunities in physical education, teachers should plan initially for complete inclusion of boys and girls, of pupils with special needs and of pupils from other ethnic minorities. From this point teachers may then 'work backwards towards the substitution and segregation of activities' if necessary for the purposes of adequately addressing pupil differences and ensuring that all pupils have equal opportunities to enjoy, learn and succeed in physical education. For example the teacher may assume that all pupils will be able to complete a ball skills circuit involving sending and receiving but may substitute larger sponge balls for some pupils who would otherwise find the task too difficult.

Drawing attention to the need to address relevant differences affecting attainment leads to the question of whether a commitment to the principle of equality of opportunity is a commitment to making all pupils the same or equal.

Is the demand for equality in physical education the demand that all should be made the same or equal?

Downey and Kelly (1986) argued that the interpretation of equality of opportunity as implying a commitment to making all people the same or equal, applied generally to society, is unrealistic and unattainable in practice. One way in which people are advantaged relative to others is in terms of their wealth. Even if there was complete redistribution of wealth as a move toward social equality, inequalities would still remain as a result of people's differing attitudes to wealth and the uses of it. 'One would have to redistribute wealth so regularly – at least daily as far as most punters and bookmakers are concerned – that the whole process would become meaningless' (Downey and Kelly 1986: 216).

Dahrendorf (1962) agreed that inequalities are a feature of any society. He illustrated this point with reference to an example of an imaginary society held together by a desire to exchange news of intrigue, scandal and general gossip. Even in this society, he believed that members would quickly become distinguished by the quality of their stories and their manner of recounting them so that a rank ordering of members would result.

While this may highlight difficulties in defining social equality in terms of literally 'making people the same', it nevertheless leaves open the question of whether a commitment to the principle of equal opportunities is a matter of *attempting* to equalise outcomes to as great an extent as possible. It is a view which allows recognition of the fact that some pupils are disadvantaged from the outset and advocates targeting resources at those pupils to allow their development to a certain (common) level rather than expending resources on those that are already advantaged. (See Gender example 7).

Gender example 7: does equality of opportunity in physical education imply a commitment to equalising outcomes?

A commitment to equalising outcomes in physical education, in relation to gender equality, might be interpreted, for example, as reducing as far as possible differences between the attainment levels of boys and girls in different activities; between the extra-curricular opportunities and involvement of boys and girls; between the opportunities for sport / dance representation; between levels of post-school involvement; between the allocation of resources to girls' and boys' physical education; and reducing differences between the proportions of male and female staff holding posts of responsibility in physical education.

Differences between the approaches of liberal feminists and radical feminists to equalising outcomes

Equalising outcomes according to measures of the kind identified above would be the goal of liberal feminists, who focus on the issue of fair and equal access for women to participate in sport, dance and exercise and to share the rewards available from such participation (Coakley 1994).

Radical feminists, however, argue that the approach of the liberal feminists does not go far enough. It is focused on increasing access to activities such as sports and games which are already 'gendered' activities and which serve as contexts for the display of dominant masculinities and reinforce the apparent 'superiority' of men. Radical feminists would prefer to see greater emphasis on activities which are defined according to the interests and values of females. This would require greater emphasis on activities such as dance in the curriculum for both males and females and more neutrally gendered activities such as outdoor and adventure activities (see Humberstone 1990) and less emphasis on those activities such as competitive sports and team games which continue to reinforce dominant masculinities.

Despite this difference of approach, liberal and radical feminists agree that females should enjoy a greater share of social rewards. The achievement of this goal might require compensatory mechanisms such as positive action strategies which direct a greater share of resources to disadvantaged groups. Physical education programmes, for example, might give additional lessons to girls in rugby to enable them to compensate for their general lack of experience in this activity, or additional gymnastics sessions to boys in segregated, non-threatening contexts.

Equality and elitism

The targeting of resources to disadvantaged groups could, however, limit the achievements of the more able to attain standards of excellence. It might be argued, for example, that opportunities for talented individuals to achieve sporting world records (e.g. the fastest human being over 100 metres) is limited if finite resources are distributed to the masses (including girls) instead of heaped on individuals capable of outstanding performance.

Few have expressed opposition to the principle of equality of opportunity, but where it has been opposed, it has tended to be for reasons such as those articulated by Nietzsche, that the pursuit of equality of opportunity may lead to mediocrity and the lowering of standards. Nietzsche (1891) believed that individuals must be allowed to be unequal if human evolution is not to be held back.

In physical education, it might be claimed that national prestige may be sacrificed if egalitarian ideals prevent talented individuals from maximising their potential.

The problem is then one of how to allocate finite resources. Most discussions of elitism focus on the problem which arises from allocating resources to the more able which may restrict the opportunities of the less able to access certain goods and opportunities. It is in this sense that elitism was viewed by Thomas and others as 'fundamentally incompatible with an ideology of equality' (Thomas 1993: 106). By privileging access for some, others may be oppressed and alienated (Dewar 1990, Evans and Williams 1989). Thomas believed the concentration of resources on the elite 'reproduces existing inequalities and legitimises these' (Thomas 1993: 110). While some children succeed, others may be labelled failures and have depleted resources because of the allocation to the more able. This 'does not bode well for minority groups or lower-ability pupils' (or girls who may be considered physically less able than boys in physical education) (Thomas 1993: 110, parentheses added). Moreover, those likely to be most successful are those who already enjoy 'the cultural competencies and resources to succeed and benefit' (Evans 1990: 162). There is an obvious tension between a commitment to the social principles of freedom and equality. Should the freedom of talented individuals to pursue excellence be constrained by a commitment to assist the less privileged?

The problem of placing too great an emphasis on 'equalising outcomes' is that the fundamentally educational purposes of physical education might be undermined in favour of 'social engineering' (O'Hear 1988). Social engineering is a process primarily concerned with changing the social make up of the population in terms of the redistribution of power and advantage. The goal of educational enterprises is not primarily one of social engineering. Educational processes should enable all pupils to learn and to develop their potential, and it is as important to extend the learning of gifted and able pupils as it is to attend to the learning needs of less advantaged pupils. The difficulty comes in ensuring that any discriminatory practices which might prevent pupils from developing their potential to the full are removed. This would help to ensure that where people have an equal capacity to benefit from physical education they are treated equally.

Equal opportunities in physical education as the opportunity to develop potential

The opportunity for all pupils to develop potential in physical education requires not only that provision is differentiated according to need but that any obstacles such as discriminatory practices, which could inhibit the development of potential, are removed. Vickerman defined discrimination as 'principally about the deliberate exclusion of individuals due to perceived differences' (Vickerman 1997: 149). It can include the open and deliberate exclusion of individuals purely on the grounds of their colour, sex or disability. Discriminatory practices can both prevent access to physical education and prevent the development of potential within those contexts. A commitment to the principle of equality of opportunity requires removal of all forms of discrimination which may limit the achievement of pupils. (See Gender example 8.)

Gender example 8: equality of opportunity in physical education and the removal of gender discrimination

Discriminatory practices affecting gender equality in physical education include:

- Practices which deny access to particular groups to develop their potential in particular physical activities, e.g. limited access for boys to develop potential in dance, for girls to develop their potential in football (Sports Council for Wales 1995).
- Giving boys priority for use of facilities over girls. The American developmental editor for Messner and Sabo's (1990) book recalled girls' volleyball being relegated to the 'girls' gym' with its low ceilings and short end lines, while the boys' basketball practice would always take priority in the newly built gymnasium. If the girls wanted use of the better facilities they had to 'practise at 6.00 a.m. or come back to school after 6.00 p.m. when the boys were done' (cited in Messner and Sabo 1990: 201).
- Making available a greater proportion of extra-curricular physical education to boys than girls and more staff assistance and support for boys' teams and events (Harris 1993: 32). This imbalance of provision was noted by OFSTED as a key issue for secondary schools: 'Extra-curricular activities play a substantial part in the extension of the curriculum but are often restricted to team games with access limited to those selected to play for teams. The opportunities for girls are generally more limited' (OFSTED 1995a: 5).
- Engaging in practices which may hinder the development of girls' physical potential through requirements to wear clothing which may be inappropriate or cause embarrassment to girls in the development of physical skills, such as skirts or leotards for gymnastics.
- Biasing the curriculum in favour of activities which are more in tune with boys' interests than with girls' interests, e.g. team games rather than aerobics (Evans et al. 1997).
- Having a greater focus on boys' physical activity achievements than girls' physical activity achievements, for example, in school assemblies.
- Setting 'easier' tasks for girls than boys (such as girls' push ups).
- Allowing the predominance of male role models in physical education and sporting contexts e.g. as heads of department for physical education, as illustrative material in school texts or on display materials and school notice boards, or as exemplifiers of skilled performers, e.g.

> professional male footballers or athletes and the stereotyping of these examples, e.g. male footballers, female gymnasts.
>
> If girls are not to be denied opportunities to develop their physical capacities in physical education to as great an extent as boys then steps should be taken to avoid discriminatory or sexist practices of this kind.

The need for effective action to remove discriminatory practices of any kind is central to the implementation of an appropriate equal opportunities policy in physical education. This is most likely to be achieved where targets are set for eliminating discrimination and where action plans are drawn up and their implementation monitored. If an equal opportunities policy is to be translated into a programme of change, it may be necesssary for physical education teachers to put in place arrangements which:

- audit current provision (such as current participation levels and pupils' perceptions of desired changes)
- set targets for change (for example, 10 per cent increase in the participation rates of girls in extra-curricular activities)
- put forward an action plan which sets specific achievement goals, deadlines for achievement and the allocation of staff for achieving the goal
- evaluate the outcome so that goals can be reformulated if they remain unachieved, and good practice shared.

The implementation of plans of this nature can help to prevent the commitment to equal opportunities in physical education being no more than empty words. (Bringing about changes in physical education is further discussed in Chapter 14.)

However, even with the removal of discriminatory practices from physical education, equality of opportunity could still fail to be realised if the problem of achieving equity and justice in wider society is not given due consideration.

Equality of opportunity in physical education and equity

In discussing the distinction between 'equality' and 'equity', Evans and Davies (1993b: 24) envisaged a state of affairs in which there could be equality of opportunity in physical education in the sense of:

- all pupils having a basic entitlement to physical education, ensured through the National Curriculum
- all pupils having access to a common physical education curriculum
- all pupils receiving as far as possible more or less the same educational experiences

- no significant differences between the distribution of measurable achievements based on sex, class or race.

Even under these conditions, equity, in the sense of whether the resulting state of affairs is just, could fail to be achieved. This is because if the common curriculum to which pupils were introduced continued to perpetuate and reinforce existing patterns of power relationships in wider society, it would fail to address an underlying injustice or inequity in wider society. There is a sense in which a commitment to equality of opportunity is lacking if the curriculum continues to reinforce inequalities in wider society. (See Gender example 9.)

Gender example 9: *equality of opportunity in physical education and the issue of gender equity*

With reference to gender relations, access to a common physical education curriculum, including access to the same extra-curricular opportunities, with an even distribution of outcomes (rewards), could nevertheless continue to confirm and reinforce patriachal relations which favour the dominance of men and subordination of women in wider society. This would be the case if, for example, the curriculum continued to be biased toward games and sports which have been socially constructed out of the values and experiences of male interests and which favour the display of attributes more typically associated with masculinity. Where the activities themselves are 'gendered' in the sense of success in those activities largely being determined by the demonstration of qualities such as aggression, competition, strength and physical prowess which are more typically associated with men than women, the curriculum will be used to confirm the superiority of males. Powerful females in sport can, of course, begin to challenge widely held gender stereotypes of femininity, but because adolescent and older males are on average more physically powerful than females, a games and sports biased curriculum tends to perpetuate a notion that male privilege in wider society is grounded in nature and biological destiny and hence functions to perpetuate patriarchal relationships between men and women.

Coakley (1994) argued that real equity lies in developing alternative sports forms which are constructed according to the values and experiences of women and of men who do not see themselves in terms of dominant definitions of masculinity. 'Some boys', as Hargreaves suggested, 'hate the images and conventions of masculine sport' (Hargreaves 1994: 154). Gender equity is not just a female issue. It requires greater access for men to participate in forms of sports that are not based on dominant definitions of masculinity. The final report of the National Curriculum Physical Education Working Group (NCPEWG) proposed that dance should be compulsory for both sexes until the age of fourteen partly to allow the questioning of 'stereotypes which limit children's behaviour and achievements; and to challenge, whenever necessary, instances of sexism and racism' (DES/WO 1991: 5).

These radical proposals, Hargreaves (1994) observed, were not adopted in the NCPE. Dance is compulsory at KS1 and KS2, but not at secondary level, at the very time when boys are consolidating a sense of masculinity. The current physical education curriculum, with its relative lack of attention to dance and gymnastics for boys during the secondary phase (OFSTED 1995b), does not comply with the proposals of the NCWGPE to offer 'a broad and balanced programme of physical education (which is) sensitively delivered . . . [to] help to extend boys' restricted perceptions of masculinity and masculine behaviour' (DES/WO 1991: 58).

Coakley believed that 'gender equity will never be complete or lasting unless there are changes in the way people think about masculinity and femininity and unless there are changes in the way sports [and physical education programmes] are organised and played' (Coakley 1994: 237, parentheses added). Changes to physical education that could occur in the interests of gender equity include the following:

- Pupils having increased opportunities to participate in less 'gendered' physical activities, such as the kind of more neutrally gendered outdoor and adventure activities studied by Humberstone (1990). These activities were found to challenge gender stereotypes, encourage greater mutual respect from both sexes, and promote co-operative relations between the sexes (see Gender example 5).
- Pupils having greater access to physical activities which challenge traditional conceptions of masculinity and femininity (for example, greater access to dance for boys; rugby for females).
- Greater awareness from physical education teachers to encourage alternative definitions of masculinity and femininity and to oppose behaviours which denigrate males and females who do not conform to traditional definitions of masculinity and femininity. For example, teachers should oppose references to males who do not excel in sports or who excel in dance as wimps. Teachers should actively discourage the questioning of girls' real 'female' status because in excelling in sports she appears to conform to a masculine identity. References to girls as 'tomboys' or 'lesbians' or as needing to be sex tested because of their high level of physical performance in sports should be opposed. Teachers should avoid reinforcing conceptions of females as weak, for example by asking for strong boys to carry the apparatus. Physical education teachers can also lessen the 'gendered' nature of sports through discouraging references which frequently associate sport with

masculinity. For example, the association of sports with boys proving themselves to be men can be dropped. Similarly, teachers should avoid encouraging such views as boys throwing correctly 'throw like a boy', boys throwing incorrectly, 'throw like a girl' (Coakley 1994). Teachers can also campaign for rule changes which lessen the emphasis on violence, strength and aggression in sport and place greater emphasis on skill and the cooperative relations necessary for competitive sport to take place. (See Chapter 9.)

Conclusion

Using gender equality as an example, this chapter has drawn attention to the different kinds of practice that can result from differing interpretations of the concept of equality of opportunity. It has been argued that a demand for equality of opportunity is not a demand for recognition that people are the same in a descriptive sense since clearly there are both biological and socially constructed differences which affect how pupils should be treated. It is necessary that pupils have access to a physical education programme if they are to have equality of opportunity in physical education but equality of access in a *de jure, de facto* or equivalence sense is not sufficient for equality of opportunity. Acknowledgement that it is as unjust to treat equals unequally as it is to treat unequals equally was taken to imply that equality of opportunity in physical education requires attending to relevant differences that may affect pupils' abilities to achieve in physical education. Where pupils differ in their capacity to benefit from a physical education programme, differentiated provision is required. This does not mean that for equality of opportunity to be an effective principle in physical education, all pupils should reach the same level. This is both unrealistic and fails to offer equal opportunities to gifted and more able pupils who are equally entitled to develop their potential as part of a programme of physical *education*, which implies that it is a programme of *learning* and not of social engineering. If all pupils are to have the opportunity to develop their potential then it is important that any forms of discrimination that might act as barriers to the development of the physical potential of groups of pupils are removed. However, even in a situation where all pupils have an entitlement to a physical education programme, all have access to a common curriculum, and the measurable progress of all groups of pupils is comparable, a genuine realisation of equality of opportunity may still fail without recognition of the need to address issues of equity. A commitment to equity seeks to prevent physical education programmes from functioning to confirm and reinforce patterns of social injustice and inequality in wider society.

Aspects of the concept of equality of opportunity are discussed further in the following two chapters in relation to pupils with special education needs and cultural diversity in physical education.

Questions for reflection

1   Identify ways in which your own experience of physical education in schools has or has not demonstrated a commitment to equality of opportunity.
2   How might current practices in physical education be improved to promote equality of opportunity? Construct an action plan to assist in the realisation of equal opportunities in physical education for a school with which you are familiar.
3   Following your reading of the following two chapters, replace the gender examples in this chapter with examples relating to pupils with special educational needs and examples relating to pupils from different cultural backgrounds.

Further reading

Carrington, B. and Leaman, O. (1986) 'Equal opportunities and physical education', in J. Evans (ed.), *Physical Education, Sport and Schooling*, London: Falmer: 265–79.

DES/WO (1991) *National Curriculum Physical Education for Ages 5 to 16. Proposals of the Secretary of State for Education and Science and the Secretary of State for Wales*, London: HMSO, Chapter 6 and Appendix A.

Evans, J. (ed.) (1993) *Equality, Education and Physical Education*, London: Falmer.

Evans, J., Davies, B. and Penny, D. (1997) 'Making progress? Sport policy, women and innovation in physical education', *European Journal of Physical Education* 2 (1): 39–50.

3 Equality and the inclusion of pupils with special educational needs in physical education

Christopher Robertson, Carolyn Childs and Elizabeth Marsden

Introduction

Pupils with special educational needs are those for whom some degree of special provision has to be made to enable them to enjoy optimum access to learning opportunities.

This chapter aims to identify some key issues in teaching physical education to pupils with special educational needs. The context for discussion of these issues is that of educational policy in the United Kingdom which currently places a strong emphasis on the development of more inclusive provision and practice. This policy is seemingly based on values and beliefs that are associated with the concept of equality. Political commitment to developing a more inclusive educational system is made clear in the Green Paper *Excellence for All Children: Meeting Special Educational Needs* (Department for Education and Employment (DfEE) 1997) and the subsequent implementation plan *Meeting Special Educational Needs: A Programme of Action* which stated:

> Promoting inclusion within mainstream schools, where parents want it and appropriate support can be provided, will remain a cornerstone of our strategy. There are strong educational, as well as social and moral grounds for educating children with special educational needs, or with disabilities, with their peers. This is an important part of building an inclusive society. An increasing number of schools are showing that an inclusive approach can reinforce a commitment to higher standards for all.
>
> (DfEE 1998a: 23)

This policy statement, though it is cautious, would appear to be saying two things about pupils with special educational needs that should be kept clearly in focus throughout this chapter. First, making provision for pupils with special educational needs is a matter of equalising opportunities in mainstream schools and that this has a moral as well as a practical dimension. Second, such provision, if well developed, should also lead to better educational attainment for all pupils. These two central planks of policy are not unproblematic as a number of commentators have noted (see, for example, Lindsay and Thompson

1997 and Sebba with Sachdev 1997), for they make questionable philosophical assertions and equivocal empirical claims. However, they are influencing the development of educational practice in significant ways and therefore warrant serious consideration. In the context of physical education this means grappling with the following practical but not simple questions:

- How can the needs of all pupils be met in mainstream physical education programmes?
- How can the educational attainments of all pupils be improved in mainstream physical education?

In addressing these questions, there are no straightforward solutions and no elixirs available to teachers. Meeting the needs of all pupils takes place within particular organisational contexts that are constraining (Wedell 1995), and curriculum content can also be weakly conceptualised (Noddings 1992). In other words, even if there is agreement on what should be done in physical education, changing ways of working to achieve new aims will not be easy, for as the philosopher Neurath remarked: 'We are like sailors who have to rebuild their ship on the open sea, without ever being able to dismantle it in dry-dock and reconstruct it from the best components' (Neurath 1983).

The pragmatic and conceptual difficulties associated with meeting special educational needs within physical education are certainly real, but they are also positively challenging. These difficulties are considered in relation to the following interlinked dimensions:

- the idea of inclusion
- moving forward: a triadic view of needs
- a curriculum for all: rhetoric and reality
- pedagogy
- embedded practice: involving the whole school.

Within each of these dimensions, the concept and struggle for equality features centrally.

The idea of inclusion

Normality and difference

The history of special education is complex. Writers such as Cole (1989) have identified a strong humanitarian strand in it, while others such as Hurt (1988) have highlighted less humane practices that have influenced developments. Yet others (Ford *et al.* 1982, Tomlinson 1982) viewed special education policy and practice in terms of segregated social control of troublesome (for example, Afro-Caribbean) children or 'useless' pupils. It is important to exercise care in interpreting the history of special education in simplistic ways. As Armstrong noted, 'it is homogeneous neither in terms of its function nor in terms of its impact' (Armstrong 1998: 45).

In describing developments in special education over a hundred years, Armstrong characterised changes in terms of long, difficult, and different paths being trodden towards inclusion. This struggle has obvious parallels with the historical battles in education about race and gender, and some of these are far from won. But pupils with special educational needs and disabilities can be identified as having a unique connection to a particular social and historical experience that extends beyond the educational, and concerning which physical education teachers should be particularly aware. Some features of this history are summarised below, and are worth reflecting on in terms of the messages they convey about pupils with special educational needs and how these messages might be translated into curriculum provision and teaching, deliberately or otherwise:

- People with learning difficulties have systematically been separated from mainstream educational, social and economic activity (Atkinson *et al.* 1997). Many people with physical disabilities and sensory impairments have similarly been excluded (Humphries and Gordon 1992). This exclusion has, at times, led to abusive social practices such as incarceration and sterilisation. The rationale for such practices has been based on inept notions of 'intelligence' and physical characteristics (Oliver and Barnes 1998). Most horrifically, this led to the killing of disabled people. The killing of those 'unworthy of life' was a clear part of Nazi genocide policy (Burleigh 1994), with strong roots in eugenic 'science', serving as an experimental precursor to the more familiar holocaust during the Second World War. Such an extreme policy towards disabled people may seem shocking and remote from the current educational and social world, and yet some of the shocking ideas and practices of earlier times still cast a light in present times. This is illustrated in the way that the body and the construct of intelligence are both defined in terms of 'norms' from which there should be no deviation.
- A recent newspaper report with the title 'Having disabled babies will be "sin", says scientist' brings the issue of normality into sharp focus. The journalist Rogers reported that a world-renowned embryologist, Edwards, speaking at the European Society of Human Reproduction and Embryology made these remarks: 'Increasing availability of pre-natal screening for genetic diseases gave parents a moral responsibility not to give birth to disabled children'. Edwards continued that 'Soon it will be a sin of parents to have a child that carries the heavy burden of genetic disease. We are entering a world where we have to consider the quality of our children' (*Sunday Times* 4 July 1999). This recent example of thinking about medical issues is not cited here to introduce a moral debate about genetic engineering; rather it is to highlight the important notion that certain intellectual and physical qualities are seen as more valuable than others, and that a lack of ability in the physical domain can be regarded as the definitive characteristic of a person.

- The idea that the body should conform to social norms has been discussed extensively by Foucault (see Rabinow 1984). It was highlighted in relation to physical education by Barton, who argued that 'physical education is the creation of and for able-bodied people' and that it 'gives priority to certain types of human movement'. He continued by suggesting that 'the motivation to participate [in physical education] is encouraged through idealised notions of "normality" (Barton 1993: 49, parantheses added). (The concept has gender dimensions of the kind discussed in Chapter 2 of this book.)
- It is this overarching normalising gaze, as Foucault termed it, that exercises significant power over individuals and wider social practices. It operates both visibly and invisibly. Educationally, what can follow from this is a construction of disability or special needs that is built on a premise of inequality. The results of this for individuals might be that a person is labelled, distinguished or set apart from others in such a way that he or she is considered socially inferior. Care and treatment (including education) are developed and legitimated on the basis of this label of social inferiority (adapted from Johnstone 1998, based on Rioux 1996). This has been the case historically, and it is certainly possible that today's educational practice still reflects such inequalities. Furthermore, the impact of such practice has important implications for individuals, shaping their experience and personality in ways that are damaging (Morris 1989). Brisenden called this the development of 'a sort of medicalised social reflex' (Brisenden 1986: 175).

Special educational needs and equality

The modern era of special education in Britain was ushered in by the Warnock Report (DES 1978). Many, though not all, of the recommendations made in the report became part of educational legislation in the 1981 Education Act. The Act outlined important educational policy for special educational needs and did so making use of arguments concerning rights and equality (Goacher *et al.* 1988). These arguments have influenced all subsequent special education legislation, including most notably, *The Code of Practice on the Identification and Assessment of Special Educational Needs* (DfE 1994a) and the national policy proposals on special education and inclusion mentioned at the beginning of this chapter. Warnock's thinking on matters of rights and equality led to the outlining of some key principles, including the following:

- Pupils with special educational needs are not different from other pupils. Indeed, many children (20 per cent) experience difficulties in learning during their education.
- Therefore, the aims of education should be the same for all pupils.
- Wherever possible, pupils with special educational needs should have these needs met in mainstream schools.

- Mainstream teachers should assume responsibility for meeting these needs.
- Pupils with special educational needs, and their parents, should be involved in decision-making about school provision and placement.
- Pupils with special educational needs should be assessed appropriately.

Putting these principles into practice during the fifteen years following the 1981 Education Act proved very difficult indeed, essentially because the political landscape changed radically during this period and there was seemingly less interest in educational equality. In this climate, and despite the introduction of a National Curriculum purportedly for all, moves towards the integration of pupils with special educational needs in mainstream schools either struggled to take root or floundered.

Difficulties in integrating pupils with special educational needs, for whatever reason, led to a reconceptualisation of the problem in the 1990s. Critique and reflection has led to the development of policy that is seen to be more inclusive, but more actively derived from the belief that equality has to be fought for. Inclusion has been characterised by Oliver (1996) as:

- being a process rather than a fixed state
- being problematic
- being political
- necessitating changes in school ethos
- involving teachers who have acquired commitment
- necessitating changes in the 'given' curriculum
- involving a recognition of the moral and political rights of pupils to inclusive education
- recognising that pupils with special educational needs are valued, and that their achievements should be celebrated
- acknowledging the importance of difference rather than sameness or 'normality'
- necessitating a struggle.

(adapted from Oliver 1996: 84)

A number of issues raised by this model of inclusion are considered in the context of physical education later in this chapter.

The link between the concept of special educational needs and beliefs about equalising opportunities was strengthened at an international level by three developments in legislation produced by the United Nations (UN). A caution needs to be borne in mind here, for not all countries either 'sign up', or adhere to, UN conventions and rules. Nevertheless, such legislation is significant, and worth describing briefly:

- *The UN Convention on the Rights of the Child* (UN 1989) Article 2 states that all rights shall apply to all children without discrimination on any ground and specifically mentions disability (that is, special educational needs).

Article 23 advocates that education should be designed in a manner conducive to the child 'achieving the fullest possible social integration'.

- *The UN Standard Rules on the Equalisation of Opportunities for Persons with Disabilities* (UN 1993). Rule 6 (of 22) clearly identifies integrated education as the vehicle for equalising opportunities, noting that countries should ensure that the education of people with disabilities is an integral part of the educational system.

- *The United Nations Education, Scientific and Cultural Organisation (UNESCO, the UN's education agency) Salamanca Statement* (UNESCO 1994). This document invites countries to respond to a framework of action based on a clear commitment to inclusive education. Point 7 is unequivocal:

> The fundamental principle of the inclusive school is that all children should learn together, wherever possible, regardless of any difficulties or differences they may have. Inclusive schools must recognise and respond to the diverse needs of their students, accommodating both different styles of and rates of learning and ensuring quality to all through appropriate curricula, organisational arrangements, teaching strategies, resource use and partnerships with their communities. There should be a continuum of support and services to match the continuum of special needs encountered in every school.
>
> (UNESCO 1994: 11)

Here, there is not only an increasing recognition of the rights of children with disabilities and special educational needs, but a description of what inclusive education might look like. The Salamanca Statement (UNESCO 1994) acknowledged that schools must change if they are to provide genuine equal opportunities for all pupils. From the perspective of physical education what might such changes entail?

It is easier, of course, to espouse the importance of equality than it is to achieve it in practice. Too often, the concept of equality is presented as being an unproblematic good in relation to special educational needs, whereas it is in fact deeply problematic. It presents difficulties of two kinds:

- Achieving absolute equality in practice will always be impossible in group teaching situations.
- It is conceptually incoherent (Berlin 1997) to believe that 'great goods' (values) like equality can co-exist with others; for example, the value that asserts the importance of the individual. (See Chapter 2 of this book for further discussion of difficulties inherent in the conflict between individual freedom and equality.)

Berlin (1997) warned against believing and acting as if complete equality can be achieved, suggesting that such idealism is dangerous, for it involves overriding other important interests. However, this does not mean that inclusive educational practice should be dismissed; rather it must be recognised that difficulties and dilemmas in schools, classrooms, gymnasiums and sports fields have to be 'lived with'. Berlin stressed that 'to force people into the neat uniforms demanded by dogmatically believed-in schemes is almost always the road to inhumanity. We can only do what we can: but that we must do, against difficulties' (Berlin 1998: 16).

Another philosopher, Williams (1981: 81) saw bridging the gap between different social and moral values of the kind being discussed here as an important part of social and personal activity.

How then, can such problems be resolved in theory and practice? One way is to reconsider the concept of special educational needs.

Moving forward: a triadic view of needs

Whether addressing the special educational needs of pupils in physical education or other teaching and learning contexts, the main task is how to go about:

> finding the optimal balance between adapting teaching and curriculum overall so it suits all learners [link to the value of equality] and accommo-dating to individual differences through differences in teaching when overall adaptations are not enough [link to the value of individual need].
>
> (Norwich 1994: 304, parentheses added)

To be able to undertake this daunting task, it is important to review under-standing of special educational needs with a view to asking whether or not it helps or hinders inclusive educational practice. The term special educational needs, since its introduction by Warnock (DES 1978), has come to mean 'all things to all people'. It has often been used inaccurately and disparagingly. A more useful triadic view of needs has been outlined by Norwich (1996). The three types of needs he described are interconnected and implicitly take account of the values of both individual need and equality:

Typology of Needs

1   Individual needs: these are unique to the individual pupil.
2   Exceptional needs: these are shared with some other pupils.
3   Common needs: these are shared with all pupils.

This view of needs represents a significant and positive shift in thinking about special education. Interestingly, it is also a typology that can be applied to other children (for example, the very able athlete, swimmer, or musician). More importantly though, it also has an important practical value. This can be demonstrated with reference to physical education in the following example.

The application of a triadic view of special educational needs to physical education

Manjula is an 11-year-old girl who attends a mainstream primary school. She has Down's Syndrome, and is making good general progress across the curriculum given that she has some learning difficulties. Her identified weaknesses as a learner are in physical education, though she enjoys physical education lessons very much.

What insights are provided to the teacher through the triadic concept of needs, and what practical pedagogical implications follow from these?

First, Manjula is an individual and her difficulties in physical education may have arisen for one, or many, reasons. Her difficulties would need to be assessed. The fact that she has Down's Syndrome may have no bearing whatsoever on the difficulties she is experiencing. Crude assumptions such as 'Down's children are good at physical activity' or 'find physical education difficult' are generally unhelpful.

Second, it may be the case that Manjula lacks confidence, or has poor self-esteem, and this is very evident in physical education lessons. In this regard she may share these difficulties with some other children in the class and none of these pupils has Down's Syndrome. On the other hand, it could be the case that Manjula does have motor difficulties that are associated with Down's Syndrome (see Winders 1997). If this is so, then a carefully differentiated programme of learning could be developed. This might be implemented at an individual level but more probably within ordinary physical education lessons that are carefully structured to take account of group needs.

Third, though Manjula is experiencing difficulties in physical education, she enjoys these lessons. Care must be taken to ensure that in addressing her needs, teachers do not deliberately or inadvertently stigmatise or separate her. Differentiated teaching must not lose sight of needs common to a group or class as a whole.

In summary, this approach to meeting needs is particularly valuable and relevant to the teaching of physical education because:

- it takes careful account of the tensions that exist between trying on the one hand to achieve equality, and on the other to meet individual needs effectively
- it implicitly respects individuals, recognising their uniqueness and their value as pupils, among others, in educational communities
- it does not simplistically ignore difficulties in learning (or health and safety matters) associated with particular disabilities, but it does not fall into the trap of assuming that only some characteristics define a pupil.

A curriculum for all: rhetoric and reality

Teaching physical education to meet educational needs in the way described in the previous section can only be effective if the curriculum also takes proper account of pupil diversity. Barton (1993: 49) suggested that the quality of the physical education curriculum should be judged against these questions:

- Is the curriculum enabling?
- Does it deal with difference from a theoretically appropriate stance?

Work undertaken to develop physical education as part of the National Curriculum (interim and final reports, Department of Education and Science/Welsh Office (DES/WO) 1990; 1991) certainly attempted to address these questions, identifying four key principles that were intended to ensure that all pupils could fully participate and learn. These principles were summarised by Sugden:

1 *Entitlement* to the National Curriculum with modifications where appropriate.
2 *Access* to be achieved by, first and foremost, the provision of appropriate and challenging programmes of study and assessment mechanisms, allowing for modification where required.
3 *Integration* to be considered as central. Pupils, even when following an adapted curriculum, should be doing so alongside their peers.
4 *Integrity* to be at the heart of physical education. It should be demanding and not trivial. Most important of all, it must be motivating and exciting educationally.

(Based on Sugden 1991: 135)

However, despite this positive outlining of educational principles, some authors have raised concerns about the exclusive nature of the National Curriculum for Physical Education (NCPE) produced in the early 1990s. Barton (1993) questioned its inclusiveness, suggesting that it overemphasised individualism and competitiveness. He also noted that it was based on outmoded definitions of disability that reinforced discriminatory practices (for example, those of the World Health Organisation (WHO) 1980). Both Coakley (1994) and Hargreaves (1994) criticised the curriculum on grounds of gender stereotyping as is made clear in Chapter 2 of this book. It is certainly possible to see parallels in their critiques and that applied by Barton (1993), to considerations of special educational needs. It should be noted in this context that feminist perspectives on physical education have as yet failed to connect with writing about physical education from a disability perspective.

With regard to the changes to the National Curriculum in the year 2000 (DfEE/Qualifications and Curriculum Authority (QCA) 1999, QCA 1999a, 1999b), there would seem to be the rhetorical promise at least, of a more flexible, less prescriptive and more inclusive curriculum. It might seem unhelpful to express doubts about the revised physical education curriculum when it is still awaiting implementation, but it is worth pointing out that in terms of both content and associated descriptions of attainment the proposals contain a number of recommendations that do more to exclude than to include all pupils. Two brief examples illustrate this. First, the Key Stage 2 Programme of Study for swimming indicates that children should be taught to swim using 'recognised arm and leg actions, lying on their front and back' (DfEE/QCA 1999: 19). This seems a laudable enough recommendation, but it excludes many children who can learn to swim without using orthodox strokes at all (Association of Swimming Therapy 1981, Sherrill 1998). Second, the early level descriptions 1 and 2 (DfEE/QCA 1999) outline target language and cognitive skills that would exclude many pupils with significant learning difficulties.

These concerns highlight the need for a more informed debate about curriculum content; one that recognises the full implications of educational inclusiveness. On a more positive note, there are many good examples of innovative physical education that could be used more extensively. A few of these are highlighted next:

Illustrative examples of innovative practice in physical education

The use of *Developmental Movement* (Sherborne 1990) for pupils in all forms of special educational provision, including both special and mainstream schools. Much innovative practice in special schools deserves to be disseminated more widely.

Innovative approaches to swimming teaching for pupils with special educational needs. *The Halliwick Method* (Association of Swimming Therapy 1981) and *the Sherrill Water Fun and Success Model* (Sherrill 1998) are methods that could be used with all children.

The utilisation of curriculum goals premised on *humanistic values* (Hellison and Templin 1991), an approach developed for use with pupils experiencing behavioural difficulties. Its application could be much wider.

These examples challenge the current content of the physical education curriculum, but they also raise issues about both the aims of physical education and teaching methods.

These practices certainly warrant greater consideration through a careful professional dialogue between specialists in physical education, teachers, including those with expertise in special education, disabled people and the QCA.

Pedagogy

The obvious starting point for an inclusive physical education pedagogy is that of differentiation. A useful typology of differentiation was outlined by Lewis (1992) and this can be purposefully linked to Vickermann's (1997) view, referred to in Chapter 2 of this book, that initial planning to teach physical education should start from a consideration of diversity and difference in all learners, so that teaching is inclusive from the beginning. Working in this way, the issue of meeting needs and doing so equitably is faced head on.

There is, though, no point in working simply on the basis of equality and carefully considered differentiation without also using effective pedagogic skills, knowledge and understanding. An underlying knowledge of applied motor development (Wright and Sugden 1999) is vital, and this needs to incorporate an understanding of impairment and motor development. The ability to be able to assess and identify pupils' difficulties is also important. Some helpful informal and formal assessment 'tools' are available to teachers. For example, Sugden and Henderson (1994) devised a useful assessment for motor difficulties associated with Developmental Co-ordination Disorder (DCD). This assessment can be used to 'screen' for problems without any specialist training. The same authors (Henderson and Sugden 1992) also devised a standardised assessment and teaching programme for school age pupils with DCD. Both of these assessment and teaching frameworks can be linked to the staged approach to assessment and intervention outlined in the *Code of Practice on the Identification and Assessment of Special Educational Needs* (Department for Education (DfE) 1994a). Another useful general assessment schedule has been developed by Knight and Chedzoy (1997) for use with pupils who have motor co-ordination difficulties, emotional and behavioural difficulties, hearing impairments, learning difficulties, physical disabilities and visual impairments. The ability to use assessment methods like these assists teachers in meeting the needs of pupils effectively. Equitable provision cannot be developed on the basis of teacher commitment alone.

Assessment, if it is worthwhile, also directly informs, and is informed by, the teaching process (Daniels 1996). The essence of good physical education teaching is that it should encourage both participation and learning (Wright and Sugden 1999). Participation can be guaranteed if detailed attention is given to pupil grouping and support, and curriculum adaptation. Planning for participation should also be informed by an understanding of needs described earlier in the chapter. Participation alone does not guarantee that learning will take place, so careful attention also needs to be given to phases, or levels, of learning (Haring *et al.* 1978; Sugden and Wright 1996); those of *understanding, acquisition and refinement, automatising, and generalising.* The pedagogic importance of these should not be underestimated, for it is easy to spend too much time teaching a pupil experiencing difficulties at the wrong level. Two examples of this are: encouraging a pupil to generalise the use of ball skills when he has not yet acquired these to any degree of fluency; and spending too long teaching a pupil acquistional skills without variation that might lead to greater refinement and fluency (learning to catch and throw a ball). The result of this might be that the pupil becomes bored and demotivated.

It is also important for physical education teachers to be able to analyse carefully the teaching context. This analysis may involve reflection on the physical and social environment and the role of the teacher, but it could also focus on the teaching task and its component parts.

Inclusive education involves complex pedagogy. Wood noted that although 'a great deal of teaching is spontaneous, "natural" and effective, deliberate teaching of groups of children in formally contrived contexts is an intellectually demanding occupation' (Wood 1986: 191).

To conclude, the boxed section below draws together some summary reflections on aspects of teaching and curriculum provision, and how it might lead to the greater equality of opportunities in physical education.

A summary of aspects of teaching and curriculum provision which may lead to greater equality of opportunity for pupils with special educational needs

- The physical education curriculum and the way in which it is taught should focus primarily on making learning possible for all pupils. This involves ensuring that the curriculum available for the majority of learners is made accessible to a wider range of pupils. It also involves adapting the curriculum and sometimes providing educationally equivalent worthwhile alternatives. Some of these alternatives may also be educationally beneficial to all pupils.
- Particular attention needs to be given to ensuring that pupils with special educational needs can fully participate in the physical education curriculum. For this to be effective, pupil grouping and support needs to be planned carefully and flexibly (Wedell 1995).
- Teachers of physical education greatly enhance the development of inclusive practice if they are genuinely welcoming and committed to meeting the needs of all pupils. For them to be able to do this confidently, they need to have well-developed knowledge, skills and understanding in aspects of pedagogy that bridge the fields of special education and physical education.
- Where appropriate, it may be necessary for teachers of physical education to consider adding to provision to make learning more accessible (such as using new teaching materials). At the same time, it may be more appropriate to reflect on ways that existing provision could be altered (for example, different use of staff support, or a change of teaching approach).
- Working with pupils who have diverse and sometimes complex needs should involve teachers in partnership learning. This implies engaging in educational dialogue with pupils, parents and other professionals. Only through such a dialogue can educationally effective inclusion be achieved (Robertson 1998).
- When the five previous points are coherently interlaced in teaching and

planning, and related to an appropriate theory of inclusion of the kind discussed earlier in this chapter, equality of provision within a physical education programme can be seen as possible.

(Adapted from Sugden and Talbot 1996)

Embedded practice: involving the whole school

Though much can be achieved in the quest for equality of provision in physical education by good quality teaching and appropriately enriched subject content, this can be greatly enhanced if, at the whole school level:

- an inclusive policy for physical education is in place
- the initial teacher education (ITE) and continuing professional development of teachers in teaching physical education to a diverse range of pupils are seen as important.

Policy

The Education Act 1993 requires schools to have special educational needs policies in place, and *Circular 6/94: The Organisation of Special Educational Provision* (DfE) 1994b) provides guidance on what these policies should include. Similarly, schools should have policies in place for different curriculum subjects, including physical education. Of course, the legal requirement to have policies in place does not guarantee that they will be good policies. Arguably, good policies should adhere to these tenets:

- policies should be *active*, and useful to teachers and other educational staff
- policies should be *communicative* to the school community as a whole
- policies should be *interlinked* (for example, the policy for physical education should connect with policies for equal opportunities, special educational needs, assessment, recording and reporting, and promoting positive behaviour).

Useful guidance on effective school policy development has been described by Palmer *et al.* (1994). Their suggested policy framework has four components:

1 Philosophy: where do we start from?
2 Principles: what should we do?
3 Procedures: how do we do it?
4 Performance: is it happening?

Each of these components requires a consideration of both equal opportunities and special educational needs. How might this framework be applied to a physical education policy? Space precludes a comprehensive response to this question, but the following example provides a brief (and partial) listing of what might be included the principles section:

Inclusive physical education policy

Principles: what should we do?

These would need to include explicit reference to:
    Whole school responsibilities
    Department and (where appropriate) responsibilities
    Positive attitudes and expectations
    Consideration of special educational needs as an integral part of
    curriculum development
    The assessment of individual needs
    Inclusion
    Support (school-based)
    Support (external advice)
    Partnership with parents
    Partnership with pupils.

(Adapted from Beveridge 1996: 68)

Careful thinking about policy principles should lead to the establishment of policy procedures (e.g. resource allocation, staff development activity) that result in the needs of all pupils being met as equitably as possible. A particularly useful feature of the four-part policy framework outlined above is its monitoring and evaluative component (performance), enabling the efficacy of inclusive physical education policy and practice to be gauged.

In the light of earlier discussion in this chapter concerning changing concepts of needs, it might in future be more appropriate for schools to replace special educational needs policies with policies for inclusive learning. Examples of these have already been developed at local education authority (LEA) (Newham LEA 1997) and school (Alderson 1999) levels. Such policies, by definition, are intended to be pervasive and to underpin teaching in all subjects. The recently published *Index for Inclusion* (Centre for Studies on Inclusive Education 2000), available in all schools, may provide additional guidance for work of this kind.

ITE and continuing professional development

Physical education teachers need access to good quality ITE and continuing professional development if more equitable and inclusive provision is to gather pace and become sustainable. In this regard, parallels can be drawn with concerns about the absence of equal opportunities provision within such programmes (Evans and Davies 1993b, Flintoff 1993), a matter highlighted in Chapter 2 of this book. Difficulties of this kind, combined with concerns about the impoverished nature of special educational needs and inclusive education provision generally within ITE (Robertson 1999a, Special Educational Needs Training Consortium 1996) reflect a failure to take proper account of the true nature of inclusive education. Two important points to note here are:

- without well-educated teachers, equalising opportunities for pupils in inclusive learning contexts will not be possible in the mid to long term
- commitment to inclusive practice requires that all teacher education, whether ITE or continuing professional development, should be inclusive from the outset.

If these points are accepted, then a serious review of teacher education, particularly in ITE is required. Within the physical education curriculum for teachers there needs to be:

- The development of pedagogic skills, a number of which have been outlined in this chapter, in theory and in practice. For further details see the suggested further reading list at the end of this chapter. The development of these skills would need to be accompanied by development of conceptual knowledge and understanding of the inclusive physical education curriculum.
- The development of knowledge, skills and understanding in collaborative working practice (Lacey and Lomas 1993). In the past fifteen years schools throughout the United Kingdom have employed increasing numbers of learning support assistants (LSAs), or classroom assistants (Clayton 1993). Optimal use needs to be made of these new professionals (Balshaw 1999; Fox 1998) within physical education teaching. Similarly, of course, LSAs need appropriate training to be able to carry out their work effectively. Collaboration skills are also important in working with a range other professionals and volunteers working with schools.
- The development of a critical understanding of disability equality issues (Cashling 1993; Oliver 1996), including the relationship between these and equal opportunity issues pertaining to gender and race. This critical understanding should also be developed through pedagogic practice, and reflection on the nature and purpose of the physical education curriculum.

If teachers, particularly those wishing to offer a specialism in physical education to schools, have completed a curriculum of the kind described briefly here, then the benefits that follow are likely to be manifold. Pupils should gain from enhanced pedagogic expertise, but so too should other members of staff who do not have such specialist skills in the physical education domain (Robertson 1999b). Sharing knowledge and expertise in this way should greatly enhance the inclusive capability of schools.

Conclusion

This chapter has considered a number of issues important to the development of inclusive physical education. It has been argued that though equality of provision for all learners, including those currently described as having special educational needs, may be a problematic ideal, it is nevertheless one worth striving towards. This striving must be located in the practice of schooling as expressed in the curriculum and its associated pedagogy. In this regard, good practice in physical education should intersect and overlap with other good practice in schools. It also needs to be reflected in school policies and the ITE and the continuing professional development of teachers through their careers. Finally, but arguably most importantly, moves towards equality in educational provision need to based on a thorough understanding of educational needs, and recent developments in thinking about the nature and meaning of disability.

Questions for reflection

1   What immediately comes to mind when you consider children with special educational needs? Does this tell you anything about your preconceptions or your concerns? How might these factors affect your approaches to teaching?
2   Does the philosophy of inclusion in physical education require more debate? Is it possible to achieve in today's National Curriculum? What are the implications for all children? Who is in the position to make change? Where is *your* responsibility in this debate?
3   In reflecting on the features of inclusion identified in the section of this chapter entitled *Special Educational Needs and Equality*, what are the implications of this view of inclusion for the teaching of physical education?
4   In relation to the section in this chapter entitled *A Curriculum for All: Rhetoric and Reality* what could be done to make the physical education curriculum more inclusive? Are there specific examples of physical education activities, not found in the current NCPE that ought to be included?

Further reading

Access to the curriculum

Kenward, H. (1997) *Integrating Pupils with Physical Disabilities in Mainstream Schools*, London: David Fulton.
Pickles, P. (1998) *Managing the Curriculum for Children with Severe Motor Difficulties*, London: David Fulton.

Developing pedagogical skills in inclusive physical education

British Association of Advisers and Lecturers in Physical Education (BAALPE) (1996) *Physical Education for Pupils with Special Educational Needs in Mainstream Education*, BAALPE, Dudley: Dudley LEA Publications.

Brown, B. (1998) 'Constructive learning in physical education', in M. Littledyke and L. Huxford (eds), *Teaching the Primary Curriculum for Constructivist Learning*, London: David Fulton.

Knight, E. and Chedzoy, S. (1998) *Physical Education in Primary Schools: Access for All*, London: David Fulton.

Pointer, B. (1993) *Movement Activities for Children with Learning Difficulties*, London: Jessica Kingsley.

Sherrill, C. (1998) *Adapted Physical Activity, Recreation and Sport: Cross Disciplinary and Lifespan* (5th edn), Madison, Wis.: Brown and Benchmark.

Stewart, D. (1990) *The Right to Movement: Motor Development in Every School*, Basingstoke: Falmer.

Sugden, D. and Talbot, M. (1996) *Physical Education for Children with Special Needs in Mainstream Education*, Leeds: Carnegie National Sports Development Centre.

Wright. H. and Sugden, D. (1999) *Physical Education for All: Developing Physical Education in the Curriculum for Pupils with Special Educational Needs*, London: David Fulton.

Inclusive schools

Alderson, P. (ed.) (1999) *Learning and Inclusion: The Cleves School Experience*, written by staff and pupils of the Cleves School, Newham, London, London: David Fulton.

Thomas, G., Walker, D. and Webb, J. (1998) *The Making of the Inclusive School*, London: Routledge.

Disability and equality

Campbell, J. and Oliver, M. (1996) *Disability Politics: Understanding Our Past, Changing Our Future*, London: Routledge.

Johnstone, D. (1998) *An Introduction to Disability Studies*, London: David Fulton.

Oliver, M. (1996) *Understanding Disability: from Theory to Practice*, Basingstoke: Macmillan.

Oliver, M. and Barnes, C. (1998) *Disabled People and Social Policy: From Exclusion to Inclusion*, London: Longman.

Swain, J. Finkelstein, V. French, S. and Oliver, M. (1993) *Disabling Barriers – Enabling Environments*, London: Sage.

4 Valuing cultural diversity: the challenge for physical education

Tansin Benn

Introduction

It is an opportune time to consider policies and practice in physical education that relate to 'race', 'ethnicity' or 'cultural diversity'. Following the much publicised death of Stephen Lawrence, apparently for no other reason than the colour of his skin, the inquiry leading to the Macpherson Report recommended that education should have a fuller role in the prevention of racism and: 'that consideration be given to amendment of the National Curriculum aimed at valuing cultural diversity and preventing racism, in order better to reflect the needs of a diverse society' (Macpherson Report 1999: para. 67).

Similarly, the Office for Standards in Education (OFSTED), using geographically-based terms to define ethnic membership for settled British communities, recently reported on *Raising the Attainment of Ethnic Minority Pupils*, focusing on those from Bangladeshi, Pakistani, Black Caribbean and Gypsy Traveller backgrounds. Despite pockets of good practice, the report found that many schools and Local Education Authorities (LEAs) are not effective in tackling underachievement by ethnic minority groups and that underachievement 'fuels prejudice and stereotypical attitudes towards minority ethnic groups' (OFSTED 1999a: 54). If the Macpherson Report definition of 'institutional racism' is accepted as:

> The collective failure of an organisation to provide an appropriate and professional service to people because of their colour, culture or ethnic origin. It can be seen or detected in processes, attitudes and behaviour which amount to discrimination through unwitting prejudice, ignorance and thoughtlessness and racist stereotyping which disadvantages minority ethnic people.
>
> (Macpherson Report 1999: 6.34)

then, the OFSTED (1999a) evidence indicates that institutional racism exists in some sectors of education.

How can the physical education profession address this issue? This chapter attempts to highlight the complexity of the debate in two distinct parts. The first part of the chapter contextualises the debate, focusing on the challenge of defining terms, examining the wider educational picture, and identifying issues of 'cultural diversity' and physical education. A focus on 'Muslim pupils' permeates the first part of the chapter and becomes the in-depth illustrative example of the complexities surrounding 'cultural diversity' and physical education in the second part of the chapter. A more interactive style is adopted in the second part of the chapter, enabling readers to reflect on and discuss key questions aimed at identifying and resolving areas of potential tension between physical education teachers and Muslim pupils. The complexity of the issues is illustrated through a particular focus on British Muslims because Muslims cross many boundaries of 'race', language and heritage, yet are united by Islam, their universal religious faith. The evidence of discrimination on the grounds of religion, in the Runnymede Trust (1997) *Islamophobia – a Challenge to Us All* and the complexity of overlapping disadvantage, with the majority of British Muslims being of Asian heritage, make this a particularly pertinent focus.

Cultural diversity: definition and context

It is not difficult to demonstrate the complexity and controversy of addressing issues of cultural diversity and physical education. Areas such as dance have been praised as a means of celebrating and valuing cultural diversity (Arts Council 1993; Brinson 1991; Semple 1993). Yet advice to British Muslims suggests that 'dance has no academic significance or value, nor does it contribute positively to meaningful knowledge' (Sarwar 1994). Teachers who encourage black youngsters into sporting success risk accusations of racism since they could be side-tracking them from more serious academic pursuits (Chappell 1995). How can teachers provide a more 'inclusive' experience for all pupils? The area is complex and sensitive, yet persistence is vital to seek deeper understanding of issues related to 'valuing cultural diversity'. It means positive action, challenge to, and change in, traditional practice if there is going to be space for difference and greater equality of opportunity.

Initially, it is necessary to understand the related issues of 'race', ethnicity and cultural diversity. Defining terms is an ongoing challenge in the attempt to achieve clarity in thinking about cultural diversity. Are we referring to distinctive groups of people differentiated on the grounds of, for example, 'race', ethnicity, religion, language, nationality, geographical location or heritage? Reflecting on terms such as 'race', ethnicity and culture emphasises the complexity of the issue.

'Race' remains in parenthesis to denote that it is problematic. The term is based on a socially constructed categorisation of people by phenotypical features and genetically transmitted traits such as skin colour (Coakley 1994: 240, Figueroa,1993: 92). This is not to underestimate the significance of reinforcing areas of social inequality, for example religion, gender and 'race' in the experiences of Asian Muslim women. The racialisation of religion cannot be ignored, particularly in relation to Islam where the majority of British Muslims are still of

Asian heritage. According to Sahgal and Yuval-Davis (1992: 15), it is a phenomenon of the post-Rushdie era, when basic human rights of 'freedom of expression' and 'religious freedom' clashed and Muslim fundamentalism fueled islamophobia in Britain.

'Ethnicity' is also difficult to define and use without contention (Jenkins 1997) but is more inclusive than 'race'. Ethnicity is concerned with culture and cultural differentiation. It concerns ways in which people usually choose to define themselves as distinctive from others. This is different from 'race' where membership is not a choice (Banton 1983, cited in Jenkins 1997: 81). Ethnic groups are included under the 1976 Race Relations Act which protects people against discrimination on the grounds of colour, race, nationality, ethnic and national origins. Ethnic groups are defined as sharing a long 'history and a cultural tradition of their own, which they and outsiders regard as characterising them as a distinct community' (Runnymede Trust 1997: 57). While Sikhs and Jews are defined as ethnic groups and therefore protected, in the eyes of the law, Muslims are not. Yet Muslims, alongside Sikhs, Jews and other 'distinctive groups,' all share the same potential for being victims of belief systems that rank different groups as superior or inferior to each other, leading to prejudice and discriminatory practices affecting the life-chances of members.

'Cultural diversity' is a more inclusive term since it is not bound by political or legal strictures. Figueroa (1993) suggested language, including dialect, and religious difference are embraced by the term 'cultural diversity'. It allows for a more open vision of cultures influenced by and influencing each other in living, dynamic 'cultures of hybridity' (Hall 1992, cited in Jenkins 1997: 30). Globalisation in one sense drives everyone in a more homogeneous direction. Yet, with increasing global cultural diversity comes the search for distinctiveness, for ways of maintaining preferred values and meanings in life 'within' groups while sharing a sense of belonging with 'other' groups.

'Culture' embraces a much wider notion than 'race' or 'ethnicity', yet is subsumed into everyday lived experiences of both. It involves shared meanings and understanding, as well as divergence and conflict, produced through interaction with other human beings. Individuals make sense of their world in relation to the meanings created by and within social groups. Attitudes, values and beliefs are passed on within cultures, but culture is dynamic, the rate and resistance to change varying in different cultures at different times. In an ethnographic sense culture means a 'whole way of life of a particular group of people . . . (when) work, leisure, family, religion, community etc. are woven into a fabric of tradition consisting of customs, ways of seeing, beliefs, attitudes, values, standards, styles, ritual practices etc.' (Hargreaves 1986: 9).

Culture can also refer to the activities, institutions and processes that reproduce systems of meaning such as education, religion, the media and the family. The survival of a culture, of maintaining a distinctive identity, is always dependent on an active process, utilising relational power within and between cultures, in the process of development.

In these macro and micro senses it is appropriate to use the term 'culture' in relation to the meanings inherent within the guidelines religion offers to its followers related to, for example, life-style, diet, dress codes and behaviour. In the same sense the term can be applied to education and physical education because they reflect and reinforce values and meanings, actively pursued in the interests of sustaining a particular world-view. The significance of culture cannot be underestimated: 'If the power of culture were acknowledged in its institutional and conceptual control, we would be nearer to explaining the power of the dominant culture in structuring the experiences of ethnic minorities' (Saifullah Khan 1987: 229).

Cultural diversity and education

At a macro level education is a dynamic institution that carries specific, inherent values and meanings and passes them on from generation to generation. At a micro level individuals cope with the 'everyday', with shaping and interpreting their lives in relation to interactions with others. The micro is not separate from the macro. They are reciprocally influenced and influencing. The experiences of any minority group reflects the wider society in which they are situated. Therefore schools and teachers have a role to play, for example in eradicating racism:

> It has often been said that schools 'cannot do it alone' against the forces of racial inequality, prejudice and social exclusion that are outside their gates but reach into the classroom. While that may be true, and offer some comfort to those schools who feel they are constantly battling against the odds, it must not become an excuse for failure to take action
> (OFSTED 1999a: 54–5)

The dilemma of moving towards greater valuing of cultural diversity is related to what Bullivant (1981) called the 'pluralist dilemma' in Western societies which results from the juxtaposition of different, but unequal, cultures within a democratic and liberal society. Education in such a society is problematic because the cultural preferences of the dominant group are legitimated through, in England and Wales, a statutory content-based National Curriculum: 'the National Curriculum attempts to homogenise the educational experiences that children receive in the state schools; it sets out to make individuals 'more the same' (Evans *et al.* 1996: 3).

Education is a facet of culture through which future generations are initiated into particular ways of knowing, values, interpretations of meaning and significance. The introduction of a content-based National Curriculum has been criticised as a symbol of the myth of monoculturalism with the potential to further disadvantage minority groups who share different cultures. Not only have aspects such as the 'subject boundedness' and hierarchical nature of the National Curriculum been criticised, but also the narrowly white and English concept of

'National' in the National Curriculum. Subject content has been criticised, for example in History, and aspects such as 'traditional British dances' that slipped into the post-Dearing (Dearing 1994) Physical Education reforms (Department for Education/Welsh Office (DfE/WO) 1995). The re-affirmation of Christian traditions were also legitimised through the Education Reform Act (ERA 1988), another demonstration of the way in which 'the British state privileges Christianity' (Sahgal and Yuval-Davis 1992: 3).

Research has indicated that children from minority cultures are differentially disadvantaged within the education system (OFSTED 1999a). Nevertheless, individuals from all minority cultures are often victims of racism from a very early age, for example the prejudice against Asian children and teachers identified by Wright (1992), and there is much current concern to improve the situation (OFSTED 1999a).

The culture of physical education

Physical education is a school subject with its own culture, based in a history that dates back to the nineteenth century. This includes values and meanings maintained and perpetuated though principles, practices and policies that permeate the subject. The established culture influences what is taught and how under the umbrella of physical education. Like any culture this is not static, as changes in dress codes in physical education during the last century reflect. Any change is the outcome of a struggle between influential 'gatekeepers' who are in privileged positions to enable or constrain new initiatives. How is cultural diversity reflected in the working parties which contributed to the re-making of the National Curriculum, and how is cultural diversity being addressed by those key people? How much change has there been since earlier reports found that 'there is little evidence that members of minority groups have much influence in . . . educational process' (Higher Education Funding Council for England (HEFCE) 1993 and 1995; Swan 1985).

Hargreaves (1986: 166) described physical education as the most culturally ritualistic aspect of the school curriculum. Implicit in what and how the subject is taught are non-verbal communication systems expressing coded messages. These include control over pupils' bodies, relating to where and how they move in space, how they 'look' via rules on dress, how bodies are 'maintained' via hygiene practices, all serving to discipline the body by exerting power over the presentation of self, actions and behaviour. Where meanings and values are differently attached by minority groups to the body, dress codes, behaviour and activity patterns, for example within Islam, there is potential for conflict.

Research on cultural diversity and physical education

Inadequacies in addressing the needs of ethnic minority pupils in physical education was recognised by OFSTED as a weakness in both secondary and primary schools (Clay 1997). In relation to research relating to ethnic minorities and physical education and sport, most attention has been on black youngsters of African-Caribbean heritage. Bayliss (1989) summarised the position at the end of the 1980s, concerning the ways in which issues of racial stereotyping in physical education and their implications for teachers were being recognised and addressed. Research on physiological and psychological differences in black athletes, subsequently discredited as scientific racism and pseudo-science, was influential (Cashmore 1996). Alongside a legacy of 'racist logic' (Coakley 1994: 243), the 'evidence' fuelled myths underpinning teacher-pupil interaction. These myths included suggestions that: African-Caribbean pupils were poor swimmers because they had heavy bones; blacks were good at sport because slavery weeded out the weak; all blacks had a natural sense of rhythm and therefore were good at dance; Asians were too frail for contact sports; and blacks were good at boxing because they could absorb a heavier beating (Bayliss 1989). The outcome for some pupils was a channelling into or away from particular sporting activities, with repercussions on academic expectations. Efforts to improve the situation rested on the 'problematic approach' which placed 'the problem for physical education' within the culture, for example within the culture of being a Muslim woman. This perspective failed to examine the appropriateness of experiences on offer, that is, to critique what was 'going on' in institutional practices. 'A commitment to equity demands that we scrutinise the nature of experiences that are distributed through the curriculum' (Evans 1993, cited in McGuire and Collins 1998: 80), and recognise the deeper racial tensions in wider society. 'It is dangerous, if not downright racist, to concentrate on culture and hope that racism will go away' (Bayliss 1989, cited in McGuire and Collins 1998: 19).

Chappell (1995) identified increasing evidence of racial stereotyping in particular sports including football, rugby union and basketball. Over-representation of blacks of African-Caribbean heritage in some sports and some positions on teams in those sports reflected wider stereotyping influencing the professional sports world as well as the attitudes of teachers. 'It is felt that teachers think (black children) are fast, strong and play with good instinct, whereas white children are thought to show qualities of leadership, intelligence and emotional control' (Maguire 1991, cited in McGuire and Collins 1998: 26).

The research evidence has shown growing awareness of the needs of particular groups. For example, evidence suggested the need for increased physical activity levels among people of South Asian origin as mortality and morbidity levels from coronary heart disease were highest among this group (Sevak *et al.* 1994). Research related to physical education and sport and Asian communities has suggested that they do not always have the same cultural significance as in the dominant culture (Figueroa 1993, Williams 1989c). Carrington and Williams (1988) found, for example, that: ethnicity accentuated the differential rates of sporting participation between males and females; that some Asian parents do exercise greater control over their daughters' participation in community sport because of cultural conflicts; and that some parents actually withdraw their children from physical education. Brah and Minas (1985: 24) reported that Asian girls often found their own 'coping strategies' to survive social conflicts. For example, one account reported the incident of an Asian girl who chose not to tell her parents about her selection for the school sports because she feared they would not let her take part. 'I wanted my parents to be proud of me, but asking them and getting a refusal was too big a risk to take' (cited in Husband 1982: 200).

Not all Asians are Muslims and not all Muslims are Asian. This is a key point. To conflate 'categories' of being Asian and Muslim tends to homogenise all Asians and fails to recognise the particular needs of those who prefer to identify themselves differently, for example as Muslims. In their study on *Raising the Attainment of Minority Ethnic Pupils* OFSTED (1999a: 4) chose particular ethnic groups based on 'geographical' not religious distinctions. Yet, in relation to identifying barriers to improving standards of attainment, within all the groups studied religion will have been differentially important to individuals. In the Pakistani and Bangladeshi groups studied the majority may have been Muslim, but not all. The two schools in the survey that collected data on ethnic minorities found that 'none of the Asian girls opts for physical education' (OFSTED 1999a: 24). This raises questions such as 'Why?' and 'Can the school make any changes that might improve the situation?' The answers might be more closely related to their religious, rather than their Asian, identity.

The findings of the OFSTED (1999a) research indicated that lack of data on the particular progress of ethnic groups is unhelpful. The failure to acknowledge Muslims as an ethnic group equally denies opportunities to collect important data, monitor and respond to specific needs and levels of attainment. De Knop *et al.* (1996) recognised the value of specific research on different ethnic groups and the particular under-representation of research into Muslims as a distinct group.

In relation to the interface of Islam and physical education, knowledge of religious requirements, and ways in which these could be met have been long recognised. Although Parker-Jenkins (1995) and Haw (1998) suggested the situation for Muslim pupils in physical education to be improving, barriers still exist for some and awareness-raising is vital to sensitise teachers to issues that could emerge where Islam and physical education meet (Benn 1996a, 1996b, 1998). Having contextualised the wider debates concerning cultural diversity and physical education, the next part of the chapter uses an interactive approach which aims to engage readers in reflection on issues and strategies for improving practice in physical education.

Focus on Muslim pupils

This section aims to highlight issues specifically related to the needs of Muslim pupils and education. Questions for discussion include a focus on 'Islam and physical education' as well as consideration of equality of opportunity in a wider arena. For example, suggestions have been made that anti-sexist policies could conflict with anti-racist policies in relation to Islam, and the sanctioning of state-supported separate Muslim schools in 1998 remains a recent breakthrough, not without controversy. In relation to physical education, Carroll and Hollinshead's research (1993), on British Muslim secondary girls in physical education, is used to provide a framework for the development of discussion points in this section. Muslim pupils in 'Borin High School' raised the following issues for consideration:

- physical education dress
- showers/changing
- Ramadan
- provision of extra-curricular activities
- dance has been added for further discussion.

Although Siraj-Blatchford (1993) criticised Carroll and Hollinshead's research, for example in failing to recognise the institutional racism that underpinned the lack of accommodation on the part of the school, the issues for consideration listed above are used as focal points for increasing awareness of the interface between physical education and Islam.

In a society committed to improving equity and the valuing of cultural diversity, any policies that force religious transgression, and therefore induce feelings of shame and guilt in some pupils, need to be re-negotiated in the interests of respecting cultural diversity and offering greater equality of opportunity to Muslim pupils. In schools, teachers should work within a 'whole-school' policy relating to equality of opportunity which includes considerations of race and ethnicity. Teachers should, where possible, work with the local community, and with support from local physical education advisers.

Since religious requirements for stricter modesty codes in Islam start at puberty, primary schools may easily presume themselves exempt from the need for such consideration. This is not the case, although there are differences in terms of strictly 'religious requirements'. It is useful to consider the following realities for primary teachers:

- puberty commences in the primary school years for some pupils
- evidence indicates that Muslim children in primary schools already have well-established ideas about their bodies and preferred practices such as separate-sex activities and privacy in changing (Benn 1996a, 1998)
- some Muslim families will be encouraging their children to lead their lives Islamically and to participate in family cultural practices that belong to day-to-day lived experiences.

It is inevitable, then, that some requests to acknowledge Islamic requirements in physical education could be made in the primary school. All teachers, therefore, need to sensitise themselves to the issues involved.

The points which follow are situations in which state and religious directives could conflict with physical education and therefore, readers may wish to consider each scenario, with the help of the *discussion questions*. First, it is useful to consider general parameters at the interface of physical education and Islam.

Is participation in physical education anti-Islamic?

Participation in physical education is not anti-Islamic. Care of the body and participation in physical activity for health and well-being is valued in Islam, equally for girls and boys (Daiman 1995, Sfeir 1985). The proviso is that Islamic requirements are met after puberty. Privacy in changing, modest clothing and single-sex lessons post-puberty are preferred, and are 'essential in swimming' (Sarwar 1994: 13). This includes the necessity for a same-sex pool environment. More problematic is the activity area of dance (Sarwar 1994). Each of these aspects is addressed under points 1 to 5 below. In reflecting on these matters it is interesting to note the following advice to British Muslims:

> Sometimes schools find that they are unable to fulfill all of the requirements of Muslim children. In such circumstances head teachers should exempt their Muslim pupils from those areas where they cannot meet the Islamic requirements. It is our experience that schools where head teachers respond positively in such situations provide more harmonious and balanced learning environments.
>
> (Sarwar 1994: 14)

What are the implications of this statement?

Traditional dress requirements for physical education

This can cause conflict for Muslim girls and boys who are required by their religion to keep their arms and legs covered, completely for girls and from navel to knee for boys, essentially from puberty onwards. 'Clothing should not be revealing or skin-tight. Muslim children should, therefore, be allowed to wear sportswear compatible with Islamic dress code' (Sarwar 1994: 12). Post-puberty some Muslim female pupils may choose to adopt the hijab or headscarf as a symbol of their faith. Many would want to keep this on in any public space or in mixed-sex company. Teachers need to consider the consequences of dilemmas faced by pupils forced to decide between breaking with religious requirements or school policy requirements. 'For the devout Muslim there is a real feeling of guilt and shame at exposing their bodies and legs, which had not been fully appreciated by the teachers' (Carroll and Hollinshead 1993: 158). What are the issues for the physical education teacher? Are there safety implications? Is it acceptable for the hijab to be worn in physical education?

Communal showers/changing

Practising Muslim pupils are not allowed to expose their bodies, even to members of the same sex, in the interests of modesty and privacy. This affects showering at secondary level and changing at primary level where mixed-sex education and classroom changing for physical education is the norm. Some schools are dropping requirements for showers, others are making it optional for all pupils, while others are rescheduling lessons to enable pupils to go straight home from physical education for a private shower. The problem of mixed-changing at the top end of the primary school, where puberty may have commenced, is more difficult to overcome with constraints on resources, facilities and staffing. How could privacy in changing be fostered at the top end of some primary schools where buildings and staffing structures do not cater for separate-sex changing? Is this a real hygiene risk? What are the advantages and disadvantages of optional showers at the end of a physical education lesson? Are there alternatives?

Ramadan

During Ramadan, practising Muslims fast for approximately one month from sunrise to sunset. Muslim pupils could therefore be going without food and drink for the whole day. Participation in strenuous physical activity at such times could be distressing and uncomfortable. As pupils sweat during activity they are unable to replenish body fluid levels until sunset. Since no water is meant to enter the mouth during fasting time, swimming could be particularly problematic. What are the implications of a physical education department not responding to those pupils who wish to fast during Ramadan? What arrangements could be made to accommodate fasting pupils during Ramadan? How could you address the swimming difficulty?

Extra-curricular involvement

It can be difficult for some Muslim boys and girls to engage in extra-curricular activities after school as they may be required to attend Mosque or contribute in other ways to family life. What strategies could you adopt to facilitate greater participation in extra-curricular activities by Muslim pupils?

Dance

Sarwar suggested that dance has no educational value since it contravenes Islamic limits on certain topics:

> these include a modest dress code, the prohibition of many types of music, the means to prevent the arousal of the human being's base feelings outside of marriage (*sexuality*), and the prohibition of free-mixing of the sexes . . . It is clear to see that dance as is generally practised is not allowed for Muslims.
> (Sarwar 1994: 13–14)

This is the most difficult area to address and one that requires further dialogue to exchange views on the educational value of dance. Does the statement correctly summarise what is 'generally practised' in dance in schools? Such questions have been asked by Muslim student-teachers who had the opportunity to participate in 'dance in education' courses. They contested the notion expressed by Sarwar (see Benn 1996a and 1996b). This is not to suggest that dance is completely unproblematic for some Muslims. Increased sensitivity can lead to planning and teaching that avoids aspects that could be offensive, for example pop music and tight-fitting lycra leotards. However, there is a need for more research into the interface of dance in education and Islam since there is no consensus on dance or music within Islam (Parker-Jenkins 1995). Dance does use the body as an instrument of expression but to suggest that all dance movements are sexually motivated, intended or interpreted is equally offensive to those committed to dance in education. How would you respond to the suggestion that dance has no 'academic significance or value nor does it contribute to meaningful human knowledge'? What themes or approaches to dance would you take in a strong Muslim community? If there were no middle way, on religious grounds, for some Muslim pupils to participate in dance or music what would be your response?

Equality of opportunity for Muslim pupils in physical education: an anti-sexist/anti-racist dilemma?

One dilemma that might be faced by teachers empowering Muslim girls through physical education/sport participation is the apparent clash of anti-racist/anti-sexist strategies. 'Empowerment to both women and Muslim culture, would cause a cultural clash' (Carroll and Hollinshead 1993: 165). This is rooted in the assumption that Muslim women have a particular, subservient role to play in Muslim communities and therefore to empower them is to move beyond the wishes of the group (see the Walkling and Brannigan (1986, 1987) Troyna and Carrington (1987) debate). More correctly, this is rooted in what has been called 'Pakistani and Bangladeshi culture' as opposed to 'real Islam' (Benn 1998). In 'real Islam' women do have particular roles, but these are regarded as equally valued to the roles of men. Choice, rights and active participation in all aspects of life is encouraged. This is not to suggest that what might be regarded as unacceptable practices have not been done to girls and women in the name of Islam but, as increasing numbers of young people, students and other scholars return to the roots of 'authentic Islam' (Madood 1992), then greater understanding of the positive position of women in Islam will spread (Jawad 1998). In British Muslim communities these issues will be differentially influential in shaping attitudes towards participation in physical activity, particularly by girls and women. What do you know about the position and rights of women in Islam? Do you think the rights of the individual should come before the rights of a 'group'?

Having looked at Islam and physical education, the next section of the chapter considers briefly the wider debate. It looks at the issue of separate

Muslim schools, then finishes by looking at open and closed views of cultural diversity.

Separatism: a way forward?

The issue of separate Muslim schools for Muslim families who would prefer to educate their children in this way has been contentious. Research has indicated that an education in a Muslim school can be more empowering for Muslim girls than an education in the state system because pupils build confidently on their preferred identity and therefore are better prepared for adult life (Haw 1998). In England two Muslim schools received state approval and support for the first time in 1998 after a long and sometimes bitter struggle. The debate revolves around issues of equity, justice and fairness. In this country Christianity and the Church have nurtured much educational provision. Many state supported schools still exist for those parents and pupils who would prefer to be educated in a faith context, such as Catholic, Church of England or Jewish. While this option remains for some faiths, what justification could be used for refusing Muslims the right to educate their children in their preferred type of school? Perhaps fear and transmissionist rather than transformative views of Muslim education, with particular concern over the education of girls, are possible reasons for the reticence to move in favour of the establishment of state supported Muslim schools. Is this equality of opportunity? Perhaps the delay in acceptance of Muslim schools is more attributable to the relatively powerless position of the Muslim community, not only in Britain but also in Europe. In his work on Muslims in Europe, Nielsen suggested that 'the Muslim communities, always a religious minority and usually also an immigrant and ethnic minority, are relatively powerless communities in the face of the majority economic, social and political structures' (Nielsen 1986: 37). What are the advantages and disadvantages of separate schools for Muslim pupils? Do you think schools supported by a religious denomination should receive state support in a predominantly secular society?

Open and closed views of cultural diversity

Finally, the Runnymede Trust report on Islamophobia (1997: 5) offered a useful framework for understanding positive ('Open') and negative ('Closed') views on Islam that underpinned interaction, attitudes, behaviour and actions. Where views of Islam were 'open', that is, where Islam was seen as a positive religion, *living, interacting, with potential for dialogue, rational debate and shared understanding*, relations between Muslims and non-Muslims could be mutually beneficial and enhancing. Where views of Islam were 'closed', that is where Islam was seen as a negative religion, *the 'enemy' of the West, intolerant, manipulative, fundamentalist, monolithic and unyielding*, relations between Muslims and non-Muslims were negatively influenced. It is possible to adapt the model, for application on a wider cultural scale, to identify attitudes capable of influencing inclusive or exclusive practices in education, including physical education. In this way individuals and institutions can reflect on their own 'positions' and work more positively towards 'valuing cultural diversity'.

Open views of cultural diversity (leading to inclusion)

Open views of cultural diversity see culture as:

- fluid to a point, diverse and progressive, with internal differences, debates and development
- interdependent with other cultures, having certain shared values and capable of being affected by and enriching them
- distinctly different but equally worthy of respect
- an actual or potential partner in joint cooperative enterprises and in the solution of shared problems
- capable of entering criticism and debate about own and other cultures.

Closed views of cultural diversity (leading to exclusion)

Closed views of cultural diversity see culture as:

- static and unresponsive to new realities, closed to debate, change or development
- separate and unable to interact with other cultures, having no shared values and not being capable of being affected by or enriching them
- inferior
- 'enemy', 'outsider', clashing with other cultures
- criticisms rejected out of hand, incapable of debate.

Few, if any, teachers would deny the desirability of striving to improve ways in which cultural diversity is valued, acknowledged and respected in education. Much has been learned through research, yet evidence also indicates there is much left to achieve. The layers of complexity make this a sensitive and political path since greater equity, and therefore a re-thinking of current systems, values and traditions, is required. This is a challenge to the whole of society and physical education has a key role. The subject's 'visibility' makes the choice of an in-depth look at the needs of Muslim pupils particularly relevant. There are no easy solutions, one reason being that issues of prejudice and discrimination are part of a wider social picture. Cultural diversity means increasing knowledge and awareness across different cultures, finding ways to respect and make room for difference. The adaptation of the Runnymede Trust's (1997) framework of 'open' and 'closed' views of culture is proposed as a guide towards positive ways of viewing cultural differences which can lead to policies of inclusion. Accusations of institutional racism or of failing to meet the needs of particular pupils are unwelcome, but that should not prevent the physical education profession from being critical of systems and practices which might be less relevant to the culturally diverse needs of children of the next millennium than to those of the last.

Questions for reflection

1 Does ethnicity restrict access to physical education, or physical education restrict access for some ethnic groups?
2 Discuss the advantages and disadvantages of a secular education system, such as France, where all religious symbols remain outside the school environment.
3 You are head of physical education in a school and have built an excellent reputation for the work of your department over the last five years. You have a request to consider dress concessions, on religious grounds, by a Muslim family that has moved into the area. How do you respond?
4 What strategies could you incorporate in your school which reflect 'valuing cultural diversity' in a meaningful and integrated way?
5 Is it possible to value cultural diversity in an education system that 'sets out to make individuals "more the same" (Evans, et al. 1996).
6 If you met stereotypical or closed views of 'difference' among colleagues or pupils, would you respond, and if so how?

Further reading

Carroll, B. and Hollinshead, G. (1993) 'Race and gender in physical education: a case study', in J. Evans (ed.), *Equality, Education and Physical Education*, London: Falmer: 154–69.

Chappell, R. (1995) 'Racial stereotyping in schools', *Bulletin of Physical Education* 31 (4): 22–8.

Figueroa, P. (1993) 'Equality, multiculturalism, antiracism and physical education in the National Curriculum', in J. Evans (ed.), *Equality, Education and Physical Education*, London: Falmer: 90–102.

McGuire, B. and Collins, D. (1998) 'Sport, ethnicity and racism: the experience of Asian heritage boys', *Sport, Education and Society* 3 (1): 79–88.

OFSTED (1999a) *Raising the Attainment of Minority Ethnic Pupils: School and LEA Responses*, London: OFSTED.

Runnymede Trust (1997) *Islamophobia: A Challenge for us All*, London: Runnymede Trust.

Part III

Issues concerned with teaching and learning

5 Approaches to teaching games

Susan Capel

Introduction

Participation in physical activity outside and post-school has been reported as being low (e.g. Cale 1997; Sports Council 1995a, 1995b; Thirlaway and Benton 1993). One reason for this may be that young people are 'turned off' physical education and report negative attitudes towards physical activity post-school (Coakley and White 1992; Sports Council 1995a, 1995b). Further, the performance of national sports teams in international competition has been criticised and initiatives have been undertaken to improve their performance (e.g. *Sport: Raising the Game* (Department of National Heritage (DNH) 1995); *Labour's Sporting Nation* (Labour Party 1996); *England, The Sporting Nation: A Strategy* (English Sports Council (ESC) 1997). Concerns about low participation and about the poor performance of national sports teams have led to questions being asked about the way in which games are taught in schools.

This chapter promotes reflection on the teaching of games in curriculum time. Consideration is given to teaching games across the whole of compulsory schooling (5 to 16 years). First, the chapter looks at what games are, then describes a classification of games. It looks at links between games in primary and secondary school before considering two different approaches to teaching games: the traditional skills-based approach; and the Teaching Games for Understanding (TGFU) approach. The chapter concludes by promoting reflection on the way forward in teaching games.

By the end of this chapter, readers should be able to:

- reflect on current practice in teaching games
- consider different approaches to teaching games and some potential advantages and disadvantages of these approaches
- use different approaches to teaching games in lessons according to aims and objectives of units of work and specific lessons.

In reflecting on the teaching of games it is first necessary to be clear about what games are.

What are games?

Games have several distinct features. They involve acquiring certain skills/techniques, using those skills/techniques and applying tactics and strategies to solve particular problems within a set of rules that provide a structure. Games have been defined as, for example,

> a struggle for territorial dominance within a set of rules (structural parameters) which includes significant strategic (cognition) and technical (action) aspects and in which coincidence anticipation is paramount. The struggle for territorial dominance is decided by a system of scoring which symbolises the extent of victory. The code of rules identifies the problem and ensures that both teams or individuals meet on an equal basis
>
> (Brackenridge 1979, cited in Almond 1986a: 73)

Classification of games

Games have been classified into different types. A number of different classifications have been identified, each with different groupings. The classification perhaps more commonly used in England is shown in Table 5.1.

When referring to games, reference is most commonly being made to invasion games. This is for a number of reasons, e.g. the content of school curricula is biased heavily towards invasion games. For example, OFSTED

Table 5.1 Classification of games

Invasion	Net/Wall	Fielding/Run-scoring	Target
Basketball	*Net*	Baseball	Billiards
Football	Badminton	Cricket	Bowls
Handball	Platform Tennis	Rounders	Croquet
Hockey	Table Tennis	Softball	Curling
Ice Hockey	Tennis		Golf
Lacrosse	Volleyball		Pool
Netball			Pub Skittles
Rugby	*Wall*		Snooker
Water polo	Jai Alai		Ten Pin Bowling
	Racketball		
	Squash		
	Some of these are played with an implement, others with hand(s); some have a focused target, others have an open-ended target		

Source: adapted from Thorpe, Bunker and Almond 1984: 71–2

found that 'in a substantial proportion of schools the curriculum over emphasises games, in particular invasion games' (OFSTED 1995a: 12). (This issue is
considered further in Chapter 7 of this book.)

Further, many of the games that are most commonly considered an important
part of the cultural heritage of the United Kingdom are invasion games, e.g.
football, hockey, netball, rugby. Games which are part of the cultural heritage,
but which are not invasion games, e.g. cricket and tennis, are however, often
included when talking about games. For example, when referring to 'great traditional sports' that are part of the cultural heritage of the United Kingdom, the
then Prime Minister John Major, in his letter that accompanied the document
Sport: Raising the Game (DNH 1995), referred to cricket, football, hockey,
netball, rugby, tennis 'and the like', as well as athletics and swimming. These
latter two are not classified as games, but may be considered important in terms
of cultural heritage.

Games do, however, need to be considered in the context of teaching in
physical education. First, consideration is given to games in primary and
secondary schools.

Teaching games in primary and secondary schools

Links between the teaching of games in primary and secondary schools are
important. A coherent and progressive games experience is needed between ages
five and sixteen, recognising physical, mental and social development of the pupils
at each stage. Primary and secondary teachers therefore need to work together; too
often primary and secondary teachers make curricular decisions in isolation.
Primary teachers need to know what pupils will be progressing to and secondary
teachers need to know the foundations which have been developed in the primary
school. This issue is considered in greater depth in Chapter 12.

Ages up to eleven are vital in the development of fundamental motor skills,
basic movement patterns and the development of attitudes to physical activity
(Armstrong 1990). Full versions of invasion games are more complex than
small-sided games (e.g. 11 *v* 11 football is more complex than 5 *v* 5, for example,
in the number of possible interactions between players). More complex games
may be overwhelming for some young pupils. Small-sided games are more varied,
and provide more opportunities to each pupil to be involved in the play, to try
things out and to develop skills. Primary teachers are responsible for laying the
foundations for pupils to be able to participate in full versions of recognised team
games in secondary schools.

Secondary school teachers are responsible for enabling pupils to play a variety
of games; to provide a foundation for pupils to make a choice about participation
post-school for recreation; and to nurture talent. They need to consider,
therefore, how best to do this for all pupils, building on the foundations laid in
primary schools.

A hierarchy of learning games skills identified by Brown (1987) recognised
development from perceptual and general body management to learning basic

techniques, to individual and partner games, followed by group games, then team games.

Read (1995) identified KS1 as the most crucial period for the development of physical competency, which she identified as containing two elements: movement competency and technical competency. She suggested that the games included in lessons should parallel the development of skilfulness as games give skill its significance. Games should be seen as worthwhile by pupils and should aid their learning. Figure 5.1 suggests how games may be employed at different ages to take account of pupils' maturation and readiness to learn.

Likewise, Coe (1986) produced a model in which children design their own games in the early years of schooling, leading into major games being played in and beyond secondary schools, i.e. games taught from ages five to sixteen are selected and arranged in an order that allows for the development of understanding. Teaching fundamental skills (e.g. throwing, catching, etc.) lays the foundation for future learning, but teachers also need to be sure that

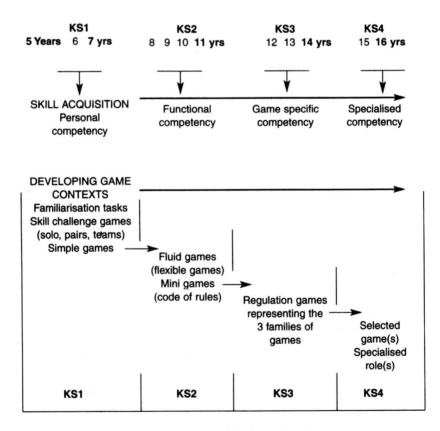

Figure 5.1 Curriculum progression in games: Key Stages 1 to 4
Source: Read 1995: 7

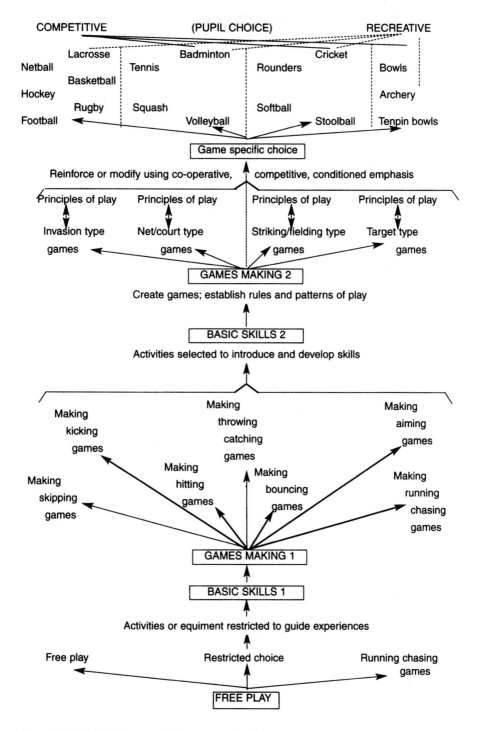

COMPETITIVE   (PUPIL CHOICE)   RECREATIVE

	Lacrosse	Badminton	Cricket	
Netball		Tennis	Rounders	Bowls
	Basketball			
Hockey				Archery
	Rugby	Squash	Softball	
Football		Volleyball	Stoolball	Tenpin bowls

Game specific choice

Reinforce or modify using co-operative, competitive, conditioned emphasis

Principles of play   Principles of play   Principles of play   Principles of play

Invasion type   Net/court type   Striking/fielding type   Target type
games   games   games   games

GAMES MAKING 2

Create games; establish rules and patterns of play

BASIC SKILLS 2

Activities selected to introduce and develop skills

Making   kicking   games

Making   throwing   catching   games

Making   aiming   games

Making   skipping   games

Making   hitting   games

Making   bouncing   games

Making   running   chasing   games

GAMES MAKING 1

BASIC SKILLS 1

Activities or equiment restricted to guide experiences

Free play   Restricted choice   Running chasing games

FREE PLAY

Figure 5.2 Model of framework for games education
Source: Coe 1986: 203

they relate the learning to the interests of the children. This model is shown in Figure 5.2.

A change of focus in teaching games may be required as pupils develop in order to maintain their interest and motivation through meeting their needs at any one particular time. Games should be chosen or designed to suit the learning and development needs of a specific group of pupils at a specific time.

Likewise, consideration needs to be given to the teaching of games at different stages. The next section of the chapter looks at different ways of teaching games. It helps to promote reflection on the question: 'In our games teaching are we, the teachers, making the best use of our resources to help all children achieve optimum potential in the playing and understanding of games?' (Asquith 1989: 76).

Ways of teaching games

One view of how pupils learn to play games is that it is like learning to read or write; basic skills or competencies must be mastered first. This raises the question of what are the basic skills required to play a game effectively. Is there a vocabulary of skills on which a game can be built? Being able to execute a specific motor skill is one competency that needs to be learned. However, analysis of successful games players shows that good motor skill is only one part of effective performance. Good games players need not only to be able to execute skills, they also need to understand the need for the skill and when it is appropriate to use it. The ability to make appropriate decisions during a game has been identified also as an important factor that discriminates between expert and novice performers (McPherson 1995; McPherson and Thomas 1989). Likewise, it has been found that novices learn to make more accurate cognitive decisions during game play faster than they learn to execute necessary skills (French and Thomas 1987; McPherson and French 1991). Thus, good games players need, for example, good motor skills, but also to understand the principles and concepts of the game, tactical awareness, decision-making skills, and to be fit.

If good games players require a number of different skills and attributes, how best are games taught at both primary and secondary level to enable these skills and attributes to be developed? Two approaches to teaching games are considered below. The appropriateness of these different approaches should be considered in relation to a number of factors, e.g. the aims for teaching games; the age of the pupils and their previous experience; the objectives of a particular unit of work and lesson for a particular age group; the skills and attributes required to play a game effectively; and content and teaching approaches which best enable these skills and attributes to be developed. It should be recognised that these two approaches are not the only approaches that can be adopted. They have been selected as they are, perhaps, the two most frequently used. Reflection on these two approaches should help to promote reflection on other approaches to teaching games.

Skills-based approach

Games lessons have traditionally followed a pattern which is repeated for each different game included in the curriculum, which is:

- warm up
- skill learning and practice
- game in which the skill learned or practised is used
- conclusion.

Mawer identified lesson phases and content as:

- a first phase which may be a warm up or introductory activity
- a second phase of development which may include skill development establishing the context for later learning
- a third phase of development extending the second stage into a game; applying knowledge/concepts learned; learning skills identified in an earlier context (such as a game)
- additional phases of development or repetition of a previous phase depending on activity, length of lesson or teaching style
- concluding activity which may take the form of a review, cooling down or calming down.

(Mawer 1995: 86–8)

Thus, in this approach, the emphasis for each game, in each lesson, is on learning a new skill or revising a skill previously learnt and then applying that in a game situation.

Teaching games for understanding (TGFU) approach

The traditional skills-based approach to teaching games puts the how (to do a skill) before the why (reasons for doing the skill). Bunker and Thorpe (1982; 1986a) developed the TGFU approach which takes account of the contextual nature of games, which, they suggested, the skills-based approach, which concentrates on specific motor responses (techniques or skills), has failed to take account of. The TGFU approach is shown in Figure 5.3.

The model starts with the game. Children are introduced to a variety of *game forms*. Their age and experience are taken into account in planning the area/space available, the number of players and equipment to be used. Pupils are presented with problems involved in playing games, e.g. creating space to attack a target while being denied space by the opposition. The long term goal is to build to the full version of the adult game. In *game appreciation* pupils learn to understand the rules of the game to be played (full game rules may be simplified), because rules give the game its shape, place constraints of time and space on the game, state how points are scored, determine the skills required

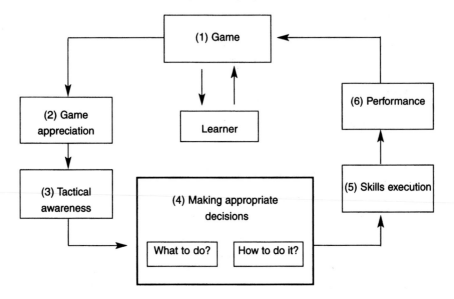

Figure 5.3 Model for games teaching
Source: Bunker and Thorpe 1986a: 10

and have implications for the tactics to be employed. *Tactical awareness* means consideration of tactics to be used, given an understanding of the rules of the game and hence an appreciation of the roles of attack and defence (e.g. ways of creating and denying space, principles of play and picking up the weaknesses of the opposition). *Decision-making* involves both *what to do* and *how to do it*. Players have to decide what to do in the continually changing circumstances of a game, e.g. recognise cues, predict possible outcomes, decide the best way to do it, and select an appropriate response. *Skill execution* is being able to produce the required movement. It includes mechanical efficiency of the movement and its relevance to the particular game situation. *Performance* is the observed outcome of the previous processes, measured against criteria that are independent of the learner and therefore classify the performance as good or poor. The appropriateness of the response and the efficiency of the technique are both important (Bunker and Thorpe 1986a: 7–10). They continued by stressing that

> the sequential aspects of the model are critical. Unlike traditional teaching approaches TGFU starts with a game and its rules which set the scene for the development of tactical awareness and decision making, which, in their turn, always precede the response factors of skill execution and performance. Satisfactory completion of the stages as outlined will necessitate modification of the game leading to a careful re-appraisal of the requirements of the new game. The cycle has begun again.
>
> (Bunker and Thorpe 1986a: 10)

The skills-based and TGFU approaches therefore take a different approach to teaching games. Each approach has advantages and disadvantages, some of which are identified next.

Advantages and disadvantages of skills-based and TGFU approaches

The skills-based approach is familiar to teachers, therefore they are likely to be more confident using it, whereas the TGFU approach is less familiar to teachers, therefore they are likely to be less confident using it

The vast majority of physical education teachers are likely to be familiar with the skills-based approach to teaching games because it has been an important part of their experience of learning to play and to teach games.

Teachers are most likely to have encountered this approach in their own experiences as pupils in school because lessons have traditionally used this approach. Bunker and Thorpe suggested that this is a

> legacy of the 'games afternoon' in which children played one major game throughout the winter terms and another in the summer. The games lesson did become more than a games 'playing' situation as the teacher saw the games lesson as a vehicle in which to develop skills.
>
> (Bunker and Thorpe 1986b: 26)

As many physical education teachers have experienced success in performing skills, they can see the need to develop skills in order to improve performance and are therefore positive about this approach. This success may have led them into teams in which the coaching they received was most likely to have been a skills-based approach.

This approach is also adopted and emphasised in lesson planning on many initial teacher education (ITE) courses, thus reinforcing this approach early in the career of many physical education teachers. Reasons for adopting this approach in ITE courses include tradition, the provision of a structure to enable students to achieve success in their early lessons, and experience. Thus, much of teachers' past experience has led them to be comfortable with, and therefore confident, using this approach.

On the other hand, teachers are less likely to have experience of the TGFU approach, and therefore may lack confidence in trying and/or continuing it. Further, they may have heard rumours about TGFU, for example that skills are not taught in the TGFU approach. These rumours need to be dispelled. To dispel rumours and to enable teachers to gain confidence they need to find out more about the approach. This can partly be achieved through reading about it. However, other support structures are also needed to provide help in what to teach and how this should be organised. For example Almond (1986b: 42–4) suggested group meetings, collaborative research and research-based teaching to support inservice courses which introduce the approach. However, such support may not be available, discouraging teachers from continuing with the approach, even if they start using it.

A further consideration is that resources are more likely to be available to support the skills-based approach. Physical education is influenced by many agencies outside the profession, school and education. One of the major influences on physical education is sport (there is further discussion about physical education and sport in Chapter 8). Many initiatives have been undertaken to improve the performance of national sports teams, particularly in traditional team games. Physical education is seen as an integral part of these initiatives. Further, National Governing Bodies of Sport (NGBs) are interested in attracting new recruits to their sport and therefore many of them have undertaken work to raise the profile of the particular sport in schools. This may result in links being established between schools and NGBs, with specialist coaching being offered in some schools. The approach adopted in teaching and coaching by these coaches and other adults attached to and working in schools is generally a skills-based approach. Further, many teachers have taken NGB awards or been involved in coaching, again reinforcing the skills-based approach. In addition, some governing bodies have produced material which is designed to assist teachers in teaching the sport. Much of this material focuses on the skills-based approach.

Thus, links with, and the impact of, sport and the various bodies associated with sport tend to reinforce the skills-based approach to teaching. Materials and resources are more easily accessible, and therefore provide support for teachers in using this approach.

It is easier to assess learning of skills rather than other aspects of games,
such as decision-making and tactics

Isolated techniques are easier to quantify and measure than other aspects important for participating in a game, e.g. decision-making or tactical play. Thus, compared with other approaches, pupils' learning as the result of a skills-based approach is easier to measure and to assess. It is easier therefore to evaluate how much pupils have learned. The current emphasis on accountability, and hence on systematic summative assessment, recording and reporting, also supports the emphasis in assessment on that which is easiest to measure. Thus, teachers may feel more confident in teaching skills, as they can assess whether the pupils have learned the skill being taught and evaluate more easily the effect of their teaching. On the other hand, the learning as a result of a TGFU approach may be less easy to assess, record and report. Means of assessing the effectiveness of a decision or a tactic need to be considered so that the outcomes of learning through the TGFU approach can be clarified.

For further reflection on the selection of what to assess being based, at least in part, on the ease by which it can be measured, refer to Chapter 6 of this book.

*TGFU encourages decision-making, which fosters pupils' curiosity and
interest, encourages them to be actively involved in their own learning, and
hence motivates them, whereas a skills-based approach does not generally
require pupils to make decisions*

Evidence suggests that the ability to make decisions is one feature which distinguishes between expert and novice players (see above); thus it is an important skill to develop. Grehaigne and Godbout suggested that tactics are an 'adaptation to the opposition' (Grehaigne and Godbout 1995: 491) and that tactical knowledge enables performers to independently construct solutions to the problems related to the configuration of a game. This requires decision-making skills. The TGFU approach to teaching games enables this tactical knowledge to be developed. It is more likely that decision-making skills will be developed through the TGFU approach because it encourages the use of teaching strategies other than didactic strategies, thereby enabling pupils to be actively involved in their own learning. Pupils are allowed to find out for themselves and to solve their own problems (Asquith 1989). Through exploration, experimentation and discovery, pupils' curiosity and interest is fostered; therefore they are more likely to be interested and to enjoy learning, which may increase motivation to learn more and to participate in the activity.

On the other hand, although other teaching styles and strategies are not excluded, a skills-based approach is often accompanied by didactic teaching styles and strategies, in which pupils are told what they have to do. Thus, pupils are not generally required to make decisions. This approach, then, is likely to hamper pupils' ability to make decisions and, hence, to achieve success in playing games.

*TGFU focuses on the child rather than the content, whereas a skills-based
approach focuses on the content rather than the child; it shows clearly who
can and cannot accomplish the skill, and therefore can be demotivating*

In a skills-based approach, less able pupils may never progress to understanding rules and tactics, making decisions and solving problems because they have not developed the skills to enable them to participate in the game. The TGFU approach recognises that not all pupils will achieve high levels of skill in games. In this approach teaching styles and strategies are adopted which accept all pupils on their own terms, with their own level of skills, so that all pupils can achieve some success (Asquith 1989). Although skills are important for playing games and are taught in the TGFU approach, they are taught when the need for them is recognised, e.g. to solve a problem or to be able to carry out a specific tactic. This approach recognises that to be able to participate at a level appropriate to the pupil, other skills are also needed, e.g. to play tennis as a recreational activity requires knowledge of the rules and tactical awareness and an ability to hit the ball; however, it does not require a high level of technical expertise. Pupils can participate in physical activity at their own level as they have an understanding of the requirements to participate. Coe (1986) indicated that many people play games post-school for social reasons or are spectators, even though they do not have a high level of skill in games. Thus, this approach is more likely to meet the needs of individual pupils.

On the other hand, in the skills-based approach, units of work and lessons are developed around the skill to be learned; a pupil either masters the skill or not. The focus is on the skill, therefore the needs of pupils can take second place. The shortcomings of games as an educational experience if poorly taught were identified by Mauldon and Redfern (1981). Further, Bunker and Thorpe observed that:

> present games teaching shows at best, a series of highly structured lessons leaning heavily on the teaching of techniques, or at worst lessons which rely on the children themselves to sustain interest in the game. . . . These approaches have led to:
> a) a large percentage of children achieving little success due to the emphasis on performance, i.e. 'doing'
> b) the majority of school leavers 'knowing' very little about games
> c) the production of supposedly 'skilful' players who in fact possess inflexible techniques and poor decision-making capacity
> d) the development of teacher/coach dependent performers
> e) the failure to develop 'thinking' spectators and 'knowing' administrators at a time when games (and sport) are an important form of entertainment in the leisure industry.
>
> (Bunker and Thorpe 1986a: 7)

Thus, they were fairly condemning of a skills-based approach to teaching. This was endorsed by Thorpe who found that 'conventional approaches to the teaching of tennis have convinced at least 80 per cent of children that they cannot play the game' and suggested that 'methods which are appropriate for small numbers of talented and motivated players in the coaching situation are unlikely to be appropriate for the physical education class of thirty children' (Thorpe 1986: 17).

Asquith (1989: 84) suggested that in any lesson there are likely to be a few pupils who will already have acquired the skill (perhaps from belonging to a club in extra-curricular activities or outside school), many who will never be able to master the skill, and the rest who will learn an isolated skill out of context. Bailey and Almond (1983) found a clear division in schools between those who can and those who cannot play games. This difference in ability is obvious to all in physical education.

> Physical actions and the success or otherwise of a pupil in accomplishing a task can be seen immediately by the rest of the class, the teacher and anyone else who is able to observe the class. To team-mates a mistake is obvious; for

example, if a pupil drops a catch and the opposition gains possession. . . . Failure in front of a class of peers can be particularly demotivating, especially as it is likely to decrease self-esteem.

(Capel, Kelly and Whitehead 1997: 108)

Failure in a particular task, in turn, may result in a sense of failure at games in general. Howarth and Bull suggested that 'interest in games often fades early for many children as they become more aware of their lack of skill and embarrassed by their failures' (Howarth and Bull 1982: 36). Stoddart reinforced this with his conviction that 'enjoyment and effective learning often go hand in hand' (Stoddart 1985: 32). Failure and consequent lack of interest may 'spill over' into other aspects of physical education and physical activity, giving a sense of incompetence, accompanied by decreased self-concept and self-esteem. This may lead to avoidance of games and competition and even to avoidance of all physical activity. (See also Chapter 9 of this book.)

Bunker and Thorpe also suggested that:

> this has led to lessons in which the game is a mere appendage to technique teaching. At worst this structure (skills-based lessons) has led to an introductory section unrelated to what is to follow, a technique section which is seen as essential by the teacher and a game which is inappropriate to the ability of many of the children.

(Bunker and Thorpe 1986c: 11)

Pupils often perceive the skill development phase of a lesson as boring, resulting in the question 'When are we going to play a game?' being asked fairly frequently.

Another disadvantage of the skills-based approach is that there is not enough time in the curriculum to practise skills to adequate levels and to play a game

Physical education time is limited in schools (e.g. a survey in 1996 showed an average of one and a half hours per week for pupils from ages six to eighteen (Editorial 1997: 157)). Although games are the dominant part of the physical education curriculum in many schools (see Chapter 7), time for teaching games is still limited. Table 5.2 shows the mean number of weeks given to different areas of activity in secondary schools (Penney and Evans 1994).

The problem of lack of time is exacerbated by the approach of teaching one game for a short period, say six weeks, and then teaching another game. In this approach there is unlikely to be sufficient time for pupils to practise skills specific to the game to be learned and incorporated effectively into the game. Teachers therefore need to be realistic about what can be achieved in the time available for games in the curriculum.

Table 5.2 Mean number of weeks given to each of the areas of activity in year 9 (KS3) and year 11 (KS4)

	Dance	Gymnastic activities	Games	Athletic activities	Outdoor and adventurous activities	Swimming
	n = 68/69	n = 63/62	n = 58	n = 61/62	n = 73/70	n = 67/65
Year 9 girls	3.6	7.4	24.3	8.9	0.7	3.5
Year 9 boys	0.7	6.6	24.9	8.9	0.8	3.2
	n = 65/67	n = 60/58	n = 48/47	n = 55/54	n = 62/60	n = 56/54
Year 11 girls	3.1	3.4	20.9	4.3	2.2	5.5
Year 11 boys	1.6	3.4	21.1	4.4	2.3	5.6

Source: Penney and Evans 1994: 11

Another disadvantage of TGFU is that there is lack of evidence as to its effectiveness

There is some anecdotal support for the use of a TGFU approach to teaching games (e.g. Doolittle 1995; Doolittle and Girard 1991; Smith 1991; Werner and Almond 1990). However, although some empirical evidence to support the use of TGFU is beginning to be generated, the evidence is mixed; for example, Lawton (1989) found no significant difference in skills and understanding between groups taught a tactical or technical approach. Turner and Martinek (1992) found no significant differences in game-playing ability, knowledge or skill between groups taught a technique or a games-centred (TGFU) approach. French et al. (1996a) found that groups taught through a skill, tactical or combined skill and tactical approach performed better than a control group on cognitive and skill components of game performance over a three-week unit. No significant differences were found for game performance measures. The results were replicated in a study over a longer period of time (six weeks) (French et al. 1996b). In addition, cognitive and skill components of performance improved from three to six weeks. Allison and Thorpe (1997) found that in comparison to a skills-based approach, a TGFU approach resulted in: teachers reporting more opportunities to observe and assess pupils and pupils being significantly more involved in planning and evaluation; pupils reporting more involvement in planning and evaluation; and pupils with lower technical ability reporting significantly higher levels of enjoyment and effort, and more positive attitudes about their ability to play the game being taught and towards physical education in general. There was no decrease in technical ability, but significantly greater increase in knowledge and tactical understanding. Mitchell et al. (1997) found that pupils taught by the tactical approach showed greater improvement in tactical knowledge than those taught by a technical approach, but that there were no differences in technical knowledge, skill acquisition or intrinsic motivation. Harrison et al. (1998) found a few differences in achievement between tactical and skill teaching but concluded that both approaches can be advantageous.

Lack of evidence and mixed results may be one reason for teachers not introducing the TGFU approach more widely in schools.

Where do teachers go from here?

This chapter has attempted to promote reflection on the teaching of games. There is little doubt that physical education teachers must reflect on and question their approach to the teaching of games in order to continue to improve both their practice and the learning experiences of pupils in physical education lessons. They should not teach as they have always done without reflecting on whether it is the most appropriate approach to teaching games.

Good games teaching is not necessarily good skills teaching. Teaching a warm up, skill and game in every lesson is not necessarily the most appropriate way to teach games to achieve the range of objectives identified for games lessons. The teaching of skills is an important part of teaching games, but when a particular skill is taught depends on a number of factors.

The TGFU approach emphasises pupils' learning to make their own decisions and solving their own problems. The emphasis is on pupils being creators of games rather than passive recipients of knowledge, and on maximising participation. The focus is on the contextual nature of games rather than on the specific skills required to play one game. However, it should be recognised that TGFU is not revolutionary (see, for example, Waring and Almond 1995). These factors can be emphasised equally as well in a skills-based approach. However, they may have been lost in the focus on skills. It may be these factors which TGFU has to offer that should be emphasised, rather than the approach itself.

Asquith asked: 'Can we, by changing the focal point of such lessons, from skills and techniques to games making and tactics, improve the environment in which learning might well take place?' (Asquith 1989: 76). This suggests an either/or situation, which reflects much of the debate about skills-based teaching versus TGFU. However, as with the skills-based approach, TGFU is not necessarily the most appropriate way to teach games to achieve the range of objectives identified for games lessons. These two approaches are not alternatives, but different approaches that may be selected at different times in order to achieve certain objectives in a lesson and unit of work. Thus, teachers should look to retain the benefits of both skills-based and TGFU approaches in achieving the specific objectives of games lessons in physical education in the curriculum.

Other approaches to teaching games have also been suggested. Much of this work is based on using specific teaching strategies with which most teachers are familiar for teaching specific aspects of games, e.g. grouping pupils in specific ways, such as mixed ability or equal ability groups, or using specific teaching styles such as those identified by Mosston and Ashworth (1994). For example, Jones (1996) reported results of research with KS2 pupils, which he described as 'the golden age of skill learning', that showed that when children are taught games using a range of teaching strategies from didactic styles to pupil-initiated approaches, as compared to being taught using mainly didactic styles, there is no decline in the performance of basic games skills. An approach selected for teaching games may not have a specific title.

As with all aspects of teaching, reflective teachers do not adopt a specific approach merely because it is the focus of topical consideration. In order to provide a coherent, progressive learning experience for all pupils, the use of any teaching approach should be planned and deliberate rather than a reaction to the latest innovation. Reflective teachers deliberately plan for a particular aspect of learning to take place, rather than allowing that learning to be incidental or left to chance. They think seriously about what a teaching approach has to offer and the impact of this on teaching and learning.

Pupils are at the centre of the learning process. The objectives for a unit of work and lesson guide teachers' selection of the approach which is most appropriate in achieving a specific objective at a specific time. However, teachers must also be sensitive to the needs of the pupils in selecting the appropriate teaching approach to achieve a specific objective; so that the material is structured and presented in a way that it is meaningful to the pupils and is therefore understood. A flexible approach to each unit and lesson is needed; aspects from skills-based, TGFU and other approaches may be used in the same lesson. There is no one right way of teaching games. 'Like all good teaching, an eclectic approach may produce the best results' (Fisher 1991: 23).

There are many other providers of games experiences for children in the United Kingdom, for example coaches and sports leaders. It is the ability to think and operate differently from these other providers by being able to select a sample of games and highlight the relationships between them and by being able to develop them with rule structures, increasing tactical complexity and greater decision-making capacity that Thorpe and Bunker (1997: 79) suggested separated the physical education teacher from other providers of games experiences. It is important that physical education teachers continue to reflect on what it is that distinguishes their role in teaching games in the physical education curriculum from the role of other providers of games experiences. If the games programme in school comprises only a 'series of separate games taught with the intention of producing good performers, then coaches may be better able to meet this need. . . . A games education should be so much more and physical education teachers have a unique role to play in it' (Thorpe 1990: 80). Teachers should be clear about the purposes of teaching games and, hence, the aims and objectives of teaching games in the physical education curriculum. It is important that physical education teachers continue to reflect on what is different about the purposes, aims and objectives of teaching games in the physical education curriculum from teaching games in other settings.

After reflecting on the teaching of games some teachers may be prompted to want to make changes in their approach. However, making change in the teaching of games, as in making any other change, is not always easy. Chapter

14 considers further how to make change in physical education.

Conclusion

It is not possible in this book to provide extensive discussion on teaching approaches for each area of activity in the National Curriculum for Physical Education (NCPE). Games were selected because of their dominance in the curriculum (see Chapter 7, for further discussion on the dominance of games in the physical education curriculum) and because it is generally accepted that games are not well taught (see, for example, Bunker and Thorpe 1986a; Thorpe 1986; Thorpe and Bunker 1986). However, this chapter should provide the foundation for reflection on the most appropriate teaching approaches to teaching activities in other areas of activity in the NCPE.

Questions for reflection

1   What is the unique contribution of physical education teachers to the teaching of games as compared with, for example, coaches?
2   What is the balance in time devoted to games, between invasion, net/wall, field/run-scoring and target games? Why? Is this appropriate?
3   What, if any, is the relationship between the teaching of games in the primary and secondary schools in which you are located?
4   What foundations should be laid in primary schools in teaching games for secondary teachers to build on? What focus should be adopted to teaching games in primary schools to enable that foundation to be established? For example should skills specific to particular major games be taught in the primary school?
5   Do you know how many of your pupils do not participate in organised games in extra-curricular, out of school or post-school and why? Is there anything you can do to change this?
6   As a physical educator are you making the best use of your resources to help all children achieve their optimum potential in playing and understanding games?
7   Why do you teach games in physical education?
8   What approach do you take to the teaching of games (skills-based, TGFU, a combination, other) and why have you adopted this approach? Do your teaching approaches enable the purposes identified in question 7 to be achieved?
9   Does your approach to teaching games need some reconsideration? If so, how can you achieve this?

Further reading

Allison, S. and Thorpe, R. (1997) 'A comparison of the effectiveness of two approaches to teaching games within physical education: a skills versus a games for understanding approach', *British Journal of Physical Education* 86 (3): 9–13.

Coe, J. M. (1986) 'Games education', *British Journal of Physical Education* 17 (4): 202–4.

Read, B. (1995) 'National Curriculum: the teaching of games', *British Journal of Physical Education* 26 (3): 6–11.

Thorpe, R. and Bunker, D. (1997) 'A changing focus in games teaching', in L. Almond (ed.), *Physical Education in Schools*, London: Kogan Page: 52–80.

Thorpe, R., Bunker, D. and Almond, L. (1986a) *Rethinking Games Teaching*, Loughborough, Leics.: Loughborough University.

The *British Journal of Teaching Physical Education* (until Autumn 1999 called the *British Journal of Physical Education*), a quarterly publication sent to all members of the Physical Education Association of the United Kingdom (PEAUK), and the *Bulletin of Physical Education* (a publication of the British Association of Advisers and Lecturers in Physical Education (BAALPE)) are good sources of articles on games teaching.

6 Formal and informal modes of assessment in physical education

Susan Piotrowski and Susan Capel

Introduction

Assessment has always been an integral part of good teaching in physical education. Effective physical education teachers identify clear learning objectives and gather evidence on the extent to which those learning objectives are achieved. Such evidence provides a basis for feedback. Feedback can be given to pupils so that sound practice can be reinforced and mistakes corrected. It also provides information to the teacher on whether learning objectives are set at an appropriate level of difficulty and provides a basis from which appropriate adjustments to the challenging nature of learning materials can be made.

Prior to the 1970s much assessment took place informally, often through careful observation in normal class teaching contexts. There was little formal reporting of assessment outcomes other than in the 'now much maligned school report' (Carroll 1994: 18). Furthermore, there was rarely an explicit focus on assessment in physical education initial teacher education (ibid.). A shift towards the use of more formal methods of assessment in physical education and a more explicit focus on assessment began in the 1970s when some physical education teachers started to campaign for the inclusion of physical education in the national examination system. This explicit focus on assessment has been reinforced more recently through the introduction of the National Curriculum and the influence of the Office for Standards in Education (OFSTED). This chapter examines some of the influences which have led to a tendency to employ more formal methods of assessment and to put a more explicit focus on assessment. While acknowledging the essential role of assessment in effective teaching and learning in physical education, a central focus of the chapter is to reflect on the issue of whether an emphasis on more formalised methods of assessment is beneficial or detrimental to effective teaching and learning in physical education.

By the end of this chapter readers should:

- understand what is meant by assessment, appreciate the significance of assessment in effective teaching and learning in physical education, and recognise that assessment can be conducted in many different ways which include the use of formal and informal methods

- be aware that during the last thirty years a shift towards the use of more formalised methods of assessment in physical education has taken place which has been influenced by a number of factors, including political influences
- recognise that there are distinct advantages and disadvantages to using more formal methods of assessment which require careful consideration by teachers in developing an appropriate assessment strategy for physical education.

To provide an informed basis for the debate which is to follow, the chapter begins with a focus on the question 'What is assessment?'

What is assessment?

In an educational context, 'assessment' can be defined as a process which involves an attempt to make 'relevant, appropriate and accurate judgements about pupils' achievements' (Department of Education and Science/Welsh Office (DES/WO) 1991: 42). These judgements are typically made by the teacher (teacher assessment), by pupils about their own performance (self assessment) or one anothers' performance (peer assessment), or by an external examining body (e.g. as in General Certificate of Education (GCSE) or Advanced (A) level physical education). The kind of judgement involved in educational assessment involves making comparisons of a pupil's achievement against pre-determined criteria (criterion referenced assessment); against the achievements of others (norm referenced assessment); or against the individual's own previous achievement in the same activity (ipsative assessment). These judgements provide evidence of the extent to which any intended learning is achieved. Such judgements are crucial to educational contexts, including physical education, where the development of pupils' learning is a defining characteristic. While learning can occur, in principle, without assessment, the progression of learning is likely to be more effective when outcomes are assessed and feedback given. The role of assessment in effective teaching and learning is explored in the following section.

Assessment as integral to effective teaching and learning

Assessment is not necessarily integral to all teaching and learning, but it is integral to those forms of teaching which are more likely, consistently, to be effective in developing learning. For example, it is possible in principle for a teacher to teach pupils a skill and for that skill to be learned by the child without anyone assessing or even recognising that achievement. The pupil could, for example, have grasped some key points from the teacher about performing a handstand. The pupil may go home, practise what he or she has absorbed and perform an unobserved handstand as a result of learning from the teacher how to position the limbs correctly. There is no denying that the teacher taught the skill and the pupil learned, even though there was no assessment of that learning. But while this may be possible in principle, in fact learning is more likely to be facilitated with greater effectiveness if the outcomes of learning are assessed. Assessment allows for the possibility of teachers forming judgements on the basis of which sound practice can be reinforced and mistakes corrected. Teaching is also likely to be more effective if it is related to the pupils' current level of attainment and what is needed if the child is to progress. Assessment might therefore be appropriately identified as being essential to good or effective teaching. This is acknowledged by a number of commentators on assessment in physical education. Robinson asserted that, 'assessment *should* be an inseparable part of curriculum planning and delivery' (Robinson 1996: 9, our emphasis). Spackman also considered 'ongoing . . . assessment of children's work in physical education is at the heart of *good* teaching' (Spackman 1998: 4, our emphasis). Dearing agreed that 'teacher assessment is fundamental to good teaching' (in SCAA 1996a: i).

Modes of assessment

Acknowledging that assessment should be integral to effective teaching and learning in educational contexts, including physical education, nevertheless leaves open the question of how that assessment should be conducted (that is, the mode of assessment to be used). Possible modes of assessment have been identified by Rowntree (1977: 119) to include: formal versus informal modes; formative versus summative modes; continuous versus terminal (final) modes; course work versus examination modes; internal versus external modes; convergent versus divergent modes; and ideographic versus nomothetic modes. These differing modes of assessment are described in detail by both Rowntree (1977) and Satterly (1981). For the purposes of this chapter, the distinction between formal and informal modes of assessment is explored in greater detail since the chapter later focuses on the apparent tendency towards the use of more formal methods of assessment in physical education.

Formal versus informal modes of assessment

'Informal assessment' can be defined as 'assessment conducted while pupils are carrying on normal classroom (physical education) activities' (Satterly 1981: 352, parentheses added) while 'formal assessment' can be defined as 'assessment conducted in situations solely for that purpose . . . usually using well-validated tests or other instruments' (ibid.: 351). While informal assessment takes place during normal individual and class learning activities, formal assessment often involves standardised testing or checks of pupils' levels of attainment under examination type conditions when periods of time are deliberately set aside for the purposes of assessing. Whereas judgements associated with informal assessment often lack 'conscious organisation or interpretation' until a situation arises where a teacher is pressed to make a verbal or written report, in more formal assessment contexts 'the teacher deliberately uses pre-set criteria and is explicitly aware of what he or she was "looking for"' (ibid.: 13).

In physical education, informal assessment is based on the continual flow of evidence within each lesson and generally relies on ongoing, observational assessment and verbal interaction. It provides information on how successful or otherwise the planned tasks, practices and teaching approaches have been in promoting pupils' learning. Formal assessments, on the other hand, tend to involve close observation and simultaneous recording of a child's achievements during time which is specifically set aside for making such judgements. Very often, as Robinson observed, formal assessment in physical education takes place at the end of a unit of work when 'the final lesson is planned around a series of tasks or activities designed to provide evidence of pupils' levels of attainment relative to the unit's learning objectives' (Robinson 1996: 15).

For the purposes of this chapter 'formal assessment' is interpreted broadly as referring to a more explicit, more systematic, more conscious and more deliberate focus on assessment which sometimes, though not always, involves the assessment of learning under examination-type conditions. Hence the more formal the assessment, the more likely it is to be separated temporally and spatially from the teaching context. This contrasts with 'informal assessment' which in this chapter is interpreted as ongoing, less systematic modes of assessment, where assessment criteria are not clearly and explicitly identified and applied to performance in a consciously, focused way.

There have been several influences which have led to greater use of more formalised methods of assessment in physical education. The following section traces the development of some of these influences.

A tendency towards more formal modes of assessment in physical education

A brief look at the history of physical education since the early 1970s suggests that there has been a tendency towards the use of more formal assessment methods. Prior to that time, any involvement of physical education teachers in more formal assessment methods tended to be limited to the assessment of achievement for sport governing body awards such as the Amateur Swimming Association (ASA) distance awards. With regard to more general practice in teaching and assessing physical education, Carroll observed that 'assessment debates and reform hardly touched physical education. Physical education teachers were largely left to their own devices in . . . assessment matters' (Carroll 1994: 2). Three main influences appear to have encouraged a move towards increased use of more formalised assessment methods in physical education and a more explicit focus on assessment. These are the influence of the national examination system, the influence of the National Curriculum and the influence of OFSTED.

The influence of the national examination system

Carroll (1994) traced the increasing use of more formalised modes of assessment in physical education to the inclusion of physical education in secondary schools' formal examination programme. Initially, this occurred in the early 1970s through the introduction of Certificate of Secondary Education (CSE) (Mode 3) syllabuses in physical education. Under these arrangements it was left to individual teachers to design and assess their own syllabuses. The subsequent development in the early 1980s of CSE (Mode 1) syllabuses in physical education (with the syllabus set and assessed externally) and the introduction of GCSE Physical Education in 1986 moved this emphasis on more formal modes of assessment 'from the individual level mode to the more institutional level' (Carroll 1994: 22). These developments have been followed by more widespread involvement of physical education teachers in A level Physical Education and Sport Studies and Business and Technician Education Council (BTEC) and General National Vocational Qualifications (GNVQ) Leisure Studies.

The following arguments have been included among those put forward in favour of the introduction of national examinations in physical education. The inclusion of physical education in the formal examination system could:

- improve the marginal status and credibility of the subject in the school curriculum
- save the subject from the threat of removal from the secondary school curriculum as raising of the school leaving age from fifteen to sixteen in the early 1970s led to an increasing emphasis on the leaving qualifications of pupils
- raise the status and morale of physical education teachers
- bring a greater sense of purpose to the work
- improve pupils' motivation levels which were sometimes lacking in more recreational programmes
- acknowledge pupils' achievement through certification
- better ensure the development of pupils' in-depth knowledge and understanding of the subject.

Early attempts to introduce more formalised methods of assessment in physical education via the formal examination system met with some resistance for several reasons including:

- formal examinations could destroy the recreational value of physical education and the enjoyment of the subject for its own sake
- difficulties in objectively assessing some dimensions of the subject (e.g. the process of learning to improve performance) might lead to a distortion of the subject through increasing emphasis on more easily measurable aspects (e.g. theoretical understanding of concepts and knowledge related to physical education)

- difficulties of comparison between activities make it difficult to achieve accurate assessment of attainment in physical education
- differences in individual development (such as physique and temperament) mean that there is no common starting point.

Some of the educational arguments mentioned above are examined in more depth later in the chapter. However, it is of concern to find that among some of the most powerful influences in the move towards the adoption of more formalised methods of assessment in physical education, through the inclusion of physical education in the formal examination system, were considerations more related to the role satisfaction and status of teachers than to the educational interests of pupils. The inclusion of physical education in the formal examination system was used for the benefit of teachers to compensate for role dissatisfaction; for role survival; to give additional challenge and stimulus to experienced teachers; and for status redefinition in bringing physical education into a more central role within the school (Carroll 1994). Tozer, in citing correspondence concerning the introduction of A level physical education, noted that most respondents who supported its introduction did so for reasons relating to 'the prestige of the subject' and 'the status of the teacher' (Tozer 1970: 37). Moves towards more formalised methods of assessment for these reasons might be justifiable if the educational climate was such that, without such desperate measures, the subject itself was in danger of being eroded from the curriculum. It is questionable, however, whether the introduction of formal assessment methods to satisfy the insecurities of physical education teachers, rather than for reasons relating to the educational interests of the pupils, can be justified.

The National Curriculum in England and Wales has also led to a more explicit focus on assessment in physical education and may also have encouraged some teachers to employ more formalised methods in collecting evidence of pupils' attainments.

The influence of the National Curriculum

The drive for accountability has influenced developments in physical education in recent years, including developments in the use of more formalised assessment methods. Broadfoot (1986) cited accountability for the use of public funds due to increasing cost-consciousness as one of the reasons for greater interest by government in education. Among the political motives underlying the introduction of the National Curriculum, with its attendant assessment requirements, were desires for greater accountability and a need to address an alleged 'widespread concern to improve standards of teaching and learning' (DES 1989b: 2.4).

A more formalised approach to assessment and the reporting of assessment addresses requirements for accountability in a number of ways. It provides greater accountability to pupils who are entitled to have their attainment assessed in ways which guide their future learning, progress and achievement. Pupils are entitled to know whether they are learning intended content and progressing at a rate comparable with their peers. A more formalised approach to assessment and reporting also provides greater accountability to parents who want to know what their children are learning and how they are progressing. In addition, more formalised assessment provides information to headteachers, governing bodies, Local Education Authorities (LEAs), industry, and the Government about the performance of pupils in particular subjects and/or schools. This enables comparisons to be made between pupils and between schools across the country.

Carroll described the National Curriculum in England and Wales, established under the terms of the Education Reform Act (ERA) 1988 as 'an assessment driven curriculum' (Carroll 1994: 131). Physical education is included in the National Curriculum as a foundation subject and shares with the other core and foundation subjects three components:

- Attainment Target(s) which determine assessment objectives and state what pupils should know and understand and what skills they should be able to perform
- Programmes of Study which define the teaching syllabus
- Assessment Arrangements which define standards of attainment.

Assessment of pupils must take place before the end of each of the Key Stages (at ages 7, 11, 14 and 16 years) and in physical education requires that teachers report the pupils' level of attainment at the end of each Key Stage to parents and other teachers with either current or imminent responsibility for the pupil. While there are no standard assessment tasks (SATs) in physical education, teachers must nevertheless focus explicitly and consciously on assessing the extent to which pupils' attainment relates to the expectations embodied in an eight level Attainment Target in the recently published draft proposals for a revised National Curriculum for Physical Education (NCPE) to be introduced in September 2000 (DfEE/QCA 1999).

It should be noted, however, that while the NCPE requires teachers to adopt a conscious and explicit focus on assessment and to make judgements of pupils' overall performance in relation to levels of attainment, there is no statutory requirement for teachers to collect evidence of pupils' attainments in any particular way. 'Decisions about collecting information, about its purpose and how it should be used, are matters for teachers working within agreed school policy' (SCAA 1996a: 21). Similarly, while teachers may wish to keep records of pupils' attainments, 'there is no statutory requirement to keep detailed records or evidence on every pupil' (SCAA 1996a: i). The NCPE does not require that teachers should adopt formalised methods of assessment which entail the use of well validated tests or other instruments or the setting aside of specific times for assessment. Nevertheless, as Carroll indicated, 'Like CSE and GCSE, the National Curriculum does mean that the teacher must be more systematic in the assessment, must be much clearer about the criteria to be used, must observe all the children more carefully, and record their actions in some way' (Carroll 1994: 8).

The move towards more explicit, more formalised assessment methods which accompanied the inclusion of physical education as a foundation subject in the National Curriculum is another example of change to assessment practices occurring in physical education in response to the need for credibility and acceptability. Physical education achieved recognition and status as a foundation subject, but along with this came the attendant requirements to meet the statutory framework which applies to all foundation subjects, and the obligation for a more explicit focus on assessment. Perhaps the essentially different nature of physical education should have been acknowledged and physical education released from more explicit, and in some cases more formal, assessment procedures. By fitting into the National Curriculum framework, increased credibility is balanced against increased requirements for assessment.

The drive for greater accountability which influenced the introduction of the National Curriculum has also led to an increase in inspections. Spackman considered the inspection process to have had an impact on assessment in physical education:

> unfortunately the pressure of inspection has created a great deal of 'hype' for teachers, and the issue of assessment is one which has dominated thinking. This has sometimes been at the expense of good planning which would have led to better ongoing assessment.
>
> (Spackman 1995: 34)

The following section focuses on the influence of OFSTED in moves towards more formal approaches to assessment in physical education.

The influence of OFSTED

OFSTED has been influential in encouraging moves toward more formalised approaches to assessment in physical education. It is important for schools to be seen to do well in the inspection process and to comply with the criteria considered by OFSTED to define good practice. During the 1990s, physical education was frequently the target of criticism from OFSTED for failing to develop sufficiently rigorous practices of assessment, recording and reporting (AR&R). For example, OFSTED reported that at all Key Stages 'in general assessment, recording and reporting in physical education are weak' (OFSTED 1995a: 11–12). Further, they reported that at Key Stages (KS) 1 and 2 'there is little evidence of systematic recording of progress by teachers against National Curriculum programmes of study' (OFSTED 1995a: 11). It was concluded by OFSTED that 'the quality of assessment, recording and reporting needs to be improved at all key stages. Teaching should be informed by the results of assessment' (OFSTED 1995a: 5). Given the powerful influence of OFSTED on provision in schools, it is not surprising that the criteria identified by OFSTED as identifying good practice with respect to AR&R, combined with criticisms that AR&R is weak in physical education, should have led to a more formalised, more conscious, more explicit focus on assessment in physical education than was hitherto the case.

In summary, in recent years, as a result of the inclusion of physical education amongst those subjects formally examined for GCSE, A level, BTEC or GNVQ certification, the introduction of National Curriculum assessment requirements, and the influence of OFSTED, physical education teachers have tended to 'become much more involved in formal assessment techniques and procedures' (Carroll 1994: 2). With concerns for the creditability of the subject in schools, along with concerns for greater accountability and pressures to raise standards of teaching and learning, teachers have had to think more about the assessment of pupils, recording their progress and attainment and reporting on these to parents, the school and governors. However, is greater emphasis on formalised assessment methods beneficial or detrimental to effective teaching and learning in physical education? The next section discusses some of the issues raised by this question. This discussion is presented so that an argument in favour of a more formalised approach to assessment in physical education is put forward first, followed by some points for discussion. These points for discussion are in the shaded sections that follow.

Issues resulting from greater emphasis on formalised modes of assessment in physical education

Does formal assessment better place the teacher to reach more accurate judgements?

As suggested in the introduction to this chapter, assessment involves 'making relevant, appropriate and accurate judgements about pupils' achievements' (DES/WO 1991: 42). In being accurate, assessments must faithfully reflect what the pupils know, understand and can do.

Reaching accurate judgements in physical education is notoriously difficult. Teachers are largely judging practical performances which by their very nature are transitory. The actions are often fleeting and there is usually no permanent record in the form of written or crafted objects for the teacher to return to in formulating a judgement. Difficulties are compounded where assessment is of an informal nature, taking place during normal class teaching. It is particularly difficult for teachers to concentrate on making accurate, observational assessments while teaching classes of approximately thirty actively involved pupils and also attending to relevant safety considerations. An advantage of using a more formal approach to assessment, where assessment may take place during periods set aside specifically for purposes of assessing, is that it enables teachers to observe pupils' attainments and to apply criteria in a more focused way than might otherwise be possible.

Furthermore, as Satterly (1981) acknowledged, the more formal the mode of assessment, the more the assessment process itself is open to scrutiny in a way that informal assessment may not be. More formal methods can help to guard against a lack of fairness.

Some points for discussion on the question: does formal assessment
better place the teacher to reach more accurate judgements?

THE SELECTIVE NATURE OF FORMAL ASSESSMENT MAY LIMIT ACCURACY

Whereas in informal assessment the performance tends to make an 'impression' on the teacher's mind, formal assessment is more of a 'construction' where the teacher is explicitly aware of what he or she is looking for (Satterly 1981). Formal assessment is inevitably selective and not all of the pupil's abilities are of equal worth in the formal assessment process. The selective nature of formal assessment may detract from giving an accurate, more rounded judgement of pupils' attainments.

FORMAL ASSESSMENT MAY BIAS THE SUBJECT AND ITS DELIVERY

In formally assessing certain attainments rather than others, formalised assessment may have the effect of emphasising that which is more easily assessable. This was seen, for example, in the emphasis given to theoretical studies in CSE, GCSE, and A level physical education. Assessment can become more focused on those aspects which are easily measurable and which, for example, lend themselves to ticking boxes (e.g. if a pupil completes a particular activity or skill successfully) or towards testing (e.g. fitness testing).

McChonachie-Smith (1991) identified a possible source of tension between capability in physical education and what is assessed. Capability in physical education can be both product (e.g. performing a well executed chest pass) and process (e.g. learning how to improve through being able to reflect on previous performance and to modify future performance in the light of such reflection or developing positive attitudes towards physical education). Both product and process can be assessed, but since it would appear less complex to focus on the outcomes of physical education as products rather than as processes, these tend to be the primary focus of attention for the formal assessment of attainment in physical education.

Similarly, some products are easier to assess than others. For example, it is easier to assess progress and the attainment of learning outcomes where the outcomes are measurable or quantifiable; such as being able to run 100 metres in a specific time, e.g. under fourteen seconds. Likewise, it is easier to assess performance of a specific motor skill, e.g. ability to throw a ball, than less tangible aspects of performance, e.g. using skills effectively in tactical play in a games situation, where a number of variables interact to determine the degree of success. Care is required to ensure that the content of physical education is not distorted to accommodate that which is amenable to measurement at the expense of equally valuable but less easily assessed components.

A further difficulty arises when one considers that there may be aspects essential to the unique value of physical education in schools which it would be impossible to assess within the limited timespan of school experience. For example, if a primary aim of physical education is to promote life-long involvement in physical activity, how can this be assessed? Shorter term outcomes must be assessed which, hopefully, will lead to this long term aim being achieved. This requires clear articulation of what encourages and what discourages pupils to participate in physical activity after they leave school, and for the physical education programme to incorporate those factors that encourage life-long participation, with appropriate learning outcomes to be identified and assessed.

As the outcomes of assessment become increasingly more public it would be easy for interested stakeholders to attach increasing value to some attainments rather than others. In being accountable to outside bodies, the content of physical education could easily be biased away from aspects such as the development of physical literacy and the encouragement of mass life-long participation in physical activity towards aspects of the subject more in keeping with the interests of these external groups. For example, a government interested in encouraging sporting prowess for purposes of national prestige, or parents interested in fostering the sporting potential of their children as sporting superstars, could easily exert outside pressure on what is valued in physical education. Evans *et al.* acknowledged that pressures on physical education teachers may encourage 'the adoption of a questionable and limited criteria of "success"', because of the emphasis on public accountability, as well as 'marketability' (Evans *et al.* 1996: 8).

Is formal assessment stimulating and motivating to pupils?

Formal assessment processes can provide public acknowledgement of pupils' achievements. This can be highly motivating for some pupils. These pupils find involvement in formal assessment contexts stimulating and motivating. Formal assessment opportunities give pupils the chance to demonstrate what they know, understand and can do. This contributes to the pupil's own self-knowledge and can be motivating.

Some points for discussion on the question: is formal assessment stimulating and motivating to pupils?

FORMAL ASSESSMENT CAN BE STRESSFUL AND DEMOTIVATING FOR SOME PUPILS

While formal assessment may be stimulating and motivating for some, it can be stressful and demotivating for others. Formal assessment can be harmful to those pupils whose results are insufficiently encouraging to motivate them to try harder and to sustain their efforts (Satterly 1981). Particularly given the public nature of physical education (Capel *et al.* 1997, Williams 1996a) it can lead to labelling, from an early age, of some pupils as 'poor' or failures in physical education. Such assessments have 'an uncanny knack of becoming self-fulfilling' (Satterly 1981) whereby pupils perceiving themselves as 'no good' consider it a waste of time to make any effort and hence continue the circle of underachievement. Pupils are far more likely to remain committed to participation in physical education if they develop a sense of competence and enjoyment (HEA 1998a). Public assessment contexts which allow for obvious comparisons of pupils, may lead pupils to see themselves as lacking competence in these contexts relative to others and may therefore withdraw from involvement (Fox 1996, HEA 1998a). This detracts from achieving important life-long participation goals in physical education – particularly for adolescent girls – who may consider that physical activity is more suited to boys who tend to outperform girls in physical contexts where qualities of strength and speed etc. are significant factors in determining success.

Does formal assessment, linked to regular recording and reporting, enable better information to be provided more consistently?

Feedback to pupils and others

Records of assessment can be used to provide feedback to pupils about their progress and achievements and to inform planning and teaching which develops pupils' learning. More detailed information can be provided to parents about how their children are doing. Also, information is available to other stake-holders, e.g. the headteacher, governors, the LEA and Department for Education and Employment (DfEE).

The recording of assessment outcomes provides comparative information which, as suggested by the DES (1989b; 6.2), can be used as an indicator of where further effort is needed, for example in relation to resources, changes in the curriculum, and staff development. Assessment results can be published, and where they are good, can be used to gain prestige for the school.

A more informed basis for progression

Reported assessment outcomes can also be used by the current and next class teacher as a basis for ensuring that the work is progressed at a rate which is suitably challenging for the pupil's level of ability. Progression and increased attainment (or capability) are expected throughout the years of compulsory schooling. In England and Wales progression is expected within and across Key Stages. Progression across Key Stages is identified in the levels of attainment and Programmes of Study. Progression may take many forms including, for example, more accurate performance of the same skill or performance of the skill under more demanding circumstances, e.g. throwing a ball to a partner unopposed which can be progressed to throwing the ball in a controlled situation, such as when there is an additional time pressure, or to throwing the ball in a game situation. (Progression in physical education is considered in more depth in Chapter 12.)

Deliberate, focused assessment, where teachers apply pre-set criteria based on their understanding of stages of progression, enables teachers to assess whether the necessary progress has been made. This can be linked to maintaining an accurate record of the progress of each pupil throughout the years of schooling. Such assessment can be used diagnostically to identify specific learning needs of individual pupils and can be used to inform planning and differentiated provision.

A more informed basis for diagnosing special needs and exceptional abilities

Focused, formal assessment methods can be used deliberately to identify learning difficulties and exceptional abilities which may require the implementation of appropriate, specific strategies (DES/WO 1991). Formal assessment of pupils prior to or on entry to a school (and at times during their progress through a school) can help to provide a base-line for identifying pupils with exceptional abilities or with special educational needs. This enables learning tasks to be matched to individual learning needs. By adopting a formal approach to assessment, it is more likely that such difficulties and needs will be picked up at an early stage, enabling appropriate action to be taken.

> *Some points for discussion on the question: does formal assessment, linked to regular recording and reporting, enable better information to be provided more consistently?*
>
> Formal assessment, well conducted, and well linked to good recording and reporting practices, does provide useful information. This information can provide a useful basis for planning well focused, progressive learning experiences for pupils in physical education. It can also be used to provide feedback to the pupils and to other interested parties. However, formal assessment processes can be time-consuming and lead to a shift from intrinsic to more extrinsic motives for participation. It may also be an alienating experience for some pupils. Physical education teachers should reflect on these matters in reaching decisions about how to gain the benefits of formal approaches to assessment while avoiding unnecessary bureaucracy and the possible reduction of physical education as a positive and enjoyable learning experience for the pupils.

MORE FORMALISED ASSESSMENT CAN BE TIME-CONSUMING AND
BURDENSOME AND DETRACT FROM VALUABLE LEARNING TIME

One of the problems associated with the increasing emphasis on formal
assessment in physical education concerns the amount of time that
might be taken up by such practices. This was noted by Satterly. 'It is not
at all clear what proportion of a school year is taken up by assessment
although it is salutary to remember that every minute spent in formal
assessment is time taken from actual teaching' (Satterly 1981: 5). This
point was also acknowledged by Robinson (1996) who noted that with
formal methods of assessment such as assessing at the end of each unit
of work, valuable teaching and learning time may be lost. She calculated
that using such methods could result in one in every six or seven lessons
being spent assessing (testing) rather than teaching physical education.
Robinson challenged those adopting formal assessment practices of this
nature to identify what such end of unit assessments tell teachers and
pupils that they do not know already. Informal assessment, on the other
hand, which takes place on an ongoing basis in a class context, does not
detract from learning and practice time.

Linked with the time-consuming nature of some formal assessment
practices is the additional burden that formal assessment practices may
place on teaching staff. Penney and Harris found that 'for many heads of
physical education, reducing assessment requirements and/or administrative demands associated with the implementation of the National
Curriculum in physical education was clearly the preferred course of
action in any revision process' (Penney and Harris 1998: 8–9).

MORE FORMALISED ASSESSMENT MAY RESULT IN PUPILS VALUING
PHYSICAL EDUCATION FOR EXTRINSIC RATHER THAN INTRINSIC
REASONS

With increasing attention given to formal assessment methods in
physical education, it is possible that what pupils value from their experiences of the subject are not the physical activities themselves and their
contribution to their overall health, enjoyment and well being, but
rather the extrinsic rewards that may be associated with the outcomes of
assessment. For example, pupils may perceive the greatest value of
assessment as the opportunity to compare their performances against
those of their peers, particularly when their levels of achievement are
seen to meet with approval from significant others such as teachers,
parents and peers. Other external measures to which value may be
attached, include objective achievements such as winning trophies or
playing for a team.

MORE FORMALISED ASSESSMENT METHODS MAY ALIENATE PUPILS

A study by Loose and Abrahams (1993) found that Year 7 pupils perceived assessment, *inter alia*, as something which lay outside themselves and which the teacher did to them rather than with them. It was the teacher's judgements of their ability that were considered to be of greater significance than their own views of their achievements and progress. Thus, pupils may be alienated from the process because it is seen as a threat rather than a support. This may be exacerbated by placing greater emphasis on more formal assessment methods. These perceptions could be overcome by using self and peer assessment, particularly through the use of reciprocal teaching methods (see, for example, Mosston and Ashworth 1994), as these provide methods of drawing 'the pupil centrally into the assessment process' (Loose and Abrahams 1993: 8) and allow pupils to practise their observation and evaluative skills (McChonachie-Smith 1991). However, such methods of assessment are not generally considered to be integral to more traditional, formal, teacher assessment mechanisms.

Conclusion

This chapter has focused on the trend towards the use of a more formal approach to assessment in physical education during the last thirty years. Some of the reasons, including political motivations, which have influenced this development have been considered. The chapter has been designed to promote reflection on whether the use of more formal modes of assessment is to the benefit or detriment of physical education and to provide a basis from which to consider how assessment practice should develop in future. Physical education professionals should not just accept current assessment practice without question but should establish their own clear views about what is worthwhile and is manageable, and then reflect on, debate, discuss and challenge existing practices where appropriate, in order to promote effective development and change.

Questions for reflection

1   If assessment is integral to everyday teaching, how can evidence be collected to ensure that there are accurate judgements of all pupils?
2   What should be the balance between formal and informal assessment in physical education and why?
3   Should assessment in schools take the form of more formalised testing? Why?
4   What are your views on whether an emphasis on assessment (particularly on assessment of theoretical aspects of physical education) should be used to give physical education credibility in the school curriculum?
5   Do you gather evidence of assessment against all the aims and objectives

stated in your physical education curriculum (including personal and social skills)? If not, which aims and objectives do you not gather evidence for, and why and how could you gather this evidence?

6　Describe the methods used in your school to gather evidence on pupils for assessment purposes. Is this range appropriate to ensure that the aims of the physical education are met?

7　How can the outcomes of assessment be recorded efficiently by providing appropriate information to enable you to make accurate reports on pupils' progress?

8　How can your assessment, recording and reporting practice be improved?

Further reading

Carroll, B. (1994) *Assessment in Physical Education*, London: Falmer.

Spackman, L. (1995). 'Assessment in physical education', *British Journal of Physical Education* 26 (3): 32–4.

—— (1998) 'Assessment and recording in physical education', *British Journal of Physical Education* 29 (4): 6–9.

Part IV

Issues concerned with the curriculum

7 Breadth and balance in the physical education curriculum

Andrea Lockwood

Introduction

Many people participate in a wide range of physical activities either in a professional capacity or in their leisure time. Physical activities in educational institutions, however, take place within the context of teaching and learning and, as physical education, they become part of the educational process. The Educational Reform Act (ERA 1988) established general principles that must be reflected in the curriculum of all pupils. Every pupil is entitled to a curriculum which is broadly based and balanced and schools must ensure not only that a broad and balanced curriculum is offered but that it is fully taken up by all pupils. When considering a framework for planning work in physical education Her Majesty's Inspectorate (HMI) stated that 'a programme of work should be designed to reflect a balance both in the kind of activity and in the processes involved in becoming more skilful, more efficient and more fluent within that activity'; and that 'a balance is also necessary between breadth and depth of content (DES 1989a: 7–8).

The context for this chapter is the introduction of the National Curriculum for Physical Education (NCPE) in 1992 (Department of Education and Science (DES)/Welsh Office(WO) 1992), its subsequent revision in 1995 (Department for Education (DfE)/WO 1995) and the NCPE for the year 2000 (Department for Education and Employment (DfEE)/Qualifications and Curriculum Authority (QCA) 1999). Within all these orders for physical education, breadth and balance in the kind of activities in the curriculum are provided through a programme of study which includes up to six areas of activity at any Key Stage; athletic activities; dance activities; games activities; gymnastic activities; outdoor and adventurous activities (OAA) and swimming activities and water safety. Participation in a range of activities should enable pupils to experience a range of processes involved in becoming more skilful, efficient and fluent in each activity.

However, it is necessary to question whether breadth and balance are actually being achieved in the curriculum. Three aspects of breadth and balance are identified in this chapter. These are:

- accessibility of all pupils to a broad and balanced curriculum
- the nature of core knowledge in physical education

- the implications of a bias towards games in providing breadth and balance in physical education.

The first aspect identified is accessibility to a broad and balanced curriculum. The National Curriculum Council (NCC 1990) identified equal opportunities as one of the cross-curricular dimensions which should permeate all subjects in the curriculum. In relation to physical education all children should have access to, and gain confidence in, all aspects of the subject regardless of their ability, sex or racial/ethnic/cultural background. There have been structures existing within physical education both before and after the advent of the NCPE that may create and maintain inequality in access to a broad and balanced curriculum for all pupils.

The principle established by law that all pupils in maintained schools should experience a broad and balanced curriculum (ERA 1988) has specific implications for the physical education teacher in ensuring accessibility for pupils with special educational needs (see Chapter 3 of this book). Additionally, equal opportunity for all pupils to participate in a subject that has traditionally been differentiated by gender requires teachers to examine carefully, when planning, not only the content but also their teaching methods (see Chapter 2). Further, equal opportunity must be afforded to pupils whatever their race, ethnicity or culture (see Chapter 4). The legal requirement not only to provide but also to ensure accessibility to a broad and balanced curriculum for all pupils is considered in depth in the chapters identified above, and is therefore not discussed further in this chapter. This chapter reinforces an appreciation of the need to plan both content and teaching approach to ensure that *all* pupils experience a broad and balanced physical education curriculum.

The second aspect focuses on the 'core knowledge' of physical education as presented in the NCPE. Before 1992 the physical education profession, through its associations and membership of the National Curriculum Working Group for Physical Education (NCWGPE) appointed by the Secretaries of State for Education and Science and for Wales to advise on appropriate attainment targets and programmes of study for physical education in the National Curriculum, tried to influence the 'core knowledge' to be included in the curriculum.

'Core knowledge' concerned with process as well as product, together with the development of personal qualities and competence was advocated (see, for example, DES/WO 1990, 1991; Dudley Metropolitan Borough 1989, PEA 1987, Sumner 1989). Although somewhat diluted, process and personal development were included in the 'core knowledge' of the 1992 NCPE (DES/WO 1992), but the 1995 NCPE (DfE/WO 1995) showed an increased emphasis on product, performance and physical skills (see, for example, Williams 1996b). The 2000 NCPE (DfEE/QCA 1999) suggests a return to a much broader base of 'core knowledge'; reflecting the pre-1992 proposals, but also increasing the emphasis on health related exercise (HRE). The teaching of HRE in the physical education curriculum is in itself an issue promoting debate and is addressed further in Chapter 11. The first part of this chapter looks at 'core knowledge' in physical education.

The third aspect acknowledges that, traditionally, games have been a major component of physical education programmes, particularly in secondary schools. A comparison of the 1992 NCPE (DES/WO 1992) and the 1995 NCPE (DfE/WO 1995) shows an increased emphasis on team games in the latter, particularly at Key Stages (KS) 3 and 4. In contrast, the draft proposals for the 2000 NCPE (QCA 1999a) prompted considerable media comment because of an apparent move away from traditional team games. For example, in the 2000 NCPE (DfEE/QCA 1999) there is no longer a requirement for games to be taught at KS4. Breadth and balance in the activities included in the curriculum, including the place of games in the physical education curriculum, are considered in the second part of the chapter.

The second and third aspects of breadth and balance identified above are considered in this chapter. Thus, by the end of this chapter readers should be able to reflect on the nature of 'core knowledge' in the physical education curriculum and consider the relationship between games and the other areas of activity in the NCPE.

'Core knowledge' and the process/product debate in physical education

Before the introduction of the NCPE in 1992 (DES/WO 1992) there was no defined view of what pupils should experience through physical education, either at the primary or secondary phase of their education. Additionally, until the mid 1980s there was a strong body of opinion that rejected the idea of formal assessment through examinations in the subject and so physical education, unlike other subject areas, did not have its content dictated, or influenced to any noticeable extent, by public examination syllabuses. (The debate about the introduction of examinations in physical education is considered further in Chapter 6.)

HMI and local education authority (LEA) advisers exercised some influence, but the physical education curriculum offered in any one school was largely dependent on the interests and expertise of the staff employed. Higher education institutions (HEIs) involved in initial teacher education had some influence through the content and mode of delivery they prioritised in their programmes. However, even here there was no consensus of opinion as to what 'core knowledge' in physical education was and how it should be encompassed in the school curriculum. Additionally, when appointing new teachers, schools were able to choose applicants whose ideologies and approach reflected their own; thus maintaining the status quo within their department. Even within the same school, the curriculum for boys and girls could be very different; the boys' curriculum often being dominated by competitive team games at the expense of the gymnastics and dance offered to girls (see Chapter 2 for further discussion of gender in physical education). These factors all contributed to a diversification in focus and in curricular content being delivered as physical education in different schools.

There were (and still are) various views about whether physical education has value in its own right or whether it should be a means of achieving other ends; whether it has intrinsic value or extrinsic value; whether it should focus on the process of learning or the product. There is a strongly held view by many that physical education should focus on that which is unique to the subject; namely promoting physical development and enhancing physical competence. Others have a strongly held view that the value of physical education is in what it contributes to the general education of pupils. (This debate is considered further in Chapters 1 and 13.

Despite these differing views, many would see the dominant emphasis in physical education being on the product; performance in physical skills and activities. This emphasis on the product, the ability to perform skills, is not new and reflects traditional practice prior to the 1980s in many schools, particularly secondary schools. However, in the late 1980s the physical education profession began to question a curriculum centred on the development of pupils' ability in particular physical activities. Different models were put forward for organising the curriculum which focused on the process of learning, including continuity and progression in learning within the subject, rather than on simply improving performance in a number of different activities.

HMI included both product and process outcomes in their statement that:

the aims of physical education are to:
- develop a range of psychomotor skills
- maintain and increase physical mobility and flexibility
- develop stamina and strength
- develop understanding and appreciation of the purposes, forms and conventions of a selection of physical activities
- develop the capacity to express ideas in dance forms
- develop the appreciation of the concepts of fair play, honest competition and good sportsmanship
- develop the ability to appreciate the aesthetic qualities of movement
- develop the capacity to maintain interest and to persevere to achieve success
- foster self-esteem through the acquisition of physical competence and poise
- develop self-confidence through understanding the capabilities and limitations of oneself and others
- develop an understanding of the importance of exercise in maintaining a healthy life style.

(DES 1989a: 1–2)

HMI also gave a framework for planning a balanced programme in physical education, stating that 'the content of a balanced curriculum is not simply a series of particular activities but rather the medium through which all the essential aspects of physical education are experienced (ibid.: 8)'. The framework provided by HMI suggested five different aspects that should be included in planning a balanced programme in physical education:

- the development of skilful body management.
- creative and aesthetic experience through movement.
- competitive activities among groups and individuals.
- body training leading to increased strength and stamina and endurance.
- challenging experiences in a variety of outdoor environments.

(DES 1989c: 8)

Emphasis was also given to the process of learning by an informal working group set up by the British Council of Physical Education (BCPE) in 1990 to produce a NCPE. Additionally, BCPE showed a concern for continuity and progression in physical education that changed with the child's stage of development. (Continuity and progression from primary to secondary school is considered further in Chapter 12.) The principles for the physical education curriculum which the BCPE report contained were that:

- the model [the physical education curriculum] should be developmental.
- the model should show clear progression.
- initiation into culturally valued activities is important.
- these activities are both vehicles and contexts of learning.
- the isolation of school from community should be reduced.
- the model should progress from a broad general base to specialism.
- there should be increasing responsibility for self directed learning.
- personal and social education should be provided for.
- the concept of safety should be addressed in all its forms.

(BCPE 1990, parentheses added)

Murdoch (1997) claimed that these principles survived the lengthy process of the production of the National Curriculum documents in the various staged reports, subsequent reduction of the National Curriculum as a result of the review conducted by Dearing (1994) and finally the School Curriculum and Assessment Authority's (SCAA 1997a) interpretation of the orders.

The process model of the curriculum was highlighted further in the three separate attainment targets for physical education (*Planning; Performing; Evaluating*), which were identified in the interim report of the NCWGPE (DES/WO 1990). These are shown in Figure 7.1.

The frameworks and models identified so far focus on the process of learning rather than on performance. However, in the 1992 NCPE (DES/WO 1992) these three attainment targets were combined into one attainment target. The single attainment target was retained in the 1995 NCPE (DfE/WO 1995) and is present in the 2000 NCPE (DfEE/QCA 1999). This raises questions as to

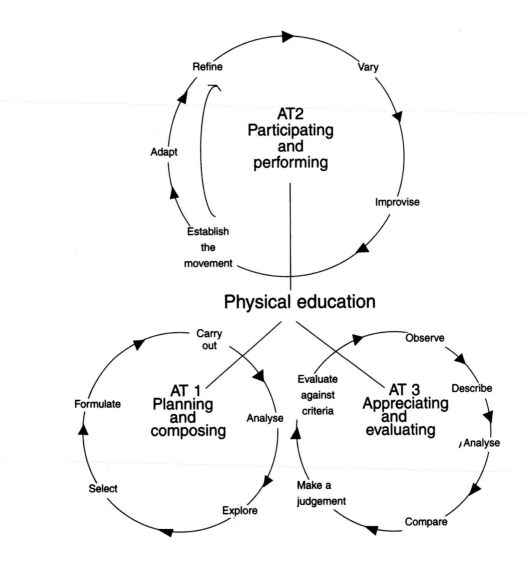

Refine

Vary

AT2
Participating
and
performing

Adapt

Improvise

Establish
the
movement

Physical education

Carry
out

Observe

AT 1
Planning
and
composing

Evaluate
against
criteria

AT 3
Appreciating
and
evaluating

Describe

Formulate

Analyse

Analyse

Select

Make a
judgement

Compare

Explore

Figure 7.1 Progressive development within attainment targets
Source: DES/WO 1990: 25

whether the process shown clearly in the interim report (DES/WO 1990) maintains its clarity when reduced to a single attainment target and whether the Programmes of Study and 1992 End of Key Stage Statements (EKSS) and 1995 End of Key Stage Descriptions (EKSD) give sufficient information on the kinds of knowledge and practical expertise required to meet a single attainment target of planning, performing and evaluating to enable the process of learning to be planned for and achieved.

It seems that on a 'process of learning-product (performance)' continuum the EKSS of the 1992 NCPE (DES/WO 1992) and the EKSD of the 1995 NCPE (DfE/WO 1995), along with the NCC non-statutory guidance for the interpretation of the 1992 NCPE (NCC 1992), with its emphasis on the development of knowledge, skills and understanding, were much further toward the product end of the continuum than the models and frameworks considered earlier.

Thus, the 1992 NCPE showed a definite bias towards a focus on product in the way that it was written, and the 1995 NCPE (DfE/WO 1995) showed a move even further towards the product end of this continuum. However, the 2000 NCPE (DfEE/QCA 1999) indicates a swing of the pendulum back once more towards the process model of physical education, viewing physical education as a subject contributing to the total growth and development of pupils, part of the wider educational process. QCA stated quite clearly that physical education is 'the process of developing pupils' knowledge, skills and understanding' and 'that it requires pupils to think as well as perform' (QCA 1999b: 1). Reference is also made to the benefits of physical activity to the development of physical and mental health and to intellectual, social and personal well-being. Increasing competence, personal confidence and self-esteem and the ability to continue learning independently are also claimed as outcomes for physical education. The addition of four clearly identifiable strands of learning in the 2000 NCPE (DfEE/QCA 1999): acquiring and developing skills; selecting and applying skills, tactics and compositional ideas; evaluating and improving performance; and knowledge and understanding of fitness and health, show a clear return to focus on the process of learning in the physical education curriculum.

Reflection on the issue of a broad and balanced curriculum in physical education requires a clear understanding of what constitutes 'core knowledge' in physical education, in order that aims can be clarified and content determined for inclusion in the curriculum. Content in physical education can be treated holistically or classified into subjects (areas of activity or themes of learning). Content in physical education can be seen as passing on tradition and culture, preparing pupils for life after school or as meeting the needs of the individual. Within the constraints of a NCPE, different approaches can be taken in delivering the Programmes of Study for the areas of activity. These approaches fall into two very different categories; a process-based approach focusing on the educational experiences to be gained, and a product-based approach focusing on the performance of the activities. In the former, activities are used to provide pupils with experiences: learning is a means to an end, while in the latter, knowledge, understanding and the improvement of performance in activities are seen as ends in themselves. Process and product are considered further in other chapters in this book; notably in Chapters 1 and 13.

Games in a broad and balanced physical education curriculum

Linked to, but separate from, the process-product debate is the debate about the balance of activities in the NCPE. The NCC stressed that 'in setting out a balanced programme it is not necessary for each area of activity to have an equal share of curriculum time provided that the Programme of Study is completed by the end of the key stage' (NCC 1992: C1). However, games have long been a major part of the physical education curriculum in many schools, particularly in secondary schools.

In 1984, a survey conducted by Hill (1984, cited in Thorpe, Bunker and Almond 1986b) found that 65 per cent or more of physical education time in schools in England was allocated to games. Since the NCPE was introduced in 1992, games have retained a central place in the curriculum.

In the 1992 NCPE (DES/WO 1992) there was some bias towards games. However, in the revision of the National Curriculum which resulted in the 1995 NCPE (DfE/WO 1995), the emphasis given to each of the six areas of activity was not equal; games were enshrined as the dominant area. In the 2000 NCPE (DfEE/QCA 1999) the balance has been redressed somewhat; most notably because games are not compulsory at KS4. The NCPE requirements in 1992 1995 and for 2000 are shown in Table 7.1.

In reflecting on the dominance of games in the NCPE Evans *et al.* concluded that the

> text of the NCPE now reinforces a very narrow and 'traditional' definition of physical education as comprising a set of separate and distinct areas of activity and openly accords the highest status to that area that has long dominated the physical education curriculum in state schools, namely, competitive team games. Nowhere does the text prompt teachers to reflect on present provision, or consider how or why they teach.
>
> (Evans *et al.* 1996: 7)

Thus games were prioritised in the NCPE, particularly in the 1995 NCPE (DfE/WO 1995). However, this is supported by tradition and the bias given by many teachers to games in the physical education curriculum, particularly in secondary schools. This tradition and bias has perhaps weighted the curriculum towards games even more than that intended by the NCPE.

Fairclough and Stratton (1997) compared data from surveys between 1974 and 1997 to assess changes in time allocated to, and the content of, physical education curricular and extra-curricular activities in secondary schools. Results showed that in 1997 games received the largest amount of curriculum

Table 7.1 The requirements of the 1992, 1995 and 2000 NCPE

Key Stage	1992 NCPE pupils were required to pursue the programmes of study for:	1995 NCPE pupils should be taught:	2000 NCPE during the Key Stage, pupils should be taught the knowledge, skills and understanding through:
KS1	five areas of activity: athletic activities, dance, games, gymnastic activities and outdoor and adventurous activities (OAA), and if the school chose to teach it in KS1, swimming.	three areas of activity: games, gymnastic activities and dance. Schools could choose to teach swimming in KS1 using the programme of study set out in KS2.	dance activities, games activities and gymnastic activities. Schools have the option to teach swimming activities and water safety based on the non-statutory programme of study.
KS2	six areas of activity: athletic activities, dance, games, gymnastic activities, OAA and swimming, unless the programme of study for swimming was completed during KS1.	six areas of activity. Games, gymnastic activities and dance should be taught during each year of the KS, with the other three areas of activity taught at points during the KS, unless the programme of study for swimming was completed during KS1.	five areas of activity: dance activities; games activities; gymnastics activities and two activity areas from: athletic activities; OAA; swimming activities and water safety. Swimming activities and water safety must be chosen as one of these areas of activity unless pupils have completed the full KS2 teaching requirements during KS1.
KS3	a minimum of four areas of activity. Games were compulsory in each year of the key stage. Swimming and other water based activities could, where schools had appropriate facilities, be undertaken in others contexts, e.g. swimming as an athletic activity, water polo as a game and sailing as OAA.	games, at least one other full area of activity (Units A + B) and at least two additional half areas of activity (Unit A) taken from different areas of activity. At least one half area of activity (Unit A) had to be taken from either gymnastic activities or dance. Games were to be taught in each year of the KS.	four areas of activity. These should include: games activities; and three of the following, at least one of which must be dance or gymnastic activities: dance activities; gymnastic activities; athletic activities; OAA; swimming activities and water safety.
KS4	at least two activities; drawn from the same area of activity or from two different areas. The same requirement for swimming applied as at KS3.	a minimum of two different activities. At least one of the two activities chosen should be a game.	two of the six activity areas.
	(DES/WO 1992: 5–11)	(DFE/WO 1995: 3–9)	(DfEE/QCA 1999: 17–25)

time throughout KS3 and KS4, followed by athletics and then gymnastics, while dance and swimming were less prominent. Traditional games such as football, netball, basketball, hockey, rugby, cricket and rounders dominated the curriculum throughout Years 7 to 11. The number of schools offering dance and gymnastics dropped dramatically at KS4. Only one-third of schools delivered courses with a focus on HRE each term. Thus the physical education curriculum in many secondary schools was based around games.

These findings were consistent with those of Penney and Evans (1994) and the Office for Standards in Education (OFSTED 1995b) who reported that between 50 per cent and 70 per cent of physical education curriculum time at KS3 was spent on games. OFSTED stated that 'in secondary schools the curriculum content often includes a strong focus on games, particularly invasion games, and this reduces the time available for other aspects of the National Curriculum' (OFSTED 1995a: 3). Further, Penney and Evans (1994) reported that more schools teach games than other areas of activity, with the balance being more biased towards games at KS4, as compared to KS3. This is shown in Table 7.2.

It seems that leaving the amount of time to be spent on each area of activity open to individual interpretation encourages the continuing dominance of games in the school curriculum, particularly at secondary level. It can be argued that although it may not be necessary to allocate an equal share of curriculum time to each area of activity, it is necessary to consider whether the right balance is achieved between the various areas of activity and activities in the curriculum. If a curriculum is biased heavily towards one area of activity, it is necessary to consider the implications of this.

One implication is that the range of processes experienced by pupils may be limited. This can be illustrated by considering the particular contribution that each of the six areas of activity makes to physical education. HMI identified these as:

> *Gymnastics* is concerned with acquiring control, co-ordination and versatility in the use of the body. It is based on natural actions such as

Table 7.2 Percentage of schools teaching each area of activity in the physical education curriculum

Area of activity	Year 9	Year 11
Athletic activities	100% (n=77)	57% (n=43)
Dance	53% (n=41)	33% (n=25)
Games	99% (n=75)	99% (n=73)
Gymnastic activities	87% (n=67)	43% (n=32)
OAA	23% (n=18)	29% (n=22)
Swimming	41% (n=32)	54% (n=41)

Source: Penney and Evans 1994: 10

jumping, leaping, balancing, rolling, pushing, pulling and swinging. . . . The actions . . . need to be combined so that children learn how to blend movements appropriately. . . . *Dance* too, focuses on developing mastery of the body. . . . it helps maintain flexibility and mobility and develops an appreciation of line, form, strength and grace in movement. . . . Most importantly the intention of dance is to use the body expressively, often to convey ideas or moods. . . . The main features of *games* are the development of motor skills, hand and eye co-ordination, tactics and strategies and the matching of this range of skills against an opponent. . . . Games invariably involve competition. . . . It is beneficial if the opportunity to learn to *swim* can be given as early as possible . . . when the emphasis needs to be on developing safety and confidence in the water. . . . At the secondary level, attention should be on improving technique and increasing the number of strokes used as well as on survival and life saving skills. . . . *Athletics* in the primary school seeks to develop children's natural capacities to run, jump, and throw without undue emphasis on competition . . . the preparation of the body for activity and appreciation of training schedules can be of value in promoting a positive attitude towards care and respect for the body. This can be translated into the practice of an active and healthy life style after pupils leave school . . . *outdoor pursuits* is dependent upon accessibility of facilities and expertise among the staff. However, much can be done at school or in the immediate area, for example, by pitching a tent or cooking a simple meal.

(DES 1989a: 9–14)

A comparison can be made between this 1989 view of the main characteristics and the distinctive contribution each of the six areas of activity makes to a broad and balanced physical education curriculum with those expressed by QCA (1999c) when defining the terminology used in the NCPE for 2000. In the 2000 NCPE (DfEE/QCA 1999), the description of each of the areas of activity has developed from the examples given by HMI in 1989 (DES 1989a) but with more detail being provided about the distinguishing characteristics of each area of activity. This clearly indicates that each area of activity has a contribution to make to a physical education curriculum that is broad and balanced (see QCA 1999c: 9–32).

A second implication concerns the view that physical education is 'sport in school', which is how many politicians would seem to define the subject. They therefore strongly support the teaching of traditional games, particularly team games, as the main focus of the physical education curriculum. Williams wrote that 'even more than the 1992 order the latest physical education order (DfE/WO 1995) reflects the dominant and central government view of physical education as virtually synonymous with sport, with priority given to traditional team games' (Williams 1996b: 20). Publications such as *Sport: Raising the Game* (DNH 1995), *Labour's Sporting Nation* (Labour Party 1996) and *England, The Sporting Nation: A Strategy*

(English Sports Council 1997) further endorse this emphasis, without due consideration of the implications for the other areas of activity or the process and personal development outcomes of education.

The implicit definition of physical education as 'sport in schools', and hence a curriculum biased towards team games is also highlighted by the media. Much media comment accompanying the publication of the draft proposals for the 2000 NCPE (QCA 1999a) highlighted the proposal for team games no longer to be a compulsory element of study at KS4. The removal of 'compulsory' was interpreted as the removal of team games themselves from the Key Stage. The fact that team games could, and most likely would, be included in the programme at KS4 for 14–16 year olds was played down. Headlines such as those warning of the decline in national standards of sporting excellence equating with the removal of team games from the school curriculum made sensational reading (see, for example, 'Schools: Less teamwork more fun' (Revell 1999: 4) or 'Playing the game could be optional' (Chaudharay 1999: 6). They made far better headlines than those identifying that pupils whose preference lay outside competitive games are enabled to choose to participate in physical activities more suited to their needs. However, the implication of this is whether physical education is and should be seen as 'sport in school'; this is considered further in Chapter 8.

A third implication concerns the view that 'education involves the initiation of children into a selection from culture and physical activities are part of that culture' (Parry 1988: 117). Games are undeniably an important part of the culture of UK society. However, if this aim of education is accepted, the question to be asked is whether the dominance of games in the physical education curriculum reflects proportionately the dominance of games over other activities in the culture and traditions of UK society.

This argument for the cultural value of activities can be extended to the whole of the physical education curriculum in the debate about 'core knowledge' in the first part of the chapter. Parry (1988) explained the intrinsic value of physical education activities by identifying them as a necessary part of the development of a human being towards an idealised conception of the person or citizen. Citing Hoberman (1984), Parry stated that: 'Underlying every conception of education there is philosophical anthropology – an idealised conception of the person or citizen which inevitably has an ideological basis' (Parry 1988: 117). Thus, arguments could be developed which could 'justify the place of physical education on the curriculum from the point of view of the individual learner and the culture into which she is to be initiated' (ibid.: 117). Justifying the inclusion of physical education in the National Curriculum through the intrinsic and cultural value of physical education activities, rather than as part of the broader educational development of the child, highlights the process of learning-product debate in determining the 'core knowledge' of physical education and how the subject should be defined.

Another issue concerning the place of games in a broad and balanced physical education curriculum relates to which games to include in the curriculum. When the wealth and variety of games is considered it is apparent that even in a games dominated curriculum it is impossible for pupils to experience all games and become competent in them all. There is an obvious need for a process of selection of games, the extent and form of which raises other questions. Is there a need to provide a games curriculum which leads to a games education which increases knowledge and understanding across the types of games available (see Figure 5.1 for one classification of types of games), or should selection be limited to a small number of games to enable excellence in performance to be developed? The former relates to a process model of core knowledge (and can be exemplified in the Teaching Games for Understanding model, see Chapter 5), while the latter relates more clearly to a product model. The latter would, no doubt, be the preference of the National Governing Bodies of Sport (NGBs), provided their game was included as one of the chosen few.

Thus, in relation to considering the place of games in a broad and balanced physical education curriculum, questions raised centre around the amount of time devoted to the teaching of games in relation to the time allocated to the other areas of activity and the implications of that on the range of processes experienced by pupils, whether physical education should be seen as 'sport in school' and whether games have greater cultural value than other areas of activity. Further questions are raised within the games area of activity itself about the breadth and nature of the games included in the curriculum. (Games are considered further in Chapter 5 of this book)

Summary

The purpose of this chapter was to enable readers to understand the importance of considering breadth and balance in developing a physical education curriculum which meets the needs of all pupils. Three aspects of the debate about a broad and balanced curriculum were identified in the chapter: accessibility to a broad and balanced curriculum; the nature of 'core knowledge' in physical education; and the balance of activities taught in a physical education curriculum (particularly the balance between games and other areas of activity). Reference was made to other chapters which cover issues of accessibility in depth but the second two aspects were discussed in the chapter. However, all three aspects are important when debating the availability of a broad and balanced curriculum for all pupils.

Questions for reflection

1 What are your views about whether physical education should be concentrating on process or on product/performance? What implications does this have for the selection of content, and of teaching approaches?

2 Does each area of activity represent a discrete area of activity and, hence,

a discrete and essential experience for all pupils? Are there any other areas of activity which ought to be included in a broad and balanced physical education curriculum and, if so, why? What would be lost if one area of activity were omitted from the physical education curriculum?

Further reading

QCA (1998) *Maintaining Breadth and Balance at Key Stages 1 and 2*, Suffolk: QCA Publications.

—— (1999c) *Terminology in Physical Education*, Suffolk: QCA Publications.

8 Physical education and sport

Susan Capel

Introduction

International sporting success is very important to Britain. The link between sporting success and national pride has been recognised by politicians. For example, in his letter accompanying the publication *Sport: Raising the Game* (Department of National Heritage (DNH) 1995) the then Prime Minister, John Major, stated that 'Sport is a binding force between generations and across borders. But, by a miraculous paradox, it is at the same time one of the defining characteristics of nationhood and of local pride. We should cherish it for both those reasons' (DNH 1995: 2). Such sentiments have been echoed by agencies with responsibility for sport. For example, in its strategy for sport in England, the English Sports Council (ESC) acknowledged that 'England – the sporting nation – takes immense pride and identity from success on the international stage (ESC 1997: 14)'. Thus, as Treadwell stressed:

> we are incredibly naive if we have not realised the international political significance in catering for giftedness in sport. Our international arenas of sport are effectively theatres of 'pseudo-war' and success at the highest level can appear to be a reinforcement of the policies, lifestyles and persuasions of any capitalist or socialist state.
>
> (Treadwell 1987: 65)

The relative lack of success of British national sports teams in international competition in recent years has resulted in much debate. Politicians and agencies responsible for sport have identified strategies to improve performance, articulated in documents such as *Sport: Raising the Game* (DNH 1995); *England, the Sporting Nation: A Strategy* (ESC 1997); *Labour's Sporting Nation* (Labour Party 1996). Many of these strategies identify an integral role for physical education. One possible reason for physical education being seen as integral to international sporting success is that many people view physical education as playing a key role in developing sporting talent. This is shown, for example, in a leading article in *The Times Educational Supplement* which rejected the practice of a comprehensive school that had introduced 'stool ball' as a game that 'allows both sexes to play and is non-competitive'. Stool ball was scorned as a game that 'is not going to help England find a quick bowler'. 'The West Indian pace attack', we were told, 'was not reared on stool ball' (*TES* 11 July 1986).

A second reason could be that many people see a decline in sport in schools as being the cause of lack of international sporting success. It was evident that John Major supported the views of many in the press and other agencies that teachers were to blame for the 'decline in sport' (Gilroy and Clarke 1997). These two reasons have been suggested as being linked. For example, Murdoch cited what she referred to as 'two current prevalent perceptions that, first, sport was in decline both within the school context and in the winning of international honours and, second, that the former was responsible in a direct way for the latter' (Murdoch 1997: 253). This may be one reason why 'many headteachers, teachers, governors, parents and children hold the view that physical education and sport are synonymous' (Murdoch 1990: 64).

But physical education and sport are not synonymous. This chapter begins by looking at some reasons why physical education and sport are seen as synonymous. It continues by considering differences between physical education and sport, starting with some definitions of physical education and sport, then articulating some of the central differences between the two. Despite their differences physical education and sport are inter-related; physical education makes a contribution to sport and sport makes a contribution to physical education. These contributions are considered in the next part of the chapter.

It is important that physical education teachers are clear about, and articulate, the differences between physical education and sport because this has implications for the future of physical education. For example, Evans suggested that 'this conceptual conflation of physical education and sport has damaged and seriously limited academic, political and public debate concerning physical education in schools in Britain and elsewhere' (Evans 1988: 175). Whitson and Macintosh asked, 'Why has the discourse of physical education today so little to do with education and so much to do with systematic production of sporting performance?' (Whitson and Macintosh 1990: 40). More practically, if physical education and sport are taken as synonymous, do schools need to employ physical education teachers? Why not simply replace physical education teachers with a number of sport coaches, each specialising in coaching their own particular activity? Thus, this chapter is designed to help physical education teachers to articulate what physical education is and its unique contribution to the education of all pupils; something which cannot be replicated by sport.

Why are physical education and sport viewed as synonymous?

The physical education profession is not sending a clear message about what physical education is and how it is different to sport

One of the major reasons for people seeing physical education and sport as synonymous is that the physical education profession is not sending a clear message about what physical education is, what lies at its core and what the differences are between physical education and sport. There may be several reasons for physical education teachers not sending clear messages. First, they cannot articulate clearly the differences between physical education and sport. This may be because they have not reflected on what physical education is, and due to there being a range of definitions they assume a definition based on their own background and experience. Thus, as 'it (is) likely that the majority of specialist physical education teachers entered the profession because of their own enthusiasm for sport and their recognition of the personal benefits and enjoyment it can bring' (Department of Education and Science (DES)/Welsh Office (WO) 1991: 7), they may not have clearly differentiated between physical education and sport and linked physical education very closely with sport. This may be exacerbated by physical education teachers including physical education curriculum time and extra-curricular activities in their reflections on what physical education is, partly because their job includes both work in curriculum and extra-curricular time. (For further consideration of what physical education is and what lies at its core, see also Chapter 13.)

It is the common-sense view of many that physical education and sport are the same

As the physical education profession does not send a clear message about what physical education is, the general public may take a common-sense view that physical education and sport are, in fact, the same. According to Leaman (1988: 97), most common-sense notions equate physical education with sport. There are a number of reasons for this, which include the following examples:

- The physical education curriculum, particularly in secondary schools, has traditionally been dominated by competitive team games and sports activities. For example, the Office for Standards in Education (OFSTED) found that 'in a substantial proportion of schools the curriculum over-emphasises games, in particular invasion games, the programme for boys is sometimes more limited than for girls' (OFSTED 1995a: 12). OFSTED found also that:

> the percentage of the available curriculum time for physical education devoted to games in the National Curriculum varied widely. Most fell within a range of 50 per cent to 70 per cent of the time at [Key Stage] KS3, but extremes included 33 per cent in one school and more than 80 per cent in another. The other three chosen areas of activity required by the National Curriculum were squeezed into what time was left.
> (OFSTED 1995b: 11, parentheses added)

The dominance of competitive team games in the physical education curriculum in secondary schools is long-standing, stemming from the traditions of the public schools in the nineteenth century. 'The strong historical tradition set in the public schools is replicated still in the minds of many and is hard to change' (Murdoch 1990: 65). More recently, the dominance of competitive team games has been enshrined in the physical education curriculum in schools in England and Wales, through the National Curriculum for Physical Education (NCPE). This reinforces a belief that physical education and sport are one and the same thing. (For further evidence of the dominance of games in the physical education curriculum in secondary schools, see Chapter 7 of this book.)

- Strong similarities in the kit worn by boys and girls for physical education and many sports reinforce the view that physical education and sport are synonymous. Further, in some schools, pupils are required to have different kit for different activities, mirroring the clothing worn to play the sport being learned, e.g. 'whites' for cricket lessons.
- The success of a school's physical education programme may be interpreted through the success of its inter-school sports teams. The difference between physical education curriculum time and extra-curricular activities is not clarified. The success of sports teams may be used as a marketing tool for the school. In addition, in an era which sees education strongly subject to market forces, it is not unusual to find headteachers and governors giving clear emphasis to the value attached to sport in their mission statements about physical education. This sends a message that physical education and sport are synonymous.

Politicians often reinforce the view that physical education and sport are the same

Politicians often see physical education and sport as synonymous. For example, the working party selected by the then Secretary of State, Kenneth Clarke, to develop proposals for the NCPE (DES/WO 1992) contained two professional sportsmen – John Fashanu (football) and Steve Ovett (athletics) – but no practising physical education teacher. In 1998 the Junior Minister for Education, Estelle Morris, speaking about the government proposals to slim down the National Curriculum in primary schools, was reported in the *Times Educational Supplement* as saying 'No subject – not sport, history or geography – has ceased to be compulsory. They were compulsory, they are compulsory and they will remain compulsory' (*TES* 3 July 1998: 6). It is also seen in various government documents: for example in *Sport: Raising the Game* the action agenda for sport in schools states that 'all schools should offer two hours per week of physical education and sport in schools' (DNH 1995: 3).

Fisher concluded that

> the pressure for a greater emphasis on traditional competitive team games in the school curriculum . . . can be seen as a feature of a political context in which tradition, order, stability and accountability are important. . . . The

demands from outside the school in the political arena and from parents have been for competition and results. . . . If traditional expectations are not fulfilled, the physical education profession is open to criticism.

(Fisher 1996: 140)

This was endorsed by Penney and Harris who concluded that 'the revision of the NCPE demonstrated all too clearly the political nature of educational reform and the inequalities of the development process in terms of "who had a say"' (Penney and Harris 1998: 5).

The media often reinforce the view that physical education and sport are the same

The media is also sometimes responsible for conflating the two concepts of physical education and sport. Murdoch cited an example of a broadcast which was introduced by the presenter as 'School sport, or to give it its proper title, physical education' (Murdoch 1990: 65). Further, the media is often quick to blame physical education in schools as responsible for national sporting defeat. This contributes to the view that physical education in schools exists for the sole purpose of developing sporting excellence.

However, physical education and sport are not the same and it is important that physical education teachers are clear about the differences. These differences are now considered; first definitions of physical education and sport are given, then some differences between the two identified.

Why physical education and sport are different

Definitions of physical education and sport

One of the problems faced in explaining differences between physical education and sport is that there is no single accepted definition of either. There are a number of definitions, or at least descriptions, of physical education and sport. Some definitions of physical education and sport are included in Chapter 1 of this book. Some other definitions of physical education and sport are provided next.

With regard to physical education, the National Curriculum Physical Education Working Group (NCPEWG) stated that:

3.1 Physical education educates young people in and through the use and knowledge of the body and its movement. It:
- develops physical competence and enables pupils to engage in worthwhile physical activities
- promotes physical development and teaches pupils to value the benefits of participation in physical activity whilst at school and throughout life
- develops artistic and aesthetic understanding within and through movement

- helps to establish self-esteem through the development of physical confidence and helps pupils to cope with both success and failure in competitive and co-operative physical activities.

3.2 Physical education also contributes to:

- the development of problem-solving skills
- the development of inter-personal skills
- the forging of links between the school and the community, and across cultures

3.3 Physical education aims to develop physical competence so that pupils are able to move efficiently, effectively and safely and understand what they are doing. It is essentially a way of learning through action, awareness and observation.

(DES/WO 1991: 5)

On the other hand, the Council of Europe in its European Sports Charter stated that:

Sport means all forms of physical activity which, through casual or organised participation, aims at improving physical fitness and mental well-being, forming social relationships, or obtaining results in competition at all levels.

(Council of Europe 1992)

To the School Sport Forum, sport covered:

- competitive games and sports . . .
- outdoor pursuits, in which participants seek to negotiate some particular 'terrain' . . .
- aesthetic movement . . . e.g. dance, figure skating, forms of rhythmic gymnastics and recreational swimming;
- conditioning activity . . . improving or maintaining physical working capacity and engendering subsequently a feeling of general well-being.

This broad interpretation allows for a range of interests to be acknowledged, and for many forms of participation to be encouraged within the provision of 'sport'.

(School Sport Forum 1988: 5)

Despite similarities in, and possible overlap between, some definitions, many people have concluded that physical education and sport are not the same. Murdoch viewed physical education and sport as 'distinct phenomena' (Murdoch 1990: 64). Further, NCPEWG identified physical education as being unique and different to sport:

Sport covers a range of physical activities in which adults and young people may participate. Physical education on the other hand is a process of learning, the context being mainly physical. The purpose of this process is to develop specific knowledge, skills and understanding and to promote physical competence. Different sporting activities can and do contribute to that learning process, and the learning enables participation in sport. The focus however is on the child and his or her development of physical competence, rather than on the activity.

(DES/WO 1991: 7)

This suggests ways in which physical education and sport are different or distinct and not synonymous. These are considered in greater depth in the remainder of the chapter.

Central differences between physical education and sport

Physical education is essentially an educational process whereas the focus in sport is on the activity

The NCPEWG (DES/WO 1991) emphasised that, in physical education the focus is on the process of learning in a mainly physical context, whereas in sport greater focus is placed on the activity and the emphasis may be placed on the end product, i.e. the performance or outcome. In the non-statutory guidance accompanying the first NCPE document in 1992 this distinction was reinforced: 'In physical education the emphasis is on learning in a mainly physical context. The purpose of the learning is to develop specific knowledge, skills and understanding and to promote physical development and competence. The learning promotes participation in sport' (National Curriculum Council (NCC) 1992: H1). On the other hand, 'Sport is the term applied to a range of physical activities where emphasis is on participation and competition. Different sporting activities can and do contribute to learning' (NCC 1992: H1).

Murdoch stressed that through participating in physical education it is important that pupils are equipped to 'continue to be engaged in the learning process even after they have left school' (Murdoch 1997: 263). She emphasised that the process of learning through planning, performing and evaluating gives an integrity to the learning of discrete activity areas and 'strengthens the uniqueness of the process to physical education' (ibid.: 267). Activities are selected for inclusion in a physical education programme for a particular purpose (see Chapter 13 for further discussion about selecting activities for inclusion in the physical education curriculum to serve a particular purpose).

This difference between physical education and sport can be illustrated by an example. Whereas a gymnastics coach, for example, might simply be concerned with producing the correct pattern of movement for a particular vault, the physical education teacher might focus on assisting the pupil to engage in a process which involves planning their approach (for example, length, speed of run up, angle of approach), performing the action and evaluating the performance (establishing the feeling, repeating the movement exactly, varying the movement, adapting the movement through repositioning the hands and so on).

The focus on the learning process may provide a knowledge of principles which assist the pupil in learning new skills.

This is linked to physical education commencing from the perspective of the child and dimensions of the child's physical learning whereas sport starts from the perspective of the activity that is to be learned. Talbot reminded us that in physical education 'the game is not the thing, the child is' (Talbot 1987). Further, Lee stressed that 'while training and coaching may be concerned with developing performance, education is concerned with developing people' (Lee 1986: 248).

Physical education involves motor skill development and need not involve sporting activities

A focus on the child requires careful consideration of childrens' needs at different stages in their development. During the early (pre-5 or nursery) years, physical activity has a base in play and playfulness. Structured support for learning through physical education assists the child to develop from this base. During the nursery and primary phases of education, physical education should encompass the learning of fundamental motor skills to form the foundation for participation in a range of physical activities. The primary years are important for helping children to gain mastery of their own bodies. Physical education is concerned with motor skill development and not just learning particular sports. Thus, the focus in physical education for very young pupils – nursery and KS1 – should not be on competing, which is necessarily involved in sports contexts, as this may be too advanced for their stage of cognitive development. The foundation provided at this stage can be the basis for 'more formal phases of participation in the activities of physical education and sport, moving from simple to complex versions' (Murdoch 1990: 73). Activities incorporated into physical education at later stages may not necessarily be sports.

Physical education is a concept broader than sport

Physical education is a concept broader than sport. Physical education encompasses sport but also embraces other physical activities which are not sports, e.g. dance. The inclusion of dance in the NCPE was supported as 'an essential part of a balanced physical education programme' (DES/WO 1990: 13). The interim report of the NCPEWG acknowledged the status of dance as a distinct art form: 'The dance as art model develops in pupils an appreciation of dance as an artistic and aesthetic activity' (DES/WO 1990: 13). Physical education also embraces physical activities which may or may not be sports, depending on reasons for participation, e.g. outdoor and adventurous activities (OAA). These activities are, or may not be, conceptually linked to competition which is inherent in sports. There are aspects of OAA that usefully form part of the learning process to enable the aims of physical education to be fulfilled, such as planning and taking part in an expedition. However, these do not constitute involvement in sport or preparation for such involvement. Thus, there is no inherent necessity that all forms of physical education should foster and promote the kind of competitive behaviour which is essential to sport.

In physical education, sports should be selected for inclusion in the curriculum for the potential they have for the learning that is to take place and not vice versa (see earlier). If the focus in physical education were only on sport there could be a narrow focus to the curriculum (for example, only rugby).

Further, there are a number of aims for physical education which can be achieved through participation in activities other than sports. One of the aims of physical education can be the aspiration for as many pupils as possible to integrate physical activity as part of their lifestyle. Some pupils may not choose to integrate sport into their lifestyle, but may choose other forms of physical activity.

Tinning identified a danger of using sport education in physical education and highlighted the need to re-emphasise the 'educational purposes of physical education' (Tinning 1995: 19). He considered that the work of physical education professionals would be

> better facilitated by reaffirming that sport is merely one medium (in physical activity) for the development of physically educated citizens. It should not be the central focus of physical education in schools. To allow physical education to be distilled to sport . . . is to sell our subject short. Certainly sport should be part of a physical education curriculum . . . but we must remember that sport is not the most reinforcing movement form for countless individuals.
>
> (Tinning 1995: 20)

Physical education should benefit every pupil in the group regardless of ability and enthusiasm for the subject; therefore an emphasis on sport and with it an emphasis on competition and competitive success (e.g. at inter-house level on a traditional sports day or at inter-school level) can result in finite resources being used for a few elite performers rather than being available to encourage participation in physical activity for all. 'If one spends a disproportionate amount of time on just a few pupils (in physical education or elsewhere) then it is only to be expected that a higher level of performance will be achieved' (Leaman 1988: 105). Many would regard such an allocation of resources as basically unfair and to be avoided in a school. Thus, 'instead of the expense of transporting a small minority of students to distant corners of the county, a lunchtime and after-school activity programme could be developed that appeals to the full spectrum of youngsters' interests' (Fox 1996: 105).

Most would agree, however, that the pursuit of excellence is important for the able performer. Physical education teachers have a role in identifying potential and enabling pupils to develop their potential, but whose role is it to develop excellence? To what degree should excellence be a focus for schools if it is at the expense of less assistance, effort, time and resources being given to the less able to help them to achieve their potential? (See Chapters 2, 3 and 4 of this book for further discussion about equal opportunities in physical education.) What role should physical education and physical education staff play in the development of excellence? As Fox contended,

> The school is not wholly responsible; as many children will take part in swimming, gymnastics, dance and other sports activities . . . Increasingly also, youngsters play sport through the club system on weekends and older adolescents are beginning to enrol in formal exercise classes and take membership at fitness clubs. An important role for schools is to make links and alliances with these alternative agencies.
>
> (Fox 1996: 106)

Thus, identification of potential may occur in physical education time, but development of that potential to achieve excellence can occur in extra-curricular time or through pupils being referred to opportunities at local sports clubs or other types of community provision. Developing potential is an integral part of the sports development continuum (ESC 1997); a framework for sporting opportunity and performance from foundation through to excellence, as shown in Figure 8.1. There is further discussion of community initiatives in physical education in Chapter 10.

Foundation
means the early development of sporting competence and physical skills upon which all later forms of sports development are based. Without a sound foundation young people are unlikely to become long-term sports participants

Participation
refers to sport undertaken primarily for fun, enjoyment and, often, at basic levels of competence. However, many very competent sports people take part in sport purely for reasons of fun, health and fitness

Performance
signifies a move from basic competence into a more structured form of competitive sport at club or county level or, indeed, at an individual level for personal reasons

Excellence
is about reaching the top and applies to performers at the highest national and international levels

Figure 8.1 The sports development continuum
Source: ESC 1997: 5

This section has shown that physical education and sport are different. However, even though they are different, physical education and sport are inter-related. Indeed, the School Sport Forum was unequivocal in its affirmation that: 'Sport and Physical Education are not the same, but they are interdependent' (School Sport Forum 1988: 7).

Physical education makes a contribution to sport and sport makes a contri-bution to physical education. Some of these contributions are identified in the next section of the chapter.

The contribution of physical education to sport and sport to physical education

The contribution of physical education to sport

There is much that physical education can offer to sport. Ways in which physical education contributes to sport include providing a foundation of basic motor skills for participating in sport. Physical education can provide the foundation level of the continuum for all pupils, on which all future sports development is based. This role is integral to the Sports Development Continuum of the ESC (1997) which is shown in Figure 8.1.

Other ways include initiating pupils into various culturally valued sports; and, linked to this, enabling pupils to make informed choices for engaging in particular sports. In physical education pupils learn to participate in sport, which enables them to make choices of sport(s) in which to participate in extra-curricular activities, out of school and post-school. This role was recognised by the School Sport Forum when it emphasised that 'Physical education prepares each child for satisfying participation in sport, through development of the necessary skills and through knowledge of opportunities available for recreation in the community' (School Sport Forum 1998: 7).

The contribution of sport to physical education

Likewise, sport has a place in the physical education curriculum. Sport is a very useful vehicle for learning in physical education and it supports the process of learning. Sport can offer a number of valuable educational experiences. For example, the sports context can provide a forum within which young people can experience success and satisfaction. They may feel successful through showing ability (often by being better than others), mastering an activity for its own sake or for the first time, being able to please others, feeling a sense of adventure, or being able to achieve as a member of a team. Pupils may be motivated to partic-ipate in sports rather than other types of physical activity included in the physical education curriculum and this is likely to have a positive effect on their continued participation in post-school physical activity (White and Coakley 1986).

However, in order for sport to contribute positively to the learning process in physical education, sports must be selected for the potential they hold for learning.

The interim report of the NCPEWG identified that 'within a programme of physical education, sporting activities such as competitive games, swimming and athletics are vehicles for education – *education through sport* – and they are also valued in their own right as worthwhile activities – *education in sport*' (DES/WO 1990: 12).

Conclusion

This chapter identified some reasons why physical education and sport are seen as synonymous. It then considered some of the central differences between physical education and sport. Although physical education and sport are different, they are inter-related and each contributes to the other. The contribution of physical education to sport and the contribution of sport to physical education were also considered in the chapter.

The inter-relationship between physical education and sport can be seen as threatening, as was recognised by the School Sport Forum, when it stated that:

> The close relationship between sport and physical education can lead to misunderstandings, some of which may be caused by unrealistic expectations. Some people in the sporting world, largely through the media, are voicing dissatisfaction with sport and physical education in schools saying, for example, that standards in performance and commitment are not as high as they should be. Tensions can arise in the other direction when behaviour in top-level sport, such as reluctance to accept decisions of umpires, violence and the taking of drugs to enhance performance, conflict with educational objectives. There is a need for dialogue.
>
> (School Sport Forum 1998: 7)

Murdoch proposed that rather than looking to polarise physical education and sport, a better way forward may be to integrate physical education and sport 'from pre- to post-school and both in and out of school in the most appropriate way' (Murdoch 1990: 72). She identified five models for the relationship between physical education and sport: Substitution model; Versus model; Reinforcement model; Sequence model; and Integration model. She suggested that the first two models have negative connotations and do not hold potential for the development of working relationships, whereas the others are positive attempts to capture the significant relationships that are considered worth developing. Readers should refer to Murdoch (1990) for further discussion about each of these models. Murdoch used the models to ask questions such as: Can and should physical education serve the needs of sport as a cultural phenomenon? Should physical education educate for sport? Does sport provide a vehicle for physical education? These questions provide a useful basis for reflection on the inter-relationship between physical education and sport.

Despite their interrelationship, differences between physical education and sport should not be ignored. Reflection on differences is important to enable their unique roles to be fully utilised. Further, it is important that physical education teachers can articulate the differences so that they are able to justify the subject to agencies such as national government; government departments/agencies such as the Department for Education and Employment (DfEE), ESC; National Governing Bodies of Sport (NGBs); local councils; school governors; headteachers; and fellow teachers (Gilroy and Clarke 1997; Peach and Thomas 1998). This justification should be based on what is unique to physical education and its unique contribution to the education of all pupils; something which cannot be replicated by sport. If physical education can be reduced to sport, this might have implications for the curriculum and for those teaching the curriculum (see also Chapter 13).

Questions for reflection

1   Should the success of the physical education programme be based on the success of the school teams? If so, why? If not, how can you articulate differences between physical education and sport to the headteacher, governors, parents and other people to ensure that the success of the physical education programme is not measured by the success of the school teams?
2   How do differences between physical education and sport affect what you do in your teaching of physical education in curriculum time and in your approach to extra-curricular activities?
3   What, if anything, do the differences between physical education and sport mean for differences between the role of a physical education teacher and that of a sports coach? Should sports coaches be employed to teach in physical education lessons? If so, how should this occur?

Further reading

Murdoch, E. B. (1990) 'Physical education and sport: the interface' in N. Armstrong (ed.), *New Directions in Physical Education: vol.1*, Leeds: Human Kinetics: 63–77.
—— (1997) 'The national curriculum for physical education' in S. Capel (ed.), *Learning to Teach Physical Education in the Secondary School: A Companion to School Experience*, London: Routledge: 252–70.

9 Competition and co-operation in physical education

Jean Leah and Susan Capel

Introduction

Despite the commitment to physical education through its inclusion as a foundation subject in the National Curriculum, debates are ongoing about what the priorities and content of the subject should be. These debates include concerns about the relative importance of competition and co-operation in the physical education curriculum. In fact, at times the place of competition in schools has been at the centre of many fierce and sometimes acrimonious debates. The debate over the emphasis that should be placed on competition and co-operation is unlikely to become less prominent in the years to come. Hence, there is a need to identify some of the issues which are raised by this debate.

This chapter begins by introducing the terms 'competition' and 'co-operation' as related to teaching and learning in physical education. Some of the recent influences on the debate about competition and co-operation are identified and consideration is given to some of the reasons why this issue remains central today. The dominance of competition in teaching physical education is then examined, focusing on some of the positive and negative aspects of competition and co-operation in primary and secondary physical education. In the last part of the chapter consideration is given to how competitive and co-operative approaches to learning can be incorporated into physical education.

This chapter does not aim to answer questions. Instead it allows readers to reflect on some of the tensions that the debate might raise and to develop their own philosophy on the inclusion of competition and co-operation in the teaching of physical education. It is recognised that this debate touches on the personal, spiritual, moral, social and cultural development of pupils and as such deserves added consideration when reflecting on the values that may be conveyed to learners in physical education.

Competition and co-operation defined

Competition may be defined in a number of ways. However, it is useful to note that the Latin derivation of the word (competere) means to strive together or 'to come together' (Sherif 1978; Siedentop 1994). Sherif suggested that

Competition consists of activities directed more or less consistently toward meeting a standard or achieving a goal in which performance by a person or by his group is compared and evaluated relative to that of selected other persons or groups.

(Sherif 1978: 82)

This definition looks only at competition against others, either individually or in groups. However, competition can also be against self, time or the environment, as the definition by Weinberg and Gould emphasised: 'The goal is to beat someone else, everyone else or an externally referenced target' (Weinberg and Gould 1995: 131). It is the outcome or product which is recognised by others that is implied in the term 'competition' and which provides the key to its meaning.

In contrast, co-operation can be viewed as the means or the process through which the learner interacts with others to achieve agreed goals. This process is one which, by definition, must mean working, learning or playing with others (Lavin 1989, Watson 1984, Weinberg and Gould 1995). In fact, the *Chambers Concise Dictionary* (1991: 225) defined co-operation as 'working together'. Orlick described co-operation in physical activities as being:

directly related to communication, cohesiveness, trust, and the development of positive social-interaction skills. Through co-operative ventures, children learn to share, to empathise with others, to be concerned with others' feelings, and to work to get along better. The players in the game must help one another by working together as a unit – each player being a necessary part of that unit, with a contribution to make – and leaving no one out of the action to sit around waiting for a chance to play. The fact that children work together toward a common end, rather than against one another, immediately turns destructive responses into helpful ones: players feel that they are an accepted part of the game, and thus feel totally involved. The result is a sense of gaining, not losing.

(Orlick 1979: 6–7)

The next section looks at some of the recent influences on the debate about competition and co-operation.

Recent influences on the debate about competition and co-operation

Pollard (1988: 111) referred to a 'moral panic' which he suggested began in the summer of 1986 following the decision of a Bristol infant school to organise a non-competitive sports day for their children. Concerns were raised in the press and by politicians that the 'traditional' values associated with participation in competitive sport were being eroded. At this time physical education teachers were accused of following a child-centred progressive approach to teaching

(Evans and Penney 1996, Leaman 1988, Pollard 1988). Shortly after this, the National Curriculum through the Education Reform Act (ERA 1988) was introduced by a Conservative government led by Margaret Thatcher, which had been in office since 1979. That government promoted a competitive market ethos and meritocracy. Hence, the term 'competition' became part of the language of education as well as of business and industry.

In the early stages of the development of the National Curriculum for Physical Education (NCPE), introduced in 1992 (Departmenr of Education and Science (DES)/Welsh Office (WO) 1992), there was explicit consideration of competition and co-operation. In 1989 Her Majesty's Inspectorate (HMI) (DES 1989a: 1) identified the development of an appreciation of the concept of honest competition as *one* of the aims of physical education. The National Curriculum Physical Education Working Group (NCPEWG), established to advise the Secretary of State for Education and Science and the Secretary of State for Wales on the content of the NCPE, acknowledged in their interim report the two sides of the debate relating to the place of competition in physical education:

> There are those who have argued . . . that competitive physical activities provided through sport have no part in the educational process and should be discouraged in schools. Others appear to think that the physical education programme should consist solely of competitive team games.
>
> (DES/WO 1991: 7)

The NCPEWG accepted neither of these views. But why? Certainly, they did not consider either position to reflect accurately what was currently occurring in schools.

In the first NCPE (DES/WO 1992), the obligation for schools to provide opportunities for pupils to be engaged in competitive and co-operative activities was identified in the non-statutory guidance. The National Curriculum Council (NCC) suggested that 'the development of interaction skills occurs when pupils increasingly . . . work co-operatively in groups; work competitively against others; help and are helped by others' (NCC 1992: D5). It also suggested that physical education could contribute to personal and social development by encouraging, for example, 'an ability to work co-operatively with others by being a member of a team or group; a competitive spirit by deciding on the most appropriate order in a relay race' (ibid.: G6). The commitment to competition and co-operation was also apparent from the criteria used by the Office for Standards in Education (OFSTED) to judge the quality of learning in physical education within the NCPE: 'The quality of pupils' learning in physical education is judged by the extent to which pupils . . . work co-operatively as well as competitively, sharing ideas and testing their skills' (DFE 1993: 43).

Learning in competitive and co-operative contexts has since continued to be a feature of developments in NCPE. The revised NCPE emphasised the development of positive attitudes by teaching pupils 'to observe the conventions of

fair play, honest competition and good sporting behaviour as individual participants, team members and spectators' (DFE/WO 1995: 2). This development was
seen to occur largely through teaching competitive team games at each Key
Stage. The End of Key Stage Descriptions identified aspects of competition and
co-operation, for example, at Key Stage (KS) 3 pupils were to demonstrate that
they 'appreciate strengths and limitations in performance and use this information in co-operative team work as well as outwit the opposition in
competition' (DFE/WO 1995: 11).

In the revised NCPE for 2000 competition and co-operation are both
included, although reference to them is not as overt as in previous documents.
For example, the importance of physical education includes the provision of '...
opportunities for pupils to be creative, competitive and to face up to different
challenges as individuals and in groups and teams. . . . Pupils learn how to think
in different ways to suit a wide variety of creative, competitive and challenging
activities' (Department for Education and Emplyment (DfEE /Qualifications and
Curriculum Authority (QCA) 1999: 15).

The dominance of competition in teaching physical education

Despite competition and co-operation both being highlighted in recent physical
education curriculum documents in England, competition seems to be prioritised,
at least in secondary schools. This is partly as a result of the dominance of competitive team games in the physical education curriculum in secondary schools
(evidence of this dominance is given in Chapter 7 of this book). There has been
considerable pressure for emphasis to be placed on competition, and particularly
competitive team games. Strong pressure has come from politicians concerned
with the performance of national sports teams and with the perceived character-
building effects of participation in competitive team games. That debate is pursued
further in Chapter 8. Another strong influence is the value placed on competition
by many secondary physical education teachers who have been successful in, or
gained high levels of satisfaction from, their own competitive experiences. They
have benefited from competitive experiences, therefore can see the value that
competition can bring to a learning environment. Shearsmith suggested that:

> the world of sport and our society have fostered the dominance of compet-
> itive practices in physical education and games. Physical education teachers
> have themselves been the so called beneficiaries of this system . . . gained
> the enjoyment/satisfaction that is intrinsic to good performance, but I have
> often felt this to be less than satisfactory if it has not been coupled with the
> success of being a winner in a competitive situation.
>
> (Shearsmith 1993: 39)

There is, therefore, a need to recognise that others, including many primary
teachers who are expected to teach physical education as well as all other

Table 9.1 Some positive and negative aspects of competition and co-operation in physical education

Positive aspects of a competitive approach	Negative aspects of a competitive approach
acts as a motivator to increase learning potential or to improve performance	does not nurture the self concept of all children
encourages children to try their best	may be demotivating to some pupils through failing to succeed
is enjoyable and satisfying	results in some pupils being perceived as 'failures'
brings about a feeling of well-being	may promote anxiety and stress through fear of failure
produces excellence	may not take account of all the pupils' potential
allows children to learn about winning and losing	can be elitist
works in harmony with the natural competitive instincts of children	focuses on the product rather than the process of learning
encourages social acceptance	favours boys rather than girls
is cathartic	could drive pupils to cheat
helps pupils to deal with competition they may meet in the adult world of work and leisure	may prevent co-operative or sympathetic behaviour
builds 'character' (e.g. loyalty, inner strength, belief in oneself, commitment and discipline)	may encourage aggressive and other anti-social behaviours
allows pupils to recognise their abilities, social strengths and weaknesses	may provide a route for developing anti-social behaviour between rival groups within a school
develops an ability to co-operate with others	can be divisive, reinforcing social divisions
provides a focus for measuring the success of, and marketing, a school	could cause tensions between rival schools
Positive aspects of a co-operative approach	Negative aspects of a co-operative approach
motivates through being non-threatening and challenging	may not be developmental and challenging for all unless taught well
promotes learning in a non-threatening manner	appeals more to girls than boys
promotes the process of learning rather than the product	teachers who emphasise co-operation may be considered 'soft'
encourages all to participate	may not be supported by school hierarchy
utilises a democratic process	
prepares pupils for life	
enables pupils to develop the ability to learn to work in groups or teams	
develops less aggressive tendencies	
is child-centred rather than subject centred	
emphasises the importance/meaningfulness of the social context in which the learner acts	
provides a unique context in which pupils can learn and demonstrate new social skills.	

curriculum subjects, may have found competition within their experience of physical education to be a negative and indeed unwelcome aspect of the subject. They may value and prioritise a co-operative approach to learning.

Positive and negative aspects of competition and co-operation

In the next section of the chapter some of the positive and negative aspects of competition and co-operation in physical education are examined more closely. These are summarised in Table 9.1.

Other positive and negative aspects have been highlighted indirectly in comparisons between competition and co-operation. For example, Johnson and Johnson (1975) considered the differences in interpersonal processes between competitive and co-operative classes. These are summarised in Table 9.2.

It is possible to expand these lists, and readers are encouraged to identify other positive and negative aspects of competition and co-operation. However, it is useful to develop a few of these points. Some of the positive and negative aspects of competition and co-operation are identified next. These have been grouped into four themes. No definite conclusions are drawn; instead, readers are invited to reflect on the issues that are raised.

Motivation

Motivation 'consists of internal processes and external incentives which spur us on to satisfy some need' (Child 1997: 44). Head noted that schools 'often

Table 9.2 Differences in interpersonal processes between competitive and co-operative classes

Competitive	Co-operative
low interaction	high interaction
mutual dislike	mutual liking
no or misleading communication	effective communication
low trust	high trust
low mutual influence	high mutual influence
low acceptance and support	high acceptance and support
no utilisation of resources of other pupils	high utilisation of resources of other pupils
attempts to mislead and obstruct others	high sharing and helping
emotional involvement of some pupils (the winners)	high emotional involvement of all pupils
low co-ordination of effort	high co-ordination of effort
division of labour not possible	division of labour possible
low divergent and risk taking thinking	high divergent risk-taking thinking
high comparison of self versus others	no comparison of self versus others

Source: adapted from Johnson and Johnson 1975

employ a system of rewards and prizes in the belief that competition will act to motivate the learners' (Head 1996: 64). However, the link between competition and motivation is complex. Competition may be motivating to some, whereas it may be demotivating to others. Likewise, some competition may be motivating, but excessive competition may become demotivating. On the other hand, co-operation may be motivating for some and not for others. Thus, both competition and co-operation have the potential to motivate and to demotivate. In this section some of the reasons for competition and co-operation being motivating or demotivating are considered briefly.

Part of the purpose of physical education is to nurture the self concept of all children. DES (1989a: 2) identified the development of self-esteem as one of the aims of physical education, to be achieved through the acquisition of physical competence and poise and the development of self confidence through understanding one's own capabilities and limitations. Those who favour the co-operative approach to learning stress that it enables pupils to feel positive and not feel threatened by what might be termed the 'conventional notion of competition' in a physical education environment and therefore is motivating. Results of research by Mitchell and Chandler suggested that 'student perceptions of non-threatening and challenging environments are powerful constructs as the strongest predictors of high levels of intrinsic motivation' (Mitchell and Chandler 1996: 48).

On the other hand, it has been suggested that emphasis on competition in physical education lessons works in harmony with the natural, competitive instincts of children, and therefore is motivating to pupils. According to some commentators, not to encourage children's involvement in competition is to subvert their true instincts (see, for example, Pollard 1988: 109). However, one key question is what type of competition, or what is the nature of competition that is motivating for children? The type of competition which is motivating is likely to be different for children of different ages and developmental stages.

HMI (DES 1989a: 11) said that competition occurs first against self ('how many times can I ... ?', 'how far can I ... ?'). Likewise, Needham suggested that in relation to young children 'any competition that exists should be with oneself rather than with others – "Is this the best I can do?" rather than "Is mine better than anyone else's?"' (Needham 1994: 158). The competition with/against self considered appropriate for young children was seen by Murdoch as motivating to them:

> Early forms of competition are more ones of having a standard or yardstick against which to measure oneself, rather than as competition in the adult sense. Each testing moment is an event in itself and a chance to test oneself, for example, 'Race you to the corner!'. Essentially they are concerned with self-mastery and bettering their own performance rather than in the beating of someone else. . . . Young children are motivated to mastery, of themselves and the objects they are playing with.
>
> (Murdoch 1996: 35)

It is only at later stages of development that competition occurs 'against a friend ("who can catch the most times?", "who can hit a target?") and then with a friend against others' (DES 1989a: 11). In contexts where competition is against others there are winners and losers. Reaffirmation of confidence in oneself as an acceptable and worthy person is awarded to winners, whereas losers are denied such self-validation.

The NCPEWG recognised 'the public nature of success and failure in physical education' to be a distinct feature of physical education that would 'demand particular thought and consideration' (DES/WO 1990: 17). To be shown to be less physically able in the highly visible and public forum of physical education may be demotivating and lead to the formation of a negative self-concept. This may occur in competition against others, but it may also occur when the competition is against self, e.g. competition may be against self to achieve a better time in a 100 metre run, but it becomes comparative when a number of people undertake the run at the same time. Williams considered this issue in relation to the wide range of physical development of pupils at KS2 at any one time

> given the public nature of the child's achievements in physical education, compared with other subjects where one's shortcomings can be concealed more easily, it is all too easy for the child who is less mature physically to be discouraged by relative failure when compared with more mature peers.
>
> (Williams 1996a: 64)

Children respond quickly and with great enthusiasm to challenges, but those who do not do as well as others quickly stop and learn to recognise that they are not as able as their peers. For example, Arnold (1968) suggested that primary children respond well to challenges when they are asked 'who can jump the highest?', rather than 'jump as high as you can'. He commented that this rivalry encourages speedy learning. However, the obvious concern with this form of competition is about those who do not jump the highest. What is the impact on them? Teachers need to be aware of the development of individual pupils as well as their diversity of ability. They also need to bear in mind that some pupils may not be as able at that time but they may well be better at another time. The problem is that the children do not know this, so their self-esteem can be damaged by such challenges.

The formation of a negative self-concept can be highly damaging as pupils can easily come to perceive themselves as 'useless'. A self perception of 'uselessness' can perpetuate what Merton (1968) described as a 'self-fulfilling' prophecy whereby persons believing themselves to be hopeless causes act upon the belief by considering that it would be a waste of time to expend any effort on the activity and consequently contribute further to the likelihood of failure. The initial negative self perception can therefore give rise to a spiralling process of under-achievement.

The consequences of negative perceptions are particularly alarming when one considers that this perception of oneself as 'useless at physical education' may result in a general demotivation and lack of effort/willingness to engage regularly in physical activity/recreation, exercise and sport in contexts other than a physical education lesson. Shearsmith proposed that:

> one possible consequence (of the dominance of competitive practices and the conveyance of a message that the degree of enjoyment/satisfaction experienced is closely associated without the degree of success achieved in competitive situations) may be that the unsuccessful have felt themselves to have no positive role to play in physical education and games and have considered physical activity to be inappropriate for them.
>
> (Shearsmith 1993: 39)

This has potential negative consequences post-school. Pupils are more likely to continue to be motivated to participate in physical activity post-school if they have enjoyed their experiences at school (see, for example, White and Coakley 1986). Individuals who do not participate in physical activity are denied the positive health benefits which research has shown to follow from a sufficient level of regular involvement in appropriate forms of physical activity (HEA 1998a, Sallis and Patrick 1994).

Emphasis on the outcome (product) or the means of achieving (process)

A process-based curriculum is one which focuses on learning as 'an active process based on the interests and unfolding mental development of each child' (Child 1997: 436). The child and his or her development are prioritised. This type of curriculum has sometimes been called 'child-centred education' and was a guiding principle of education in the 1960s and 1970s. However, 'the 1960s and 1970s professional ideology of child-centredness' has gradually been supplanted (Pollard and Tann 1993: 25). One result of this may be less emphasis on process-based models of learning and greater emphasis on the product.

A product-based curriculum emphasises the ends (competitive achievement, results, winning and winners) rather than the means (the process of learning) (Hellison and Templin 1991: 47). In physical education the product includes 'Specification of the ideal technique, breaking down the skill into its component parts, recognition of its spatial, temporal and force characteristics . . . .as central for the learning/teaching process' (Connell 1989: 104). There is emphasis on testing pupils to see if they have mastered the skill and hence if they have reached the objectives. Therefore, summative assessment is important.

Focus on the product can distract pupils from thinking about the skills being practised. This was a concern expressed by HMI : 'Concentration on this [the competitive] element can distract pupils from thinking about the skills being practised and so can impede learning. The major emphasis for young children should be on sharing and working together' (DES 1989a: 11, parentheses added). Connell highlighted this point when she asked 'Where is the learner in motor learning?' (Cornell 1989: 104). It also prevents co-operative approaches to work being emphasised. This is a disadvantage because many areas of employment require people who are able to work/co-operate with others. The importance of a co-operative approach to learning for the sake of our industrial future was emphasised by Hutchinson, who suggested that 'to educate for an interdependent and ecologically sustainable future implies doing it through co-operative group work rather than individualistically competitive learning environments' (Hutchinson 1996: 206).

It has been suggested that the change to a focus on the product rather than the process of education may partly be a result of the emphasis on the market in education (Evans *et al.* 1996: 7). The market/capitalist economy, as found in contemporary Britain, is based on competition. Encouraging competition is 'a key element of the individualism that underpins free-market capitalism and consumerism' (Evans and Davies 1988: 14) and 'competition is regarded as being a necessity both for economic growth and for the smooth running of our capitalist system' (Pollard 1988: 121). Competition in school, and particularly in physical education, is considered by some to prepare children for their place in society. Children learn the value of competition. They can be motivated by achievement in a way that will enable them to make a valuable contribution to British society. Thus, competition in schools is 'legitimated as preparing children for the cut and thrust of their future lives' (Pollard 1988: 121).

This focus on competition can result in pressure being placed on some physical education teachers to produce winning school teams; to emphasise competition and competitive team games in physical education lessons; and to focus on a product-based physical education curriculum. In such a climate, emphasis on co-operation in lessons and on a process-based curriculum could be seen negatively by the school hierarchy.

The effects of competition and co-operation on moral and social development/behaviour

The suggestion that competition is character-building and purges participants of antisocial and immoral tendencies has been promoted for a long time. For example, Dean Farrar (1889) suggested that 'even from your games you may learn some of those true qualities which will help you to do your duty bravely and happily in life' (quoted in Simon and Bradley 1975: 148). It has been supported in the NCPE through the statement that 'pupils can learn to appreciate the concepts of fairplay, honest competition and good sporting behaviour' (e.g. DES/WO 1990, 1992; DfE/WO 1995). Harrison supported the view that 'Competitive games . . . allow teachers to positively enhance the moral and social development of individuals' (Harrison 1998: 5).

However, positive 'character-building' outcomes of competition do not occur naturally. In addition, some authors have suggested that not all competition is character-building. Intense competition can lead individuals to attach value to personal achievement and winning and, sometimes, unacceptable forms of behaviour can result. These forms of behaviour may include cheating, reluctance to share and to assist others, hoping for the failure of others in order to enhance their own chances of victory, failure to empathise with others and to be concerned with others' feelings (e.g. Pollard 1988, Sherif 1973).

Harrison suggested that whether or not character-building occurs is 'entirely reliant upon the manner in which the activity is taught. It is this which will make it have a positive effect' (Harrison 1998: 5). Child illustrated this when he emphasised that in classes

> in which specific qualities or abilities are regarded as being of more value than others in absolute terms . . . the stress is often on achievements rather than on the effort which children may have made; the ethos is often competitive rather than co-operative; the success of some children is made possible only at the cost of the relative failure of others. The overall effect is to marginalise some children while the work of others is praised and regarded as setting a standard to which other children should aspire.
>
> (Child 1997: 98)

Fox suggested that 'the predominance of competitive team sport in the curriculum makes it unnecessarily difficult for teachers to help many youngsters experience a sense of personal improvement and fulfilment' (Fox 1992b: 51), which is linked to motivation (see earlier).

Thus, emphasis in physical education on competitive achievement may result in some children learning to regard themselves unfavourably, or to resent and oppose the values being emphasised. However, it is possible for a climate to be created in which

> many different qualities are valued and where children are encouraged to challenge themselves to improve their own performance. . . . One of the ways of establishing such a climate is to encourage children to evaluate their own work and to set their own personal goals.
>
> (Pollard and Tann 1993: 70)

Lavin emphasised that 'studies . . . have pointed to the conclusion that children who learn co-operatively – compared with those who learn competitively or independently – learn better, feel better about themselves and work better with each other' (Lavin 1989: 181). He suggested that co-operative learning groups can play a significant role in developing team success, but that care has to be taken as to how the group is structured and the nature of the task. He stated that 'it involves creating "positive interdependence", structuring childrens interactions so that each depends on and is accountable to the others' (ibid.: 181).

Some authors (e.g. Duda and Huston 1995, Duda, Olson and Templin 1991) found that response to competition was linked to the goal orientations of the person. People who had a task orientation to learning (when the task or learning goal is important and success is defined as personal improvement) were more likely to endorse fair play in sport. On the other hand, people who had an ego orientation (when the ego or performance is important and success is defined as outperforming others) were more likely to adopt unfair or illegal means of achieving their goals.

Reaction of boys and girls to competitive and co-operative activities

Gill (1993) suggested that there are gender differences in the response to competitive processes. This was supported by Eccles and Harold (1991), who found quite strong differences in attitudes of boys and girls to sport. They suggested that although these differences emerged at a very young age they were the result of gender socialisation rather than natural differences in aptitude. Further, 'the evidence is that a sense of competition works more effectively with boys than girls' (Head 1996: 64). This was supported by Carlson (1995), who reported that one negative factor in perceptions of girls who felt alienated in gym class was excess competition. Likewise, Browne (1992) reported that one reason that girls do not choose physical education is that it is too competitive. In addition, Tannehill *et al.* (1994) suggested that physical education, with its characteristic emphasis on competitive games, is often discrepant with the values and interests of female pupils, who may be less interested in aggressive confrontations and more inclined to seek opportunities to learn, participate, co-operate and enjoy activity.

In a study of the influence of the physical education learning environment, Mitchell and Chandler (1996) found that boys scored significantly higher than girls on intrinsic motivation, perceived competitiveness and perceived organisation. They scored significantly lower on perceived threat. This led Mitchell and Chandler to suggest that challenging and non-threatening environments are particularly important for girls. They also suggested that teachers should be aware of potential gender differences in the way pupils perceive the learning environment and recognise that some teaching strategies may be particularly applicable to girls.

On the other hand, Hastie (1998) found that girls enjoyed the competitive aspect of a sport education unit. Further, Salisbury and Jackson suggested that 'there are many boys who hate the humiliating, pressurising climate of team games but who would enjoy getting involved in personal challenges' (Salisbury and Jackson 1996: 214). They recognised that traditional team games have a place in the physical education curriculum but suggested that there should be an expansion of co-operative games which can cater for the diversity of interests of boys and girls. In an attempt to improve teaching in physical education there is a view that activities should be taught in mixed groups. But do mixed activities work? (This issue is discussed further in Chapter 2.)

Competition *versus* or *and* co-operation?

There are positive and negative aspects of both competition and co-operation, a few of which have been identified. However, as with many issues, there are no clear, easy answers. Neither competition or co-operation is good or bad (Arnold

1968, Martens 1978, Stein 1988); nor is the physical education curriculum based on one to the exclusion of the other. Physical education involves learning in physical skill contexts which are both competitive and non-competitive. Competition and co-operation are not mutually exclusive; they coexist within the physical education curriculum. Both competition and co-operation are integral aspects of learning in all aspects of physical education. Likewise, competition does not preclude co-operation; for example, in competitive team games players need to work together co-operatively as a team to perform successfully and to beat the other team. A precondition of playing a competitive game is to work co-operatively with opponents in order to play according to the same rules. A pupil trying to better the distance that he or she can throw a ball or the time that he or she can balance in a handstand is competing against self. Likewise, activities considered to be co-operative such as outdoor and adventurous activities may have a competitive element, e.g. against self or the environment.

Child provided a relevant synopsis of the debate on competition and co-operation:

> Research into the relative merits of co-operative and competitive methods in class has not been particularly illuminating. To begin with, we have the dilemma of encouraging both co-operation and competition within the same teaching systems. The only generalisation which emerges from the mass of research is that in none of the studies does competition yield more effective learning than co-operation. Nevertheless, the one thing that seems certain is that both devices are valid motivators. Provided the level of competitive antagonism is not too high, performance appears to be improved. Where the stakes are very high, children opt out or resort to cheating. . . . The matter of social motives such as dependence, affiliation and desire for approval also have a great deal to do with encouraging children to participate in co-operative ventures.
>
> (Child 1997: 61)

Finally, Murdoch emphasised that

> after playing an after school football match, the children cannot remember the score to tell their parents. The game, participation and having fun are more important than the score or the winning or losing. Competition is intrinsic to many physical education activities. In striving for achievement in these situations the way in which success and failure are defined and the way in which the child attributes the reasons for that success or failure can either sustain the child's interest and participation or cause them to withdraw.
>
> (Murdoch 1996: 35)

Competition and co-operation in physical education are both important. However, the positive aspects of competition and co-operation do not happen by chance; they have to be planned deliberately in specific aspects of the physical education curriculum; units of work or lessons.

Conclusion

It is evident that the debate about competition and co-operation in physical education is one that is likely to remain contentious. Society, through our politicians, local councillors, parents, sporting agencies and others will continue to exert a range of pressures on physical education, including pressure to emphasise the competitive aspects of physical education. Therefore, it is important that physical education teachers are able to articulate the value and place of competition and co-operation in the physical education curriculum.

Barrow and Millburn highlighted that:

> An interesting question remains: how is it that in a world that is highly competitive, with schools that are in fact in competition, and in the absence of any overriding reason why they should not be, educationalists none the less creep around as if there was nothing to discuss, since this obviously unpleasant practice is foreign to us?
>
> (Barrow and Milburn 1990: 59)

Questions for reflection

1   Reflect on your primary and secondary school education. From the earliest age note when you were aware that you were in competition with others in your school or from other schools (at this stage try to consider more than just a physical education context). From these notes, can you identify your feelings about being involved in competitive situations? Were you always successful? How did you respond to winning and losing? How did your 'opponents' respond? Did your attitude towards competition and competitive situations change over time from primary to secondary school? For example, did you find that at some point you rejected the idea of competition or did you enjoy competition throughout your time at school? Compare your responses with those of another student teacher. Is how you experienced the notion of competition and your perception of its positive or negative effect the same as or different from that of another physical education teacher? Indeed, it is highly likely that your views will be different from other people, but do you choose to socialise with people who, like you, have enjoyed a positive experience of learning physical education and in particular respond well to competition in many of its forms? What does this mean for you as a physical education teacher?

2   Are children likely to deal with competitive learning at KS1? Is this the best time to be developing these traits or should there be other aspects that need to be learnt before competitiveness? Should the emphasis given to

competition and co-operation in the physical education curriculum change with the age of pupils and, if so, how?

3   All too often competitive approaches in physical education are related to games and athletics and co-operative approaches are related to outdoor and adventurous activities, the development of group sequences in gymnastics or group work in dance. What value is there in introducing an element of personal goal-setting in activities such as gymnastics and outdoor and adventurous activities, which, as Gill (1993) suggested, is a positive use of the competitive approach to learning?

Further reading

Orlick, T. (1979) *The Co-operative Sports and Games Book: Challenge Without Competition*, London: Writers and Readers Publishing Co-operative.

The *British Journal of Physical Education* (now the *British Journal of Teaching in Physical Education*) had a specialist section for the Primary age phase entitled *Primary Focus*. This journal regularly supplied competitive and co-operative ideas that have been successfully tried out by teachers of KS1 and KS2 pupils.

10 Working with the community: a necessary evil or a positive change of direction?

Mike Waring and Peter Warburton

Introduction

The purpose of this chapter is to raise a number of issues associated with the topical and somewhat uncertain relationship between physical education and the 'community'. This relationship means different things to the diverse range of agents and agencies (all of which are considered to be working collaboratively); however, it is not the purpose of this chapter to provide the reader with the 'way it should be'. Instead, an outline of the context and the nature of the key issues is highlighted. In taking such an approach it is possible to appreciate the principles behind the political and subsequently the practical agenda. By grasping an understanding of the relationship between the political and practical agenda it should be possible to develop practice to address, and so direct, this agenda for physical education teaching and teachers so that it becomes an educative process rather than a political product. The reader should be able to identify the political climate in which physical education is presently being manipulated by a sporting agenda. Having established the broad framework, some of the wider issues and implications associated with this political agenda and policy framework are explored relative to key national initiatives in schools and the community. It is the structure and consequent nature of the impact of these initiatives (independently and together) that are important as it is through them that the agenda is set and the place and role of physical education is determined.

The political climate in which physical education now exists

Warburton (1999) commented on the potentially alarming lack of coherence in vision and policy of different government departments in spite of the fact that central to the Labour government's rhetoric and its manifesto is the development of sport in schools and the determination to enhance the status of sport at both local and national level. Central government, not only the present Labour but also the previous Conservative administration, has recognised the potential for physical education in schools to service its political agenda. Consequently the development of policy has had a political 'games' rationale

rather than an educational rationale (Evans and Penney 1995). This was reinforced by Kay (1998) who highlighted the heavy influence placed by the Central
Council for Physical Recreation (CCPR) on central government in the interests
of the National Governing Bodies of Sport (NGBs) in the formulation of *Sport:
Raising the Game* (Department for National Heritage (DNH) 1995) and its focus
on elite elements of sport and games rather than education. Therefore, *Labour's
Sporting Nation* (Labour Party 1996) merely perpetuated the essence of those
initiatives presented by the previous administration in its policy paper *Sport:
Raising the Game* (DNH 1995). Both of these papers, along with the introduction
of National Lottery funding, have meant significant changes for what has been
referred to as 'school sport'.

It remains to be seen how the government's recent strategy document *A
Sporting Future for All* (Department for Culture, Media and Sport (DCMS)
2000) will impact on schools. A five-part plan targetting improved school facilities, 110 specialist sports colleges, 600 sports co-ordinators, out-of-school
activities and support for elite athletes aged 14 to 18 years will have its limitations. The sports colleges alone will get to less than 10 per cent of the school
population, and a sprinkling of co-ordinators may have little impact on primary
schools. The problem for the elite athlete may come at 18 years. The strategy
document, itself expounding the value of partnership, hardly acknowledges the
existence of further and higher education institutions, and certainly does not
give them a role in supporting the ongoing development of the elite athlete.
This is evidence once again of a lack of joined-up thinking in the 'school sport'
debate.

Most professionals in the field of education would rightly prefer the term
'physical education' to sport, however, the government clearly sees physical
education and sport as seamless or as one and the same thing (Smith 1999) and
when pushed refers *only* to sport. (See Chapter 8 for further discussion of the
physical education/sport debate.) It is this obsession with the promotion of
'sport' that the world of physical education needs to have most concern about.
This is a significant element that permeates all of the issues raised throughout
this chapter. The nature of policy impacts on the nature of provision of physical
education in and between the school and the community setting. Unfortunately,
the lack of cohesion over the demands of, and changes to, physical education
between key government departments and agencies such as the Department for
Education and Employment (DfEE) and the Teacher Training Agency (TTA) is
a further considerable cause for concern.

Changes in physical education: a contradiction?

Recent changes in physical education go much deeper than philosophical arguments over terminology. The Labour Party (1996) stated that central to its
intention to reverse the decline of sport in schools is a determination to see that
primary school teachers are given the key role of ensuring that all children experience physical activities. It is a general principle that few, if any, would disagree

with, and as such the support of the school setting should be used to continually remind the Government of its agenda and to fight for a broad, balanced curriculum with the teacher at the heart of the delivery. Unfortunately, the compulsory nature and dominance of games throughout the National Curriculum for Physical Education (NCPE) (for example, 50 to 70 per cent of available curriculum time at Key Stage (KS) 3 is spent on games (Office of Standards in Education (OFSTED) 1998a; see also Chapter 7)) contradicts the notion of a broad and balanced curriculum. This will not change with the NCPE 2000 (DfEE/Qualifications and Curriculum Authority (QCA) 1999). Competitive games activities are compulsory throughout KS1, KS2 and KS3 and although pupils have a chance to choose other activities at KS4, the government expects schools to continue to provide competitive team and individual games for pupils who wish to take up this option (DfEE/QCA 1999). However, the TTA (1998) appears to appreciate the centrality and importance of the teacher in the whole process when it established the *National Standards for Subject Leaders*, claiming that it is the quality of teaching which is significant in the development of each child.

However, given the government's apparent commitment to the school setting and what the TTA (1998) has set out in the *National Standards for Subject Leaders*, it is a contradiction that in September 1998 the programmes of study for physical education at KS1 and KS2 were suspended until at least September 2000. Primary schools are still required to teach physical education but may decide what they teach and how often they teach it (DfEE 1998b). OFSTED inspection teams are no longer required to report on the physical education curriculum content, being limited to commenting on lessons seen and extra curricular provision (OFSTED 1998b). This raises the question: what about the monitoring of provision and nature of the links with community if OFSTED is removed? The reasons for the removal of reporting on physical education by OFSTED become clearer when one considers the government's definition of sport and the aims and framework for its development established by organisations such as Sport England.

Significantly, there are myriad interrelated issues associated with the initial teacher education (ITE) of both primary and secondary physical education teachers. Not least of these is the number of hours dedicated to physical education ITE in the primary age range. OFSTED reported averages of 23 hours (range 7.5–60 hours) in primary Postgraduate Certificate in Education (PGCE) physical education and 32 hours (range 7.5–90 hours) in three or four year undergraduate courses (OFSTED 1998c). This is further endorsed by Her Majesty's Inspectorate (HMI) findings that suggested that teaching in physical education is weak in one fifth of all primary schools. In evaluating primary physical education programmes in Wales, HMI indicated that while two-thirds of lessons observed were satisfactory or better, the lessons were often delivered by teachers who had received a specialist course in physical education as part of their ITE course (Morgan 1997). Evidence indicated that primary PGCE and undergraduate students studying physical education at foundation course level had inadequate subject knowledge, limited understanding of progression and a weak grasp of assessment (OFSTED 1998b).

There appears to be a contradiction here in the intention of policy and the actual means to achieve it. This is further exacerbated by the fact that there has been a significant decline in in-service support through a decline in the number of advisers for physical education. This undermines the call from the physical education profession to increase (especially in the primary sector) the amount of continuing professional development, particularly with regard to new initiatives. Not only do school teachers require information on initiatives, but they also need help to identify where they require further help (Hooper 1998). The diversification into sport and sport science by higher education institutions (HEIs) with a general movement away from ITE has led to a further reduction in the level of support for the student teacher. Two-thirds of a PGCE student teacher's time is school-based. With such an organisation there are implications regarding the potential inconsistency in the nature and range of experiences which the student teacher receives, as well as the quality and differentiated nature of such experience. In addition, there is the issue associated with the undergraduate experience and knowledge base which student teachers have to draw upon during the PGCE year. In their movement towards more sports science undergraduate courses, many HEIs may not have satisfactorily considered whether there is an appropriate route through the degree course to enable students to embark on a career in teaching. This is changing slowly. However, even when this issue is acknowledged and more appropriate routes are developed they tend to focus on coaching and not on teaching. Add to this the ever-increasing demands of the National Curriculum, with its drive for improvements in literacy and numeracy against national performance indices, the inevitable increase in bureaucracy and the requirements of OFSTED, it is hardly surprising that physical education at all Key Stages, curricular and non-curricular, is under pressure and there is a vicious circle of decreasing pedagogical content knowledge. All these factors create many contradictions and a 'no win' situation for the appropriate development of physical education in schools.

Moving towards 'real' collaboration and partnership: fabrication through necessity?

Few people would disagree with Gilbert's (1998) belief that partnership in physical education can be truly successful only if it sits within an overall vision for the development of young people, sport and physical activity. However, as has been alluded to earlier, appreciation of the importance of breadth in the physical education curriculum receives little recognition from those who at present support and drive government policy: the very policy that influences and drives the development of practice in school and the community. It should also be noted that the definition of physical education is one that the physical education profession has itself been debating for many years and continues to debate on a number of levels (Woodhouse 1998). However, there are fundamental aspects associated with breadth, balance and the central nature of pedagogy which can be generally agreed by the profession.

Since the introduction of the NCPE the notion of partnership has been an important component highlighted in National Curriculum documentation (Hardakre 1998). It is against this background that the community setting has recently moved into greater focus, becoming increasingly central to the delivery of physical education. The government may advocate the central role of schools in this process, but the reality is somewhat different.

The overall, but not necessarily the big picture

The remainder of this chapter reviews key community initiatives that at present are impacting on physical education programmes in schools and the way in which these relate to wider issues associated with a political agenda and supporting policy framework. The community in this context refers to anyone involved in the promotion of physical education and sport in schools. In considering these initiatives and the partners involved, it is a concern that few people have an understanding of all that is happening. Change is taking place at great pace and the channels of communication may have fallen short of what has been required. Those responsible for the delivery of physical education in schools may lack information because it is not 'education' that is instigating the changes but rather new found 'partners'.

Instigating change

Who are the key partners within this contemporary climate for the promotion of partnerships and strategic alliances within the development of sport in England? They include:

- Sport England
- Youth Sport Trust (YST)
- Departments of: Culture, Media and Sport (DCMS); Health; Education and Employment (DfEE)
- Health Education Authority (HEA) (*Young and Active*)
- NGBs
- local authorities.

Many of the new community initiatives in physical education and sport are innovative, generally well considered and appear, at least in the short-term, to be effective. As has been stated, Sport England has taken centre stage by introducing many of the new developments. Where they are not prime movers, their control of overall funding means that they are able to influence the thinking of NGBs and local authorities in their work with young people. Therefore, the focus for the remainder of this chapter is Sport England (the English Sports Council).

Sport England: a key player

More People involved in sport; *More Places* to play sport; *More Medals* through higher standards of performance, is the corner stone of the comprehensive sports development process of Sport England. This process is developed through links with the four elements of the sports development continuum; Active Schools, Active Communities, Active Sports and World Class England. Figure 10.1 is the model presented by Sport England (Sport England 1999). It illustrates the way in which Active Schools are expected to underpin Active Communities, Active Sports and World Class England. Such initiatives might be seen on a developing continuum of maintaining and increasing involvement in sport for young people, with a view to enhancing excellence. Participation, learning, performing and excelling in sport are encompassed in all the initiatives, but there are different emphases given to them in different initiatives. This highlights and reinforces the essential interrelationship between the initiatives (and consequently those agents/agencies involved). The notion that everyone has a stake in the development of physical education and sport at all levels and guises is significant and one that continually needs to be emphasised and reinforced.

It is envisaged that real partnership, supported at all stages by Sport England, will deliver the programme. It is useful to consider at this point the previously highlighted political agenda and the contradictory elements within it and their impact on the nature of the school physical education curricula, as well as what and how such a sports development programme will reinforce it. Active Schools underpin all three of the other initiatives and the related products and services. These include:

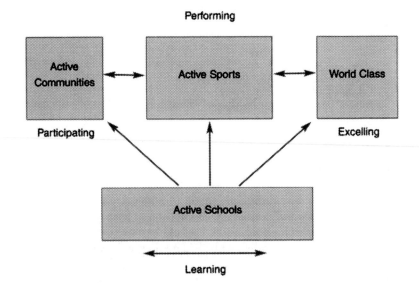

Figure 10.1 Sport England's sport development programme (*The Wider Picture*)
Source: Sport England 1999: 5

The TOPS Programme

This is a joint venture between the YST and Sport England. The programme includes intiatives such as TOP Play, BT TOP Sport, TOP Gymnastics, TOP Athletics, TOP Outdoors, BT TOP Swimming, Fit for TOPS, Champion Coaching and TOP Club. While many of these are school-based initiatives, they are also delivered extensively as community packages. Schools themselves are encouraged to set up clubs within the community initiative. The TOPS programmes vary in what is on offer in different places, but all provide teaching cards and training and many supply high quality equipment.

Evaluations have shown that the standard of training is generally high, although it is often not delivered by teachers/advisers and is limited to four hours. Research undertaken by Owen (1999) and Lewis (1999), however, showed that there is a lack of communication between schools and between schools and communities borne out of a lack of time and interest. The evidence would appear to suggest that while schools are prepared to accept resources that are directly beneficial to them, they have less interest when it comes to developing partnerships; the latter being rather too much like hard work in an already overcrowded educational agenda. Hunt's (1998) comment that the emerging national picture is both piecemeal and fragmented in terms of the evaluation of the TOPs programmes identified the need to conduct more immediate and co-ordinated monitoring and evaluation programmes. These need to be conducted on a local level (in addition to a national longitudinal evaluation) so that they can then be used to inform the national picture over and above the superficial level of number of schools, community sites and children which most of the literature to date has focused on, and the difficult situation generated by the demands of the NCPE and OFSTED. However, a contradiction arises, as highlighted earlier, associated with the continuing professional development of teachers. One of Hunt's (1998) recommendations resulting from her evaluation of the TOPs programmes was that more training for teachers is necessary in order to develop teachers' skills of observation, understanding of games principles and knowledge of games play. Additional time is unlikely to be freed up for teachers.

Another important issue is that the TOPs programmes are largely games focused and games are only one element of what might be considered part of a broad and balanced physical education experience for children. Again, the political agenda can be seen to have the potential to undermine the educational agenda given that teachers may be generally ill informed, or may not have the inclination due to other commitments, to check the nature of such initiatives.

Fourteen million pounds has been allocated to the TOPs initiatives. Only half of this is government funded, with the rest having to be found from private funding. This is clearly a significant amount of money but pales into insignificance with the government's announcement in January 1999 that it is to give £120 million to the development of music in schools. Conceivably the physical education profession might need to ask itself, in addition to the nature of the marriage of music's educational agenda and the government's political agenda, what has the music lobby done in conjunction with the community context to achieve this amount of funding within its subject, and can the physical education profession learn anything?

Coaching for teachers

This is a joint initiative between Sport England and the National Coaching Foundation (NCF) supported by the Physical Education Association of the United Kingdom (PEAUK) and the British Association of Advisers and Lecturers in Physical Education (BAALPE). This is a programme providing opportunities for teachers to improve their coaching and teaching skills, particularly in the extended curriculum, by attending NGB awards/courses. In reality, given the limited hours offered in ITE many may use the content to support their lesson delivery and much of the material may be new to them.

Sportsmark and Sportsmark Gold

This comes under the umbrella of Active Schools. It is the third year of the scheme that rewards secondary and middle schools that evidence quality physical education and sports programmes which recognise evidence of community involvement. Its existence is a consequence of the political agenda reinforced by *Sport: Raising the Game* (DNH 1995). Sportsmark was intended to be a relatively easy development in the short-term to evaluate and demonstrate the effectiveness of government policy. Useful statistics generated as a result of this programme were the nature and extent of: extra-curricular provision for young people; competition opportunities for young people (curricular and extra-curricular); coaching qualifications of teachers and adults other than teachers (AOTTs); and links with local sports clubs. However, the programme underwent a review in its third year in an attempt to make it more 'user friendly' for schools. Spencer outlined elements of the revised scheme:

- includes a statistical survey of provision, but with flexibility for time issues (100 minutes' curriculum time for Sportsmark), expectations of pupil take-up of extra-curricular activities and in breadth and balance
- takes into account the particular context of the school transport issues, lack of staff and facilities, young people with special needs, pressures for pupils not to take part resulting from examinations, and so on. The opportunity is given to explain the context in general and with regard to the specific criteria
- allows middle schools which are deemed secondary schools to apply
- asks for two referees who know the school and can verify and support their application
- gives credit for post-16 programmes, General Certificate of Education (GCSE) and Advanced (A) level provision, Community Sports Leaders Award (CSLA) and TOP link and other leadership courses

- provides guidance on such areas as school-club links, teachers' and AOTTs' qualifications, other sport-led initiatives and what kind of 'evidence' a school should be bringing together to present a case to a validator.

(Spencer 1998: 224)

As part of the Active Schools programme Sportsmark should, in theory, enable more co-ordination of physical education and sport initiatives within and between schools and the community. However, schools still need to remind themselves constantly of why they are making and developing links with clubs and the community, and where other Sport England programmes like Coaching for Teachers fit into an 'educational agenda'. BAALPE, in conjunction with Events of Excellence, validates the Sportsmark award scheme. On the one hand, this may be positive in that physical education can reinforce and apply the educational agenda. Conversely, it might be seen as the physical education profession validating a political agenda which it does not agree with.

Active Mark and Active Mark Gold

This is the primary school equivalent of Sportsmark and Sportsmark Gold and as a scheme has yet to be launched. It is different from the secondary school award as its focus is on helping with the long-term planning and delivery of a primary school's physical education curriculum. To achieve the award, schools have to evidence community links offered. The award has a preliminary national target of 1,000 in its first year.

Challenge Funding

This is based on a two-year programme which is aimed at developing school-club links. Lessons have been learnt with this scheme, hence its renaming as 'Sportslink' and its priority within the small grants lottery funding programme awards for all. This revised scheme offers funding for coaching qualifications, new start-up equipment and club recruitment.

Millenium Festival Awards for All

These were introduced in October 1999, aimed at involving groups and schools. No partnership funding is required. It also remains to be seen how after-school clubs funded through the new opportunities fund (the sixth good cause of the National Lottery) will impact on additional sporting opportunities for the young.

Clearly, the issues highlighted and discussed in this chapter are relevant to all phases of education. Even though initiatives may be principally primary or secondary based it remains essential that physical education teachers are aware of the entire range of initiatives impacting on practice if they are:

- to be a significant part of it
- to be a valued and influential component of the agenda, not only in the delivery but also in the formulation and evolution of future policy and practice, which fundamentally provides each child with a positive, developmentally appropriate, broad and balanced experience establishing lifelong access to physical activity on a number of levels and in a number of roles.

If physical education teachers remain vague, confused or unaware of these politically, financially and pedagogically significant community initiatives which are being driven by a strong and not always educationally supportive political agenda, physical education, as well as the teaching profession, will find itself continually being reactive. A proactive stance which can be used positively to manipulate the political agenda to suit and promote physical education's educational agenda has to be generated.

Questions for reflection

1   The nature and extent of the dissemination of information and associated materials is a significant feature in the development of community initiatives within physical education. Who are the key agents and how are they contributing to a redefinition of physical education and sport within this country?
2   Consider the relatively recent movement towards predominantly school-based ITE courses. What are the likely implications of this for the quality of physical education teaching in school and the development of extra-curricular and life-long physical activity? What are the advantages and disadvantages of such an arrangement relative to (a) the primary sector (b) the secondary sector?
3   Given the movement towards the community and the many sound initiatives being led by the world of sport impacting on young children, what should be the immediate agenda for the physical education profession if it is to secure quality physical education teaching in schools?
4   Why have governing bodies of sport bought into these new partnerships and who stands to gain the most: the child, the community, the school or sport? (Remember that at the centre of any sound physical education programme is the child.)

Further reading

English Sports Council (1997) *England the Sporting Nation: A Strategy*, London: English Sports Council.

Health Education Authority (1998a) *Young and Active: A Policy Framework for Young People and Health-Enhancing Physical Activity*, London: HEA.

Office for Standards in Education (1998d) *Teaching Physical Education in Primary Schools: The Initial Training of Teachers*. London: Office of Her Majesty's Chief Inspector of

Schools in England. OFSTED Publications Centre.

—— (1999b) *Initial Teacher Training Inspected: A Summary Report of Secondary Subject Inspections Physical Education (1996–98)*, London: Office of Her Majesty's Chief Inspector of Schools in England: OFSTED Publications Centre.

Physical Education Association of the United Kingdom (1998) 'Mission Statement', *British Journal of Physical Education*, 29 (2): 4–7.

Qualifications and Curriculum Authority (1998) *Maintaining Breadth and Balance at Key Stages 1 and 2*, London: QCA.

11 Physical education, health and life-long participation in physical activity

Susan Piotrowski

Introduction

The potential of physical education to contribute to health-enhancing behaviour has long been acknowledged. Indeed, at the beginning of the twentieth century, the role of physical education programmes 'to maintain, and if possible, improve the health and physique of the children' was identified by the Board of Education as 'the primary objective of any course of physical exercise in schools' (Board of Education 1905: 9). This health focus was emphasised and retained until after the Second World War when attention began to shift more towards self-discovery and the acquisition of physical skills (Sleap 1990). The early 1980s saw a revival of a focus on health as an objective for physical education initially through the growth of the health-related *fitness* curriculum (Fox 1996). Physical fitness has been defined by the Health Education Authority (HEA) as 'a set of attributes that people have or achieve that relates to their ability to perform physical activity' (HEA 1998a: 2). These attributes include the components of physical fitness identified by Bird (1992) as muscular strength and endurance, the condition of the cardiovascular system, the mobility of the joints and flexibility, and co-ordination. Fox (1996) suggested that by the late 1980s it came to be widely realised that physical fitness has a strong genetic component and that the process of *exercise* was far more important to the determination of current and future health. Consequently, 'health related exercise (HRE)' became the favoured terminology. 'HRE' has been defined by the HEA as

> physical activity associated with health enhancement and disease prevention. The teaching of health related exercise would typically include the teaching of knowledge, understanding, competence and motor skills, behavioural skills, and the creation of positive attitudes and confidence for life-long participation in physical activity.
>
> (HEA 1998a: 2)

HRE is the term adopted within the National Curriculum for Physical Education (NCPE) for work associated with health and physical fitness. Under current NCPE arrangements it is a requirement for physical education to address the health needs of pupils across all four Key Stages (ages five to sixteen years). It is a 'general requirement' of physical education programmes to promote physical activity and healthy lifestyles (Department for Education (DFE)/Welsh Office (WO) 1995). The role of physical education in developing health-enhancing behaviour continues to be emphasised in the revised NCPE for 2000, in which content relating to fitness and health form an integral part of the Programme of Study at each Key Stage (Department for Education and Employment (DfEE)/Qualifications and Curriculum Authority (QCA) 1999).

The relevance of a health focus within the physical education curriculum is now widely accepted. However, research evidence indicates that in order for participation in physical activity to have long term as well as short term health benefits, it is necessary for individuals to engage in life-long participation in physical activity. A major challenge for teachers of physical education concerns how to make a positive contribution to the goal of life-long participation.

In seeking to address this issue, the chapter focuses specifically on *how* HRE should be presented in schools if it is to contribute toward achieving this goal. Specifically, attention focuses on three key issues:

- What is the role of HRE in the curriculum? Is it predominantly to develop fitter pupils or to encourage interest in physical activity for life-long participation?
- How should HRE be delivered in schools if it is to make a positive and effective contribution to life-long participation in physical activity? Is it through discrete units of work focused on HRE or through permeating the teaching of other activity areas with an ongoing focus on HRE?
- How can physical education best contribute to the development of healthy lifestyles which include regular participation in physical activity? Does an effective health focus in physical education require a whole school approach to promoting physical activity, along with an integration of this focus with other health promoting initiatives within the school setting?

As a basis for reflection on these issues, initial consideration is given to the short term and possible long term health benefits of physical activity for young people (aged five to eighteen years).

Physical activity and the health of young people (5–18 years)

Physical activity has important consequences for the health of all age groups, including children and adolescents (Bird 1992). Research evidence points to both short term health benefits which follow from regular involvement and the possibility of longer term benefits through the development of positive attitudes towards involvement in physical activity which may affect participation patterns in adult life.

Short term health benefits from regular involvement in physical activity

There are short term health benefits for pupils which follow from their regular involvement in physical activity (Sallis and Patrick 1994). These benefits include: enhanced bone mineral density (Cooper *et al.* 1995, Grimston *et al.* 1993, Slemenda *et al.* 1994, Valimaki *et al.* 1994, VandenBergh *et al.* 1995, Welton *et al.* 1994); reduced risk of obesity (Bar-Or 1994); reduced risk of coronary heart disease (CHD) (Sallis and Patrick 1994) (the early stages of CHD have been observed in children as young as five years old (Kannel and Dawber 1972)); improved blood fat profiles (Boreham *et al.* 1997, Craig *et al.* 1996); lower blood pressure (Armstrong and Simons-Morton 1994, Gutin *et al.* 1990); and improved psychological health through improved self-esteem and the reduction of stress, providing of course, that the physical activity itself is not stress inducing such as may occur in some intensely competitive contexts (Blumenthal *et al.* 1980, Calfas and Taylor 1994, Folkins and Amsterdam 1977, Gruber 1986, Ledwidge 1980, Seals and Hagberg 1984, Steptoe and Butler 1996).

Possible long term health benefits for pupils from regular involvement in physical activity

The positive effect of physical activity on bone mineral density and the reduced risk of osteoporosis later in life is one of the long term health benefits of participation in physical activity (HEA 1998a). However, health benefits of physical activity largely derive from current participation levels in physical activity (Bar-Or 1994) and hence for physical activity to have long term health benefits it is important that patterns of engagement in regular physical activity are maintained throughout the life cycle. Current evidence, however, indicates only a 'moderate relationship between the amount and type of physical activity in childhood with that in youth' (HEA 1998a: 5) and, drawing on Malina's (1996) evidence, suggests only 'low levels of tracking from youth into adulthood' (HEA 1998a: 5). This is a matter of concern particularly when cardiovascular disease remains Britain's biggest killer – accounting for 50 per cent of all deaths – and that the risk of cardiovascular disease is associated with insufficient levels of physical activity (British Heart Foundation 1996). It is therefore a major challenge for those involved in physical education to find ways of promoting positive attitudes towards participation in physical activity which lead to continued participation in adulthood.

Levels of involvement required for health benefits to follow for young people

For health benefits to follow from participation in physical activity, it is important to engage in *regular* physical activity. It is important therefore to know what frequency, duration and level of intensity of physical activity is required for the desired health benefits to follow for pupils in schools.

Until recently, adult fitness guidelines of a minimum of three periods of twenty minutes per week of aerobic activity to maintain an effectively functioning cardio-respiratory system were used for children. For example, the United States National Children and Youth Fitness Study used the adult fitness guideline to define appropriate physical activity for children as:

> exercises involving large muscle groups in dynamic movement for periods of twenty minutes or longer, three or more times weekly, at an intensity requiring 60 per cent or more of an individual's cardio-respiratory capacity
>
> (Ross and Gilbert 1985: 49)

Such intensive activity levels for children have recently been questioned in the light of evidence suggesting that children do not favour or respond well to high intensity physical activity (Corbin *et al.* 1994, Epstein *et al.* 1991). Harris and Cale (1997) suggested that the model put forward by Corbin *et al.* (1994), 'The Children's Lifetime Physical Activity Model', was appropriate to provide the 'most up to date scientific guidelines' for minimal and optimal levels of physical activity for children if health benefits are to follow from their involvement' (Harris and Cale 1997: 59). The revised guidelines, proposed by Corbin *et al.* (1994), recommended two distinct types of physical activity corresponding to minimum and optimal levels of involvement if health benefits are to follow. The minimum level of physical activity was suggested to involve half an hour daily of physical activity where the energy expenditure is 3 kcal/kg/day. This level of energy expenditure was considered to occur through 'lifestyle physical activities' of the kind involved in childhood games and activities, walking or cycling to school, or physical tasks around the home. The optimal level of involvement was suggested to require moderate to vigorous physical activity (MVPA) where the recommended level of involvement is one hour daily of physical activity with energy expenditure of 6–8 kcal/kg/day. Types of physical activity which require this level of energy expenditure include those which use large muscle groups and require at least as much effort as brisk or fast walking. This emphasis on the benefits of moderate rather than vigorous physical activity is reflected in the recommendations for the level and type of physical activity proposed for young people by the HEA:

Recommendations for young people and physical activity

Primary recommendations

- All young people should participate in physical activity of at least moderate intensity for one hour per day.

- Young people who do little activity should participate in physical activity of at least moderate intensity for at least half an hour per day.

Secondary recommendation

- At least twice per week, some of these activities should help to enhance and maintain muscular strength and flexibility and bone health.

(HEA 1998a: 3)

In order for health benefits to follow from these levels of engagement in physical activity it is not considered necessary, according to recent expert opinion (HEA 1998a), for involvement in the recommended duration of physical activity to be undertaken in a continuous fashion. Participation in the recommended levels of physical activity may be 'in a continuous fashion or accumulated intermittently throughout the day' (HEA 1998a: 3).

Research by Armstrong and Welsman (1997) has shown that most children and adolescents do engage in at least half an hour or more of moderate intensity physical activity on most days of the week. However, patterns of involvement vary widely between individuals with some children and adolescents being very active, while others are inactive (HEA 1998a).

Physical education lessons have the potential to contribute to meeting pupils' physical activity needs. There is evidence of this happening, particularly in the USA (Pieron *et al.* 1996, Shepherd *et al.* 1980, Simons-Morton *et al.* 1988). For physical education to meet physical activity needs, the curriculum must be 'appropriately designed, delivered and supported' (HEA 1998a: 6). However, there is evidence that in many physical education lessons children and adolescents remain insufficiently active to benefit their health (Armstrong 1990, Faucette *et al.* 1990, Sleap and Warburton 1994, Warburton and Woods 1996).

While it is important for physical education to make a useful contribution to pupils' participation in recommended levels of physical activity, it is equally important, in the interests of pupils' long term health, that children and adolescents develop positive attitudes to life-long participation in physical activity. This latter goal can be affected by the way in which HRE is presented to pupils. Fox acknowledged that 'the way exercise is presented to youngsters may carry important implications for future activity patterns and consequently their health and well-being as adults' (Fox 1996: 102).

In reflecting on the question of how HRE can be presented most effectively to youngsters, the next section of the chapter focuses on the role of fitness testing in schools in the context of considerations relating to the promotion of life-long participation in physical activity.

Fitness testing versus the development of positive attitudes towards life-long participation in physical activity

Research conducted by Harris (1995) in secondary schools found that most HRE programmes focus on stamina, suppleness and flexibility and include fitness testing. Fitness testing was a compulsory component of the physical education curriculum in 62.6 per cent of 1,000 secondary schools surveyed by Harris (1995). She reported that the most common tests were: a time/distance run; the Multi-Stage Fitness Test; a 'sit and reach' flexibility test; sit ups/curl ups. A fifth of the schools in Harris's study also included skill-related fitness tests. About a third of heads of department in the study stated that the results of the fitness tests were sometimes reported to parents. The emphasis placed on fitness testing suggests that many HRE programmes have 'retained a fitness and performance orientation rather than one that is more activity and health focused' (Harris 1995: 31).

Armstrong and Welsman have drawn attention to the prevalent use of fitness testing in secondary school physical education programmes in both the UK and the USA. They reported that,

> Despite a change in emphasis from physical fitness to physical activity in physical education programmes in both the United Kingdom and the United States and regular challenges, over the last decade in the United Kingdom and in the United States, most secondary schools in both countries include compulsory fitness testing within their physical education curriculum.
>
> (Armstrong and Welsman 1997: 256)

The evidence shows that fitness testing is commonly employed in secondary school health-related programmes. Some of the reasons for this focus may be as follows.

- Teachers recognise that part of the rationale for encouraging young people to engage in regular physical activity is to optimise physical fitness (HEA 1998a). Fitness tests may therefore be used to assess the extent to which they are successful in achieving this goal.
- Fitness tests provide pupils, teachers, parents and others with knowledge of results of pupils' performance and of their progress over time. The value of this information is acknowledged by Biddle and Biddle, 'Fitness testing can be usefully employed if pupils can learn something from the tests and monitor themselves over time to see changes in their physical selves' (Biddle and Biddle 1989: 72). (However the authors are careful to qualify this remark by pointing out that it is 'the *process* of activity that has health benefits and not necessarily the *product* of achieving a high score on the fitness test').
- Knowledge of results from fitness tests may be motivating, particularly for those pupils who score well on the tests or see improvement in their scores over a period of time. Such pupils may be motivated to increase their activity and fitness levels.

- Fitness testing provides objective measurement and assessment. This fits neatly with the requirements of those physical education departments committed to more formal methods of assessment, recording and reporting. It is also possible that pupils attach greater significance to fitness as a result of this being a formally assessed component of the curriculum. Increased importance tends to be attached to those areas of the curriculum that are assessed (see Chapter 6 for further discussion of issues relating to formal assessment).

However, as Harris acknowledged, fitness testing 'is a controversial issue in educational settings' (Harris 1998: 31). Some of the reasons for the questionable status of fitness testing in schools concern: doubts about the suitability of the tests used (Armstrong and Welsman 1997); the questionable educational value of some approaches to fitness testing (Harris 1998); and the potentially damaging consequences of some of these approaches for long term participation in physical activity. For the purposes of this chapter, attention is focused on this latter concern.

Fitness testing and pupil motivation to participate in life-long physical activity

An issue of particular concern is whether fitness testing is conducive to achieving health goals in physical education. The research evidence referred to earlier in the chapter has shown that 'the important factor for health is the encouragement of physical activity as a behaviour rather than concentrating on the development of fitness as an outcome' (HEA 1998b: 3). Although there are some *long term* benefits from participation in physical activity by children and adolescents (e.g. for bone mineral density and the reduced risk of osteoporosis in later life), it is not necessary to perform high intensity activity in order to gain health benefits. Most health benefits (reduced risk of chronic diseases in adulthood) require regular involvement in physical activity at a moderate level throughout the life cycle. The inclusion of fitness testing will be detrimental to health goals if it negatively affects motivation to participate in life-long physical activity.

As mentioned above, some pupils score well on the fitness tests, which can be motivating. By implication, though, some pupils do not score well. Pupils who do not score well can become labelled as incompetent, especially if scores are compared between pupils. This can have damaging consequences for the motivation of pupils who do not score well to continue involvement in physical activity. As emphasised by Fox, 'the competent increase their commitment and the social system works to exclude and ostracise the incompetent' (Fox 1996: 96).

If fitness testing was to have this effect on some pupils who come to perceive themselves as incompetent this would be particularly worrying. Such pupils are likely to see themselves as not suited to physical activity and may look to withdraw from involvement. This would be damaging to the long term health needs of such pupils, who need to be motivated to engage in regular physical activity throughout the life-cycle. Research evidence (Duda 1987, Klint and Weiss

1987) has shown a consistent relationship between feelings of competence and involvement in physical activity.

Another way in which fitness testing can have a negative impact on pupils' motivation to engage in current and future involvement in physical activity concerns the potentially damaging effect of fitness testing on pupils' enjoyment of physical activity. Fitness tests can be an unpleasant, negative experience for pupils where they are compulsory, where use is made of exhausting maximal tests or where they cause embarrassment. Many pupils dislike exhausting and painful forms of exercise. Fitness testing sometimes involves measuring body composition. This can be embarrassing and humiliating for some pupils if publicly measured. Harris's study of approaches to HRE in secondary schools found over one-third of schools making use of skinfold callipers and weighing scales and prompted Harris to wonder how 'sensibly and sensitively the subject of weight management is being delivered' (Harris 1995: 32). More recently, Harris explicitly acknowledged the potential of fitness tests to have a negative effect on pupils' engagement in physical activity: 'Fitness tests can be demeaning, embarrassing and uncomfortable for at-risk sedentary children and can represent a negative experience that could turn children "off" rather than "on" to exercise' (Harris 1998: 32).

Where fitness testing does result in a negative experience for pupils, this is likely to have a damaging effect on life-long participation in physical activity. Enjoyment is identified by the HEA (1998a) as a particularly important determinant of young people's participation in physical activity.

The achievement of physical activity related health goals relies on understanding the determinants that affect life-long participation in physical activity. As discussed above, competency and enjoyment have been identified as two key determinants. Drawing on recent research evidence, other psychological determinants of young people's participation in physical activity identified by the HEA (1998a: 5) are: feelings of control and autonomy; confidence; positive attitudes towards physical activity; the formulation of personal goals which focus on personal effort and improvement; and perceptions of increased benefit and decreased barriers (e.g. costs) to participation in physical activity. Social and environmental determinants of young people's participation in physical activity include: family and peer group support; access to appropriate environments; and the influence of gender and socio-economic inequalities in broader society. In evaluating the usefulness of any particular approach to HRE in schools it is important to find approaches which maximise those psychological and socio-environmental determinants known to significantly influence participation in physical activity and minimise any known barriers to participation.

The next section of the chapter considers another issue relating to the way in which HRE programmes are delivered in schools. This concerns the possible impact on life-long participation in physical activity of either a permeation model or the use of discrete units of work to deliver the content of HRE.

Permeation versus discrete units of work for HRE

A permeation model of HRE has been interpreted by Almond and Harris as 'teaching HRE solely through the activity areas' (Almond and Harris 1997: 27). It is the approach to HRE favoured by both the NCPE (DES/WO 1992, DFE /WO 1995) and the Office for Standards in Education (OFSTED 1995a). An approach to HRE through discrete units of work, on the other hand, involves the inclusion of HRE in the physical education curriculum as a separate area of focus. It is this latter approach which is preferred by many secondary school physical education departments. Cale reported that despite HRE not being a separate activity area within the NCPE, 'many schools are nonetheless delivering it [HRE] through focused modules' (Cale 1996: 9). Inspection findings from Wales (OHMCI 1995) showed that 80 per cent of secondary schools were developing HRE courses, often as part of a modular approach. Almost half (43.7 per cent) of the heads of department in a survey by Harris (1995) thought that HRE at KS4 needed to be delivered through specific units of work if the specific requirements of the NCPE were to be met effectively. In Northern Ireland, HRE is a compulsory unit at KS4 (Gilbert 1998).

These conflicting views raise for consideration the issue of how HRE can be delivered most effectively in schools. According to Almond and Harris (1997) there is currently insufficient research evidence to suggest one approach to be preferable to the other. Referring specifically to the permeation approach, they found it 'particularly frustrating to hear key physical educators proclaiming that permeation is the "right" approach'. They asked 'Where is the evidence to support this point of view?' (Almond and Harris 1997: 27). Almond and Harris urged the physical education profession to generate evidence-based practice to protect from the prejudices of personal points of view.

In the absence of research evidence, it is nevertheless possible to address the issue of whether to approach HRE through permeation or discrete units of work by reflecting on the relative merits of the two approaches in relation to the following key considerations:

- effective communication of a comprehensive body of knowledge relating to HRE to meet the statutory requirements for HRE in NCPE
- effective use of time for addressing NCPE content relating to all areas of activity and HRE
- the effectiveness of the approach in encouraging life-long participation in physical activity.

Effective communication of a comprehensive body of knowledge relating to HRE

Harris provided useful identification of the type of knowledge, understanding and skills that one would expect to be developed through a comprehensive programme of HRE. Harris's identification of the knowledge base for HRE as

The Knowledge Base of HRE

The knowledge and understanding component of HRE focuses on:

- the short-term and long-term effects of exercise on predominantly the cardiovascular and musculo-skeletal systems;
- awareness of opportunities to be active in the local community (including the home);
- understanding associated with planning, implementing and evaluating a balanced exercise programme.

The skills component should enable pupils to:

- feel competent in the exercise setting through having a sound foundation of basic physical skills;
- learn behavioural skills such as setting realistic goals and establishing support networks;
- experience positive exercise sessions in which they achieve progress over time, and are helped to feel comfortable and confident.

(Harris 1995: 15)

detailed is clearly linked to developing the knowledge, skills and understanding that are likely to engender positive attitudes to life-long participation.

If this body of theoretical and practical knowledge is to be communicated effectively to pupils, it is necessary that teachers themselves are well informed, have good understanding of the knowledge base and feel confident to teach this area. Teachers also need sufficient time and resources to develop this body of knowledge.

A concern of those opposed to the treatment of HRE through permeation when the NCPE was first introduced was that an approach to HRE through permeation, rather than the designation of HRE as a separate area of activity, may negatively impact on the preparation of teachers to deal effectively with this aspect of the curriculum. Fox raised this concern: 'Without a formal programme of study there is a grave danger that exercise and fitness education will be given lower priority at a time when it needs more help than the well established areas' (Fox 1992a: 11).

In not giving HRE the status of a separate area of activity, Almond and Harris (1997) noted that resources for teaching areas of the NCPE have barely touched on HRE. Similarly, given the time constraints in initial teacher education (Carney and Armstrong 1996, Evans *et al.* 1997, Piotrowski and Capel 1996) and the limited support for continuing professional development in physical education in the context of other curriculum priorities (e.g. the National

Literacy Strategy and the National Numeracy Project in primary schools), it is unlikely that there has been time to focus on aspects of the physical education curriculum which go beyond the statutory Programmes of Study. It may be for this reason that Almond and Harris (1997) found that some teachers had experienced difficulties in knowing how to deliver the HRE aspects of the curriculum. As a theme of the curriculum, heavily dependant on the permeation model, HRE may have become a 'casualty within the system' (Rowe and Whitty 1993, cited by Harris 1995: 30).

Further difficulties for a permeation model relate to the difficulties of communicating a coherent body of knowledge if the approach lacks the necessary planning and structure to reinforce knowledge across the areas of activity. The National Curriculum Physical Education Working Group (NCWGPE) (DES/WO 1990) favoured an approach to HRE through permeation but nevertheless warned that permeation would not be successful unless there was a planned approach to the reinforcement of knowledge and concepts of HRE. Without this, important messages could be lost. Drawing on findings from OFSTED, Harris suggested that there has been 'minimal planned permeation through the areas of activity and that Her Majesty's Inspectors (HMI) have witnessed little of what they consider to be good practice' (Harris 1997b: 10). Furthermore, evidence from Harris's (1995) own research showed that despite over 80 per cent of physical education heads of department claiming to be delivering HRE through the areas of activity, much of this was unstructured. She believed this state of affairs to beg the question 'as to whether a degree of lip service is being paid to the delivery of HRE' (Harris 1995: 30). Thus the contribution of physical education to health is implicit: 'more incidental than planned' (ibid.: 25). If the permeation model is to be used effectively, teachers will need, as Almond and Harris suggested, to 'engage in a mapping process which illustrates how HRE concepts have been highlighted and reinforced across the curriculum' (Almond and Harris 1997: 27). Without this mapping there is the danger that communication of an appropriate body of knowledge for HRE will be impaired through lack of coherence, relevance, progression and even consistency if more than one member of staff is involved in delivering the content of HRE across the curriculum (Harris 1995).

With appropriate planning it is possible that one of the advantages of the approach through permeation – that of the reinforcing concepts across a range of activity areas – could be realised. Another strength of the permeation approach is that it provides a range of contexts within which to emphasise the different but complementary contribution that participation in the various areas of activity can make to health. This is explicitly recognised in the proposals for the NCPE:

> Each area of activity lends itself to the reinforcement of certain health related exercise concepts. For example, gymnastics and dance each provide a suitable medium in which to reinforce the knowledge base and experiences associated with flexibility and muscular strength and endurance;

games experiences can contribute towards an understanding of cardio-vascular health; both swimming and athletics can contribute to an understanding of cardio-vascular health, flexibility and muscular strength and endurance; and outdoor and adventurous activities provide a test of the application of this knowledge in various and rapidly changing conditions and contexts.

(DES/WO 1991: 63)

This advantage may be lost where an approach to HRE through discrete units of work is used. One of the criticisms made by OFSTED (1995a) of the provision of discrete units of work on HRE is that the approach can lead to little being done to reinforce considerations relating to health enhancing physical activity across other units of work. Similarly, the School Curriculum and Assessment Authority (SCAA) expressed strong concern where HRE is delivered through 'short units (of approximately six weeks' duration) [which] do not allow achievement to be bedded in and built upon and serve only to fragment and distort the curriculum' (SCAA 1997b: 18).

Whether HRE is approached through discrete units of work or permeation, it is essential to plan how that approach can communicate a well structured, coherent body of theoretical and practical knowledge which allows for the rein-forcement of key concepts across the various areas of activity. Attention should also be given to the practical problem of how to make most effective use of the time available for communicating this knowledge.

Effective use of curriculum time for physical education

Effective communication of an appropriate knowledge base for HRE takes time. The average time allocated to physical education in the curriculum of schools in the UK is ninety minutes per week, which is less than many other European countries (Armstrong and Welsman 1997, Harrison 1998). During this time teachers must teach the statutory programmes of study (areas of activity) at each Key Stage. Where discrete units of work related to HRE have been adopted, inspection findings (OFSTED 1995a) have shown this to reduce the time available for other areas, thus raising the possibility of a negative impact on achievement in these other areas. This finding has high-lighted the time pressures teachers face in helping pupils to reach an appropriate level of achievement within the areas of activity. In so doing, it also raises questions as to whether there is sufficient time to communicate effectively the knowledge base for HRE through the areas of activity. Research by Harris (1995) found that less than one third (29 per cent) of the physical education heads of department who responded to a questionnaire distributed to 1,000 secondary schools considered that the specific NCPE requirements for HRE could be delivered through the areas of activity at Key Stage (KS) 3. At KS4 only 18 per cent of heads of department felt that National Curriculum requirements for HRE could be delivered through the areas of activity. This finding probably reflects the concern of these heads of department to have sufficient time to cover the amount and complexity of the content of HRE for KS3 and KS4.

The implications of the approach adopted for life-long participation in physical activity

A concern to encourage life-long participation in physical activity was partly responsible for the NCWGPE recommending an approach to HRE through permeation. They noted that 'all activities of the physical education programme provide experiences through which pupils can be helped to appreciate how exercise can enhance fitness'(DES/WO 1990: 7). The areas of activity were seen to provide opportunities for addressing health and fitness concerns in the context of pupils' participation in meaningful and enjoyable physical activity. Such meaningful and enjoyable involvement was thought likely to encourage pupils to continue their participation in physical activity in extra-curricular and/or outside school and post-school. In order for the goal of life-long participation in physical activity to be realised, it was considered important that pupils acquire the skills and confidence to find joy and satisfaction in cultural activities such as football, netball, hockey etc. for which there are opportunities for participation in the adult sporting world. The intention of the NCWGPE was that through approaching health concerns through permeation, pupils would be motivated 'to extend their participation and develop life-long habits of interest and involvement' (DES/WO 1990: 8). Armstrong and Welsman supported this approach, arguing that 'although the provision of high-activity content should be an important component of physical education lessons it is much more important to build a foundation of motor skills and to make children's early activity experiences enjoyable in order to foster future participation' (Armstrong and Welsman 1997: 254).

A danger of approaching HRE through discrete units of work is that it may encourage 'detailed recommendations and rigid prescriptions for young people (which) may have a demotivating effect and make physical activity unattractive for young people (Laventure 1998: 34). Focused attention on high-intensity exercise may be 'at the expense of the type of activity the general public are more likely to take on board' (Fox 1996: 98). Hence, such regimes could be detrimental to the goal of life-long participation.

If an approach to HRE through discrete units of work is accompanied by a narrow interpretation of HRE as 'vigorous activity' this can lead to 'undesirable practices such as a "forced" fitness regime, directed activity with minimal learning or pupil involvement . . . arduous testing, and/or dull, uninspiring drill' (Harris 1997b: 11). Fitness testing is also more likely to be associated with such an approach. Of course, an approach to HRE through discrete units of work need not carry negative implications. However, teachers need to think carefully about the presentation of suitable content if the knowledge base for HRE is to be communicated in a way which helps to achieve the goal of life-long participation in physical activity.

Combining discrete units of work with a permeation approach to HRE

This discussion raises complex issues about the most appropriate and effective method for approaching HRE within the physical education curriculum of schools. A possible solution is to adopt an approach which addresses the theoretical and practical knowledge base of HRE through combining discrete units of work with permeation of other areas of activity. This is an approach already adopted in many of the secondary schools included in Harris's (1995) study. The advantage of this approach, according to Harris is that it highlights 'key concepts and experiences in focused units in physical education, integrating the knowledge base through the physical education activity areas, and creating vital links with other aspects of health education within the wider curriculum' (Harris 1995: 30).

In drawing attention to the advantages of combining discrete units focused on HRE with permeation of other activity areas in this way, Harris also touched on a further issue. This concerns the need to integrate a focus on HRE with other aspects of health education in the wider curriculum if physical education is to make a real and genuine contribution to meeting the health needs of children and adolescents. The following section broadens the discussion beyond a consideration of how to address the current physical activity needs of pupils and how to foster positive attitudes to life-long participation in physical activity within physical education lessons. Instead, the discussion moves to broader considerations of how the whole school environment (e.g. through the Active Schools initiative) could be used to promote participation in recommended levels of physical activity and create sound habits of participation in physical activity that are continued after leaving school. Linked to this, consideration is given, later in the following section, to a more holistic focus on pupils' health where attention is given to physical activity needs within the context of other aspects of health education such as diet, substance abuse, smoking and cleanliness. A holistic approach of this kind involves a settings-based approach of the kind encouraged by the World Health Organisation (WHO 1985). It is an approach which finds its expression in many primary and secondary schools in the form of Health Promoting School initiatives.

A holistic approach to health related physical activity

The Active Schools Initiative

Earlier sections of the chapter have shown that expert opinion strongly supports a recommendation for young people to participate in half an hour to one hour per day of physical activity of moderate intensity, depending on their current levels of participation in physical activity (HEA 1998a). Furthermore, it is considered that it is not necessary for this activity to be performed in a continuous way to have a positive effect on health. It is not necessary, therefore, to attend to children's physical activity related health needs by introducing a daily session of vigorous activity for all children. Indeed, as Armstrong and Welsman warned, recommendations for a daily session of vigorous activity 'need to be viewed with caution because children's resistance to participation in regimented, compulsory exercise is well documented' (Armstrong and Welsman 1997: 254). How then can the physical activity needs of pupils be addressed most effectively? This section considers whether pupils' physical activity needs are best addressed through a focus on these needs within the whole school/community environment rather then focusing more narrowly on the content and delivery of health related content within physical education lessons.

Schools have a significant role to play in helping pupils to engage in recommended levels of physical activity, both through physical education programmes and through the wider role of the school. The role of the education sector in promoting physical activity was identified by the HEA as relating to:

- the planning, delivery and support of the curriculum in health education and physical education;
- the delivery of whole-school approaches to promoting physical activity;
- developing sustained links with providers in the local community.

(HEA 1998a: 8)

Specifically, in fulfilling this role, the HEA recommended that 'Schools should enable young people of all ages to take part in physical activity, both in physical education curriculum time and at other times' (ibid.).

The Active Schools initiative is designed to achieve this objective. It is a concept which involves an understanding of the importance of physical activity promotion and the design and implementation of a policy that increases the physical activity levels of pupils and staff. The approach is intended to develop positive attitudes towards physical activity and habits of engagement in physical activity throughout the life-cycle (Fox 1996). The potential contribution of curriculum physical education is acknowledged, as are the contributions of other dimensions of school experience. These include: active transport to and from school (e.g. through walking or cycling); active play at break and lunch times; pre-school, lunch time and after school clubs and activities.

However, to have maximum impact on pupils' health in addressing their health-related physical activity needs, it is important to integrate a focus on physical activity with consideration of other factors affecting the health of the school community. For example, while there is strong support for the potential health benefits of engagement in physical activity, these potential health benefits are threatened in the presence of other health risk factors such as smoking or substance abuse. Noakes et al. (1984) reached this conclusion after studying marathon runners. He found that while exercise had the effect of reducing the risk of chronic disease (such as CHD) it did not provide complete immunity, especially in the presence of other risk factors such as smoking. The Health Promoting School initiative introduced by the WHO (1985) takes this broader approach. It considers pupils' physical activity needs alongside other pressing health concerns such as reproductive health, HIV/AIDS prevention, alcohol and drug abuse prevention, emotional health, smoking and CHD.

The Health Promoting School Initiative

'The health promoting school is a holistic concept embodying the promotion of health within the whole school environment' (Holland 1995: 2). In this approach the whole ethos of the school should convey its commitment to health with emphasis given to health matters both within and beyond the taught curriculum. Physical activity related aspects of health provide an important focus within health promoting schools along with a focus on other health concerns. The health focus of such schools includes aspects relating to the wider school environment such as the provision of healthy school meals, a healthy tuck shop, encouragement to take suitable precautions for protection against the sun's harmful rays in bright sunshine, the provision of cycle racks and helmet storage areas and so on. Furthermore, the health focus applies to the whole school community (including pupils, teaching staff and support staff) and to families and others in the wider school community.

The Health Promoting School initiative is based on a settings-based approach to health promotion of the kind first encouraged by the Ottawa Charter (WHO 1986). It is an approach which underpins public health movements which have developed internationally, e.g. Healthy Cities and Health Promotion in the Workplace. A settings-based approach to pupils' physical activity needs recognises that both personal and environmental factors have a part to play. For example, insufficient involvement in physical activity may be attributable to a personal lack of motivation and/or there could be environmental causes which restrict involvement such as a lack of safe walkways and cycleways for pupils to transport themselves to and from school.

A settings-based approach to health promotion belongs to a community approach to health which places emphasis on community participation. Community members are empowered to make their own decisions and bring about changes which are of benefit to their own health and those around them. Baric (1992) cited research by Abdelgadir (1991) which suggested that approaches which enable people to control and improve their own health are likely to have a lasting effect. Abdelgadir's study of Sudanese villages found that empowering community members with the responsibility for their own well being, and equipping them with the competencies for dealing with problems within their own limits, had a positive influence on the lasting effect of community changes. Similarly, research by Holland (1995) found a clear correlation between pupils' involvement in action to improve the health promoting practices of a school (e.g. pupils' involvement in developing a healthy tuck shop) and pupils' awareness of the importance of a healthy environment. If pupils can be involved in making decisions which increase their involvement in regular physical activity, this could have a lasting effect on positive attitudes towards life-long participation in physical activity.

Factors affecting the success of Health Promoting School Initiatives

The success of integrating physical education into health promoting school initiatives depends on the formation of productive partnerships between physical educationists, other staff within the school and others within the community such as parents, health educators and health promotion units. Laventure drew attention to recently established inter-agency groups which 'have as their starting point, the promotion of health related activity to local communities' (Laventure 1997: 29). He suggested that there are 'already examples of partnership approaches between teachers of physical education and local physical activity and health promotion specialists'. Laventure identified a challenge for physical education to develop new and exciting professional relationships between physical education, the exercise sciences and health promotion, to take forward these holistic approaches to pupils' health.

The success of health promoting school initiatives also relies heavily on 'designated and committed co-ordinators and school cultures that value health' (Harris 1995: 30). This was confirmed by findings from three small scale case-studies of Health Promoting School Award winning primary schools (Piotrowski 2000). The headteacher of one of the award winning primary schools acknowledged the school's health education co-ordinator as the key to the success of the scheme: 'She [the health education co-ordinator] keeps the children enthusiastic who enthuse other members of staff which keeps the whole thing going along'. The availability of time to co-ordinate a health promoting school approach and to link with parents and external agencies including health professionals is vital to the success of a health promoting school approach to pupils' health. The commitment of the headteacher and senior members of staff within a school is also vital to the development of a school culture that values health. (The importance of support from senior staff within the school for bringing about complex changes is discussed further in Chapter 14.)

Conclusion

Research has shown health benefits to follow from regular participation in appropriate levels of physical activity throughout the life-cycle. This chapter has considered how different approaches to HRE in schools may affect the potential of physical education to contribute to the goal of life-long participation in physical activity. For example, where fitness testing is employed, as it is in many secondary school programmes of HRE, it was argued that this may impact negatively on life-long participation in physical activity if approached in an inappropriate or insensitive way. Similarly it was suggested that discussions of whether to adopt an approach to HRE through a permeation model or through discrete units of work should keep in mind the possible impact of the approach on life-long participation in physical activity. The chapter also raised for consideration the question of whether important health goals are more effectively achieved through the inclusion of physical education in more holistic approaches to physical activity and to pupils' health in general through such initiatives as the Active School and the Health Promoting School.

The chapter has served to prompt reflection on the issue of *how* HRE should be delivered in schools if it is to make a positive contribution to the goal of life-long participation. This is a complex question to which there are no easy answers. Indeed, Almond and Harris believed it to be 'incumbent on inspectors, advisers and lecturers to adopt a neutral role and to demonstrate a variety of ways in which HRE can be delivered in order that teachers and students can make informed judgements for themselves' (Almond and Harris 1997: 27). This chapter has been designed to contribute to this process by providing a basis from which to reach informed judgements of this kind.

Questions for reflection

1   How should HRE be delivered in the physical education curriculum? How is it approached in your school (or a school with which you are familiar)? What changes, if any, would allow for a more effective contribution to the goal of life-long participation?
2   Should HRE focus on developing fitness or on achieving the goal of life-long participation and why?
3   Should health related aspects of the NCPE be delivered through a permeation approach, through discrete blocks or a combination of these approaches and why?
4   How should the physical education department be contributing to a whole school approach to health as encouraged through the Active School or Health Promoting Schools initiatives?

Further reading

Armstrong, N. and Welsman, J. R. (1997) *Young People and Physical Activity*, Oxford: Oxford University Press.

Fox, K. (1996) 'Physical activity and the active school', in N. Armstrong (ed.), *New Directions in Physical Education: Change and Innovation*, London: Cassell.

Harris, J. (1997b) 'Good practice guidelines for HRE', *British Journal of Physical Education* 28 (4): 9–11.

Health Education Authority (1998a) *Young and Active? Policy Framework for Young People and Health Enhancing Physical Activity*, London: HEA.

12 Progression and continuity in physical education between primary and secondary school

Will Katene

Big School
(*through the eyes of a 10 year old*)

Big, black iron gates
Very imposing
Inside, are there any mates?
Friendships closing

Once you go up to that school
You'll be changed
Mature, tough, smart but cool
Childhood's re-arranged

No more in Mrs Wild's class
No more just one teacher
A mass of swirling shapes to pass
The secondary creature
                              (Jordan 1958)

Introduction

The transition of pupils from primary to secondary school is probably the greatest source of discontinuity in the education of pupils. For pupils there is the excitement of setting out on a new stage of their school career, the prestige of 'growing up', learning new subjects, meeting a variety of specialist teachers and having specialist facilities (e.g. laboratories, purpose-built gymnasium, playing fields/pitches) and equipment. However, there are a number of changes to be made, for example, change from: being the oldest to being the youngest in the school; being with the same teacher for everything to having specialist teachers; being with the same group/class for everything to (possibly) being with different groups (depending on organisational arrangements, e.g. streaming, setting, banding); and using modified/smaller equipment to using full sized equipment. Thus, the prospect of joining a 'big school' remains a daunting experience for many pupils. Pupils' initial concerns and anxieties may include getting things wrong, getting lost in a large school, arriving late to lessons, turning up in the wrong place, forgetting to bring the correct equipment or kit, being frightened of strict teachers and/or being bullied by older pupils. Indeed, there are some who still operate traditional rites of passage designed to make new pupils aware of the fact that they are 'novelties' (Ruddock, Galton and Gray 1998). For some pupils these new situations and experiences can be very stressful and can even cause sickness and ill-health.

For teachers there are many challenges, including helping pupils to overcome their fears, helping them to make a smooth and relatively straightforward transition from primary to secondary school and achieving progression and continuity in the curriculum. The efforts of primary school teachers will be in vain if the progress pupils have made is abandoned at the age of eleven, with an unrelated fresh start: the practice in some secondary schools due to the erratic nature and process of transfer reports. However, the opportunity is available for secondary school teachers to promote continued development of pupils, based on their knowledge of the pupils' experiences in the primary school.

Her Majesty's Inspectorate (HMI) stressed the importance of curriculum continuity between primary and secondary schools when they stated that: 'The 5–16 curriculum is constructed and delivered as a continuous and coherent whole, in which the primary phase prepares for the secondary phase and the latter builds on the former' (HMI 1989: 23). Schools are adopting a wide range of transfer structures and procedures to combat pupils' fears and anxieties, to meet the challenges and to achieve a smooth and straightforward transition. Ruddock *et al.* (1998) suggested that the great divide between primary and secondary education is now more easily and commonly bridged by schools showing initiative in their transfer structures and procedures.

Physical education is an area of the National Curriculum which requires particular attention to be paid to the transition from primary to secondary school in order to avoid Year 7 pupils being overcome by, for example, 'enormous' sports halls, 'real' cricket bats, 'proper' gymnastics equipment, physical education kit, showers and physical education subject specialists. Thus, attention has been paid by some writers to improving the quality of physical education provision in the transition between primary and secondary schools (see, for example, Boniface 1990, Hepworth 1999, Williams 1997). Murdoch pointed out that 'the call is for the secondary school physical education specialist to embrace the complete 5–18 age range . . . and to contribute, in conjunction with primary school teachers, to the continuity and progression that are so essential' (Murdoch 1990: 73).

This chapter considers ways of enhancing progression and continuity in physical education provision in the transition between primary and secondary school between Key Stage (KS) 2 and KS3. A range of approaches, supported by some examples of ways of implementing each approach, is discussed, together with some benefits and constraints of each approach. By the end of this chapter readers should understand some of the structures and procedures that may be adopted to enhance progression and continuity of physical education provision in the transition from primary to secondary school.

Definition of key terms

In considering how the transition from primary to secondary school is supported and managed, it is important to understand the meanings of the following key terms: *transition, progression* and *continuity.*

A dictionary definition of *transition* is 'a passing or change from one place, state, condition to another' (Thompson 1995: 1482). This can be applied to schools as 'the supported movement of pupils between classes, teachers and schools' (Canterbury Christ Church University College (CCCUC) 1998: 10).

The terms *progression* and *continuity* are frequently used interchangeably. Dictionary definitions do, however, make clear distinctions between the two:

- *Progression:* 'the act or an instance of progressing' (Thompson 1995: 1093)
- *Continuity:* 'the state of being continuous; an unbroken succession' (ibid.: 289).

Likewise, use of the terms in educational contexts also shows clear distinctions. *Progression* 'occurs through interactions between teacher and pupil which move pupils through a sequence of increasingly demanding activities with the aim of achieving a development in learning' (CCCUC 1998: 10). Teaching and learning experiences are ordered so that pupils progress, each successive element making appropriate demands and leading to better performance.

Continuity in an educational context is 'based on communication between teachers which ensures the planned provision of teaching and learning to facilitate pupils' continuous development' (CCCUC 1998: 10). Continuity is about maintaining progression so that pupils perceive their learning as being continuous.

The next section of the chapter considers progression and continuity of pupils' learning experiences within the National Curriculum for Physical Education (NCPE).

The influence of the National Curriculum in England and Wales

The National Curriculum has contributed towards establishing curriculum continuity by giving schools a map which the National Curriculum Council (NCC) described as:

(a) providing a clear framework for the curriculum for all schools;
(b) requiring all teachers to build on work undertaken in previous years;
(c) requiring that schools build on work undertaken in previous Key Stages;
(d) providing a common language for the curriculum for all schools;
(e) calling for assessment both within and at the end of each Key Stage which informs decisions about work at the next stage; and
(f) requiring that the achievement of individual pupils be recorded.

(NCC 1989)

In the NCPE, programmes of study establish what pupils should be taught at Key Stages 1, 2, 3 and 4 and provide a useful framework for planning schemes and units of work.

> The knowledge, skills and understanding in the programmes of study identify the aspects (or core learning strands) of physical education in which pupils make progress:
> - acquiring and developing skills;
> - selecting and applying skills, tactics and compositional ideas;
> - evaluating and improving performance;
> - knowledge and understanding of fitness and health.
>
> (DfEE/QCA 1999:6)

When evaluating and improving performance, links should be made between acquiring and developing skills, selecting and applying skills, tactics and compositional ideas and knowledge and understanding of fitness and health.

Table 12.1 shows progression and continuity in pupils' learning, at the end of each key stage, in the acquiring and developing skills strand. The attainment target

> sets out the knowledge, skills and understanding that pupils of different abilities and maturities are expected to have by the end of the key stage. The attainment target consists of eight level descriptions of increasing difficulty, plus a description for exceptional performance above level 8. Each level description describes the types and range of performance that pupils working at that level should characteristically demonstrate. . . . In deciding on a pupil's level of attainment at the end of a key stage,

Table 12.1 Progressions in acquiring and developing skills at each Key Stage

KS1	Pupils should be taught to: a) explore basic skills, actions and ideas, with increasing understanding b) remember and repeat simple skills and actions with increasing control and coordination.
KS2	Pupils should be taught to: a) consolidate their existing skills and gain new ones b) perform actions and skills with more consistent control and quality
KS3	Pupils should be taught to: a) refine and adapt existing skills b) develop them into specific techniques that suit different activities and perform these with consistent control.
KS4	Pupils should be taught to: a) develop and apply advanced skills and techniques b) apply them in increasingly demanding situations.

Source: DfEE/QCA 1999: 16–23

teachers should judge which description best fits the pupil's performance .... each description should be considered alongside the descriptions for adjacent levels.

(DfEE/QCA 1999: 7)

Cooper (1995) suggested that principles of progression, such as *difficulty* and *quality*, should be considered. He further suggested that small incremental progressions and providing practice and repetition should be recognised as a means to progressive learning in all physical education lessons. Furthermore, NCC (1992: D3–D4) provided examples of how pupils can progress in the *difficulty* and *quality* in performing a skill (see below). Progress in the *difficulty* in performing a skill may be achieved by pupils:

- developing a variety of movements within a task
- finding different ways of performing a task (e.g. in passing a ball to a partner)
- transferring travelling and manipulative skills from one NCPE area of activity to another (e.g. travelling and jumping in gymnastic activities could meet part of the Programme of Study at KS2 and in athletic and dance activities could meet part of the Programme of Study at KS3)
- gaining strength (e.g. increasing personal performance in athletic activities, swimming activities and water safety and health-related exercise)
- using less space (e.g. improving games skills when working in a restricted area).

Progression in *difficulty* may also be achieved by working from, for example:

- single to multiple actions (e.g. combining a run, a jump and a roll into a controlled sequence)
- simple to complex knowledge of a specific activity (e.g. learning more advanced techniques in the long jump and knowing how to analyse and improve performance).

Progress in the *quality* of performance can be identified through tasks requiring, for example:

- improved form and tension in gymnastic and dance performances
- better hand and eye coordination in striking/fielding games, such as cricket or rounders
- increasing control of the body in developing an effective and efficient swimming stroke
- increasing knowledge and understanding in the mechanical principles of the discus throw.

Progress in the *difficulty* and *quality* of a performance is closely related to the age, physical and motor development, maturation, ability and previous experience of pupils. Pupils' motor development, competence and control passes through a series of changes or phases that take place over time:

- Phase 1: The period of infancy.
- Phase 2: The early childhood period.
- Phase 3: The middle childhood period.
- Phase 4: The pubertal and post-pubertal phase (Murdoch 1996: 28–32).

Further, the quality of pupils' later achievements in specific activities depends upon the degree to which early phases of development are fully experienced. This was emphasised by McChonachie-Smith (1993), who argued that educators have consistently failed to recognise that, particularly in the early years, manipulative skills and motor control are as much core skills as the literacy skills of reading, writing, speaking and listening, and numeracy.

The four phases link very closely with KS1 to KS4 of the NCPE. Thus, pupils' physical development demands different emphases on different activities at different times. This should make it possible for teachers to plan for progression and continuity in pupils' learning across the Key Stages. Some of the NCPE activities can be pursued in depth only when fundamental motor skills have been developed. Thus, in the primary years, the emphasis should be on dance, games and gymnastic activities to enable basic movements and skills to be developed to progress to recognised forms of games and athletic activities in the secondary years (DES/WO 1991).

Table 12.2 gives an example of tasks for gymnastic activities to illustrate ways of addressing issues of progression and continuity in the physical education curriculum between each Key Stage.

Table 12.2 An example of progression across Key Stages in gymnastics

KS1	Make up a three phase sequence including three still balances which are joined together by travelling. Make sure the travelling is in different directions and at different speeds.
KS2	Create a pair sequence using apparatus and floor including four balances, two of which must be shared, linked by travelling actions. The sequence should include actions involving flight, balance, variety of body shape, rotation and inversion.
KS3	Using a theme of flight, produce a sequence in groups of three or four, which makes use of a variety of ideas including supported, aided and self-initiated flight. Make use of floor and apparatus and compositional principles related to relationships and space.
KS4	As an individual or in a small group produce a sequence using apparatus or the floor which meets specific technical and choreographic criteria decided on by yourself or taken from another source. Develop the work for performance with an awareness of audience.

Likewise, progress and curriculum continuity is also related to pupils' cognitive, social and emotional development. This results in pupils generally moving from:

- dependence to independence in learning;
- performing given tasks to being able to structure their own;
- using given criteria to judge others' performance to developing their own criteria to evaluate their and others' performance;
- simple tasks to difficult and complex ones; and
- natural movements to skilful/artistic technical performance.

(DES/WO 1991: 27)

Thus the introduction of the NCPE has identified progression and continuity across the school curriculum and has thereby increased the potential for progression and continuity in pupils' learning experiences. However, progression and continuity will not happen in practice unless it is thoroughly and meticulously planned. The next part of the chapter considers different approaches to planning for progression and continuity in the transition from primary to secondary school.

Approaches to transfer between primary and secondary school

Ruddock *et al.* (1998) identified five approaches in which schools structure their transfer procedures in the transition of pupils from primary to secondary school:

1 curriculum continuity approach
2 administrative approach
3 pedagogic approach
4 pupil-centred approach
5 approaches which give priority to exploring and explaining the purpose and structure of learning.

In this chapter the first four of these approaches are considered in relation to physical education. However, the fourth of these approaches has been renamed 'the social and organisational approach'. For each approach a description is given, supported with examples of how it may be implemented in physical education, along with some potential benefits and constraints of each approach.

Curriculum continuity approach

Description of the approach

Benyon suggested that curriculum continuity refers to the:

transitions pupils experience from one stage of schooling to another; it can refer to the curricular experiences which teachers try to provide for the pupils through a school year; and it can refer to the transitions within a school as children move from class to class.

(Benyon 1981: 36)

Achieving continuity requires the planned provision of teaching and learning to facilitate continuous development or progress of pupils. Ruddock *et al.* (1998) identified as features of the curriculum continuity approach, the exchange of material and teachers, or involving pupils in projects that start in Year 6 and end in Year 7, in their new school.

How curriculum continuity may be put into practice in physical education

It has been shown above that progression and continuity are explicit within the NCPE. However, curriculum continuity between primary and secondary school does not automatically follow. Means of establishing curriculum continuity need to be considered explicitly. A number of different approaches may be adopted, focusing around establishing a collaborative partnership between primary feeder schools and the local secondary physical education department. This could take several different forms:

- Secondary physical education teachers teach Year 6 pupils before they arrive at the secondary school and/or Year 6 teachers teach and/or observe Year 7 classes to clarify understanding of the secondary curriculum.
- A named secondary physical education teacher is identified who is given time to act as a coordinator or liaison officer between the secondary school and primary feeder schools. This teacher visits primary school physical education lessons, attends staff meetings, arranges joint meetings and organises paperwork to support continuity between KS2 and KS3.
- Year 6 teachers/physical education curriculum coordinators and secondary physical education teachers meet regularly to share knowledge and expertise of the NCPE areas of activity, to share ideas or jointly plan and develop a curriculum to provide continuity from Year 6 to Year 7 (including the development of curriculum consistency across primary feeder schools as well as continuity with (and within) the secondary physical education department). This should be beneficial to all concerned: primary and secondary teachers can learn from each other. This could lead, for example, to work on a common school and/or physical education policy document, to arranging for Year 6 and Year 7 pupils to work together on an aspect of the physical education curriculum (Williams 1997). Other outcomes may include, for example, the development of a standardised policy on assessment, recording and reporting procedures or the production of guidance and exemplification materials which support and encourage appropriate curriculum continuity.

- A joint professional development day is held between the secondary physical education department and primary feeder schools which enables teachers to exchange ideas about the teaching of the subject. This may include sharing schemes and units of work and lesson plans, which enable teachers to develop knowledge and understanding of the curriculum across KS2 and KS3. They may also share or exchange ideas about the use of materials and resources, e.g. how information and communications technology (ICT) and other resources can be used creatively and innovatively to improve teacher effectiveness as well as to enhance pupils' learning experiences.
- Pupils begin some activities in Year 6 which they continue into Year 7, or activities are planned to be developmental from Year 6 to Year 7.

Bell (1992) found that many primary feeder schools have enjoyed the policy of receiving their secondary physical education teachers for a substantial input into classes all the way through primary school and especially in Years 5 and 6. Physical education curriculum coordinators have also enjoyed time with lower secondary school physical education classes, and on occasions have led the teaching of physical education in such classes. He suggested that such strategies should maximise the sharing of expertise between primary teachers and secondary physical education teachers, providing professional development for both sets of teachers and enabling curriculum continuity to be achieved.

Benefits of this approach

One benefit of this approach is that by enhancing progression and curriculum continuity, pupils' learning experiences in physical education can be maximised and pupils motivated to strive for higher standards. Planning for continuity prevents pupils from revisiting and repeating the same curriculum material and enables a progressively more challenging curriculum to be taught, retaining interest and motivation, especially in the transfer from primary to secondary school. Galton (1999) found that up to 40 per cent of eleven year olds fail to make satisfactory progress during Year 7, and one in fourteen pupils actually 'unlearns' basic skills which seemed secure at the end of primary school. Although Galton was not looking specifically at physical education, such failure to progress and/or unlearn basic skills may be prevented in physical education through planned curriculum continuity.

The potential to retain pupils' motivation in physical education is especially important in promoting an active lifestyle which, in turn, is critically important for the future health of the nation's population. The Health Education Authority (HEA) policy framework *Young and Active* pointed out that 'an appropriately designed and supported physical education curriculum can enhance current levels of physical activity' (HEA 1998a: 6) and improve physical development in young people.

Constraints of this approach

The National Primary Centre (1994) found that both primary teachers and secondary physical education teachers are not delivering a broad range of activities comprising the NCPE, since they are tending to bias the curriculum towards games teaching (Chapter 7 of this book discusses the dominance of games in the curriculum). There may be many reasons for the limited range of activities offered, including a lack of confidence in teaching specific activities due to limited subject knowledge, and lack of continuing professional development opportunities as the level of support from, for example, Local Education Authorities (LEAs) has been reduced (Durham LEA 1996). Further, limited physical facilities in many primary schools, such as the lack of a purpose-built gymnasium, playing fields/pitches and limited equipment for a range of activities, may make it difficult to offer a range of activities.

The National Primary Centre (1994) also found that primary and secondary school teachers are not collaborating closely with one another in order to develop a progressive and continuous physical education curriculum. There may be several reasons for this. For example, both primary and secondary teachers have been subjected to enormous change in recent years. These changes have created real pressures for teachers and may have impeded real progress and development in physical education as a whole, and curriculum continuity in particular. Clearly, the recent focus in primary schools has been on raising standards in literacy and numeracy with government initiatives such as the National Literacy Strategy and the National Numeracy Project. This may result in mornings largely taken up with literacy and numeracy work, which results in limited time for physical education as well as many facilities (particularly the school hall) left unused. However, this is potentially at a very high cost to a balanced curriculum and to curriculum continuity in physical education. Many primary and secondary physical education teachers are 'fighting for time' for physical education, resulting in limited collaboration between primary feeder schools and secondary physical education departments. Moreover, there are serious implications of time for primary school physical education when the school hall is needed for a multiplicity of activities (e.g. lunch, assemblies, Christmas productions), as well as for physical education lessons. Time is at a premium in many schools and there is insufficient time for teachers to meet formally and informally to discuss ideas and share good practice on curriculum continuity and progression.

Administrative approach

Description of the approach

According to Ruddock *et al.* (1998), the administrative approach prioritises the exchange of information, usually at the level of the individual teacher, or brings primary and secondary schools together in a working relationship to inform and develop good practice. For example, pupils' records of achievement, school reports and special educational needs information are transferred from primary to secondary schools.

How the administrative approach may be put into practice in physical education

If primary feeder schools and secondary schools share in-depth knowledge of Year 6 pupils, the transition of pupils from primary to secondary school can be made as smooth as possible. There are a number of ways in which information can be exchanged, for example:

- Primary feeder schools and the secondary physical education department exchange ideas, information about assessment, recording and reporting procedures and about individual pupils and their specific needs.
- The outcomes of Year 6 assessments are shared. The value of the information may be enhanced if a standardised policy on assessment, recording and reporting procedures is developed and used across both the primary feeder schools and the secondary school.
- Primary feeder schools provide effective records on each pupil, which enable secondary physical education departments to plan a programme to meet pupils' individual learning needs.

Benefits of this approach

If secondary physical education teachers have access to information concerning their pupils' achievements in the primary school they are better able to plan a progressive and continuous physical education curriculum to meet the needs of individual pupils. This could be achieved, as suggested by the Inner London Education Authority (ILEA 1988), by designating a key person within the secondary department who would brief colleagues and keep them informed about developments and discussions between associated schools.

Constraints of this approach

First, the transfer of information does not in itself ensure that it is used effectively; teachers have not only to receive good quality information, but also have to value it and be able to use it effectively. In a survey of 215 schools Galton (1999) found that only one in three respondents had confidence in the information that they sent to other schools, and even fewer (26 per cent) had confidence in information received.

Second, there are challenges in assessing, recording and reporting children's movement abilities. Office for Standards in Education (OFSTED 1995a) inspectors reported problems with assessment, recording and reporting in both primary and secondary school physical education. They also reported few examples of systematic monitoring and evaluation taking place in physical education in secondary schools. Further, they gathered evidence that assessments are not used to inform planning and so learning in physical education is not continuous or progressive. With few accurate assessments of pupils' development and abilities, many primary teachers are unable to record and report effectively and secondary physical education teachers have frequently adopted a 'fresh start' policy with pupils entering Year 7 (Howarth and Head 1988). This may be seen as inappropriate and frustrating for pupils who begin Year 7 with good motor skills and yet find themselves in lessons which fail to challenge their level of ability. Learning how to use the process of assessment and the transfer of information which is central to the administrative approach, to inform planning is, therefore, an important skill in both primary and secondary physical education teaching. One way of achieving this is for primary and secondary physical education teachers to collaborate closely with one another in order to develop jointly methods and instruments of assessing, recording and reporting so that at transfer time, secondary schools are able to understand and act upon records of achievement/development of pupils entering Year 7. Thus, repetition, revision and non-challenging lesson planning will be minimised.

Pedagogic approach

Description of this approach

This approach gives priority to exploring and explaining the purpose and structure of learning in a new setting. It recognises pupils' needs (and capacity) to develop a language for thinking about learning and about themselves as learners (Ruddock *et al.* 1998). One approach, the pupil-centred or process model, is used in this chapter to illustrate how the pedagogic approach may be put into practice in physical education.

How the pedagogic approach may be put into practice in physical education

Clearly, pupils should always be the centre of the educational process and physical education should be a medium through which both primary teachers and secondary physical education teachers can enhance pupils' learning experiences in physical education. However, whether learning is enhanced depends largely upon the teaching approaches and strategies adopted.

In some schools there has been a move from a teacher-centred to more pupil-centred learning. The teacher-centred approach includes a predominance of teacher focused and directed work, including copying the teacher (as in the command style of Mosston and Ashworth 1994) and a focus on a traditional skills-based approach to teaching (see also Chapter 5 of this book). It is product or outcome orientated. Pupil performance is often assessed on completion of a unit of work. On the other hand, a pupil-centred approach focuses on the pupils' learning rather than on the teacher. It is more process-orientated and it actively involves pupils in their own learning and development within physical education, rather than being passive recipients of teacher directed knowledge and skills. A pupil-centred approach is designed so that pupils see learning as theirs. They are guided through the learning experience rather than learning being dictated by others. There is a focus on problem-solving and decision-making by the pupils (individually, in pairs, groups or whole class).

In order for the pupil-centred approach to be effective pupils have to learn how to manage their own learning. Problem-solving and decision-making skills need to be taught and pupils given the opportunity to practise such skills in order to become effective in using them. For this approach to be successful, secondary physical education teachers must recognise and build on the approach started in primary school. This requires shared understanding of an approach to teaching physical education through a process model, coordination through, for example, meetings between primary and secondary teachers, joint continuing professional development, joint curriculum planning and development, and joint teaching in both the primary and secondary schools.

Benefits of this approach

Laventure (1992) acknowledged that many young people do not continue to participate in physical activity once they leave school. There may be many reasons for this, but the teaching strategies and approaches adopted by teachers in many physical education lessons may result in pupils regarding their learning experiences negatively. Fox believed that 'teaching style and method of delivery hold the key to success' (Fox 1992b: 51). New/different approaches to teaching and learning (e.g. pupil-centred approaches) may overcome this issue and encourage more people to participate once they leave school.

One reason that pupil-centred approaches may encourage participation post-school is that pupils' individual needs are recognised in their physical education experiences at school. Pupils are encouraged to think about their learning, and hence about their strengths and weaknesses and what they like and dislike. Emphasis on problem-solving and decision-making in lessons may better enable them to make decisions about post-school participation. Laventure argued that

> through a pupil-centred development of the individual child, from fundamental movement and body management skills to the development of more specific skills within a range of contexts, young people eventually will not only become competent in activities but in addition possess the necessary skills, knowledge and attitudes to make informed choices about the value of such activities that will enable them to have active lifestyles.
> (Laventure 1992: 190)

Constraints of this approach

First, without effective coordination there may be problems of discontinuity between teaching and learning in primary and secondary schools. This may be exacerbated by general assumptions that different teaching styles are adopted by primary and secondary physical education teachers, based on different philosophies of how children learn. Some may argue that primary teachers teach *children* and secondary school teachers teach *subjects* (Benyon 1981). Effective coordination may be difficult to achieve due to lack of time and/or motivation.

A second possible constraint in this approach is the adequacy of teachers' knowledge in areas of activity in the NCPE. Without adequate knowledge and understanding of the NCPE areas of activity, teachers may lack confidence in planning, teaching and assessing pupils' progress and attainment, resulting in lack of innovation, creativity and imagination in trying to implement a range of teaching and learning strategies. This may result in teachers using didactic methods of teaching at the expense of other ways of teaching and learning. This may limit pupils' learning experiences and may result in pupils being insufficiently challenged and motivated, with a possible consequence that lessons lack progression and continuity.

Social and organisational approach

Description of this approach

This approach concentrates on preparing pupils for the social turbulence of transfer to help them to cope with the social and organisational novelties of the new school (Ruddock *et al.* 1998).

Some concerns of pupils about transferring to secondary school are identified in the introduction to this chapter. It is not surprising, therefore, that many initiatives to help pupils transfer from primary to secondary school have focused on social, administrative and organisational issues. The School Curriculum and Assessment Authority (SCAA 1996b) noted that the standard of pastoral care in preparing pupils for the social turbulence of transfer and helping them to cope with the organisational structures of the new school has been very high, with well planned and organised induction programmes for Year 6 primary pupils to ease their transition to secondary schools.

How the social and organisational approach may be put into practice in physical education

There are a number of approaches that schools may take to prepare pupils for the social turbulence of transfer and to help them cope with different social and organisational arrangements in the secondary school. These include:

- Arranging for Year 6 pupils to work in a secondary school. Initially this may be for one day. A small, achievable move such as this may be perceived positively and benefit pupils. It enables them to learn something of the layout of their new school and to meet some of the other pupils who will also be transferring. It also prepares them for having a different teacher for each subject rather than one class teacher for all subjects. If the visit includes a physical education lesson, pupils are able to experience an aspect of the KS3 physical education curriculum taught by a specialist physical education teacher and are able to use specialist facilities and equipment.

- A single visit may lead to planning a programme of visits from the beginning of the school year, formulating a timetable of workshops for Year 6 pupils, with staff involvement across schools.
- Year 7 pupils may return to their former primary schools and share their experiences of being in a 'big school'.
- Primary teachers may be invited to secondary schools to talk with both teachers and pupils after they have settled in.
- Secondary physical education teachers may visit Year 6 to talk to pupils about expectations in the secondary school and to prepare pupils for transfer.

Primary and secondary physical education teachers should consider how they can make the transition as smooth as possible and how learning can be continued with the minimum amount of disruption. Secondary physical education teachers need to consider how they can make new pupils feel at home and how they can protect pupils' personal confidence and sense of well-being.

Benefits of this approach

An approach which prepares pupils for the different social and organisational arrangements in the secondary school can help to alleviate any concerns that there may be. Any activities which prepare Year 6 pupils for the move to secondary school are likely to be beneficial. For example, some Year 6 physical education lessons organised and delivered by secondary physical education teachers in the secondary school can provide a valuable experience for the pupils. Pupils are able to see the physical education facilities and to gain familiarity and confidence with what will be expected of them in Year 7, including being taught by a specialist physical education teacher. This gives them a greater preparedness for life in the secondary school.

Second, by attending to social and organisational aspects of the transfer from primary to secondary school, and particularly enabling Year 6 pupils to spend time in secondary schools, may help to dispel rumours from older pupils and/or siblings that some secondary physical education teachers are strict, which can be very 'off-putting' to new pupils. Indeed, helping pupils to overcome any fears or dispelling unhelpful rumours can aid their social and psychological preparation for life in the secondary school and may support other efforts to assist the transition between primary and secondary schools.

Constraints of this approach

Many secondary schools have made strenuous efforts to smooth the transition of pupils from primary to secondary school by focusing on the social, administrative and organisational structures and making pupils feel less lost in the 'big school'. However, it may have been at the expense of other aspects of the transition, including not ensuring progression in pupils' learning experiences in physical education lessons and, therefore, not sufficiently attending to pupils' progress and achievement.

Summary

Beer (1988) suggested that the coordination of the total experience of a child from early school to the completion of an honours degree must be planned. This chapter has looked at planning for progression and continuity in physical education in the transition between primary and secondary schools. Hargreaves, in pre National Curriculum days, recognised:

> that the break should be made as natural and as easily as possible and that the utmost care should be taken to ensure that the next five years (or more) of secondary schooling are based on the foundations laid in the six years of primary schooling.
>
> (Hargreaves 1984: 25)

Although the NCPE is now in place and provides a guide to curriculum continuity and the progression of learning experiences across the curriculum, the sentiment of Hargreaves's remark is still true today. The transition from primary to secondary school needs to be well planned. Planning requires the best possible liaison and close links between primary and secondary physical education teachers. This requires time to be devoted to it by the teachers concerned.

However, one possible problem with emphasising greater liaison and collaboration to achieve progression and continuity may be that it is perceived to undermine teacher autonomy. Raymond (1998) argued that professional autonomy is highly valued and moves towards continuity between primary and secondary physical education can seem a threat to teachers' autonomy. However, she pointed out that, while endeavouring to preserve a teacher's natural flair and personal approach, pupils' learning experiences must be given priority.

In this chapter the influence of the NCPE in progression from 5–16 was discussed before identifying a number of different approaches which could be adopted for progression and continuity in physical education in the transition between KS2 and KS3. Although four different approaches were considered separately in this chapter, they are closely interrelated and methods of putting each approach into practice may be the same across a number of approaches. In addition, the interaction of all four approaches is vital to the process of progression and continuity in physical education and particularly in the transition between primary and secondary schools. No single approach is going to be the most effective way to cater for progression and continuity; several or all of these approaches need to be used together to achieve effective progression and continuity in the transfer from primary to secondary school. Further, what will work in any one situation depends on a number of factors, including the schools and their transfer structures and procedures, the headteachers, primary and secondary physical education teachers and their ability to work together collaboratively. In addition, local conditions, facilities, expertise and policies have a bearing on the type of curriculum that can realistically be offered in both primary and secondary schools in any given area.

However, there is little research into the effectiveness of different approaches to achieving progression and continuity in the transition from primary to secondary school, nor in progression and continuity in physical education provision. Following a survey of 215 schools Galton (1999) concluded that schools need to be provided with tried and evaluated strategies which can be adapted for their particular circumstances, and that more research is needed into how to help pupils at transfer.

In the absence of such research evidence, it is important that readers reflect on this issue and work towards achieving progression and continuity for pupils in physical education in the transition between primary feeder schools and the secondary physical education department.

Questions for reflection

1   What structures and procedures are in place to aid progression and continuity between KS2 and KS3 in the school in which you are working? How effective are they? What, if anything, can be done to improve the procedures?
2   How do accurate and consistent records of what pupils are achieving in KS2 inform pupils' secondary physical education teacher? Can the information and/or communication of these be improved? If so, how?
3   Do you get the opportunity to observe another age group, either in your own school or in another phase of schooling? If so, what have you learned from this? If not, what could you learn?

Further reading

Boniface, M. (1990) 'Primary school PE and the implications for curriculum continuity across the school divide', *British Journal of Physical Education* 20 (2): 301–3.

Galton, M. (1999) 'Primary/secondary transfer: Left behind in secondary transit', *Times Educational Supplement* (3 September): 4.

Hepworth, N. (1999) 'Continuity and progression: Key Stages 2 and 3', *Bulletin of Physical Education* 35 (1): 23–35.

Howarth, K. and Head, R. (1988) 'Curriculum continuity in physical education: a small scale study', *British Journal of Physical Education* 19 (6): 241–3.

National Primary Centre (1994) *Continuity and Progression: Critical Issues Affecting Teaching and Learning with a Particular Emphasis on the Transition Between Primary and Secondary Schools*, Oxford: National Primary Centre.

Ruddock, J., Galton, M. and Gray, J. (1998) 'Lost in the maze of the new', *Times Educational Supplement* (20 November): 19.

School Curriculum and Assessment Authority (SCAA) (1996b) *Promoting Continuity Between Key Stage 2 and Key Stage 3*, Middlesex: SCAA.

Stoker, A. (1991) *Liaison and Transition at Key Stages 2/3: A Resource Pack for Teachers in Primary and Secondary Schools*, Lancaster: Framework.

Williams, A. (1997) 'Continuity and staff development: Key Stage 2 – Key Stage 3: A Mid-Wales approach', *Bulletin of Physical Education* 33 (2): 39–43.

The author wishes to acknowledge the contribution made by Dr Elizabeth Marsden to some of the ideas developed in an early version of this chapter.

Part V
Conclusion

13 Re-reflecting on priorities for physical education: now and in the twenty-first century

Susan Capel

Introduction

This chapter begins by reminding readers what physical education is and what lies at its core. The chapter then considers priorities for physical education, within the context of the unique contribution that the subject makes to the curriculum. In the third part of the chapter consideration is given to changing priorities for physical education over time. Attention is given to the influence of physical education teachers' own values regarding priorities for the subject, based on reasoned reflection and within a societal context. A brief historical background is then given. Finally, the chapter encourages readers to consider priorities for and content of physical education in the twenty-first century in order for the subject to make as full a contribution as possible to the education of all pupils.

What physical education is and what lies at its core

When asked what physical education is, the response from many people, including many physical education teachers, is often a list of activities that comprise a physical education curriculum rather than a definition of the subject. However, in order to justify its place in the curriculum, the subject must be more than a list of activities in which pupils participate. If physical education is only a list of activities, there are other people (such as coaches) and other places or contexts (such as extra-curricular activities, community sport provision) which can provide opportunities for pupils to participate in those activities. As Thorpe and Bunker reminded us in relation to games:

> The physical education teacher, in selecting a sample of games, must high-
> light the relationships between them and must develop them working with
> rule structures, increasing the tactical complexity and greater decision-
> making capacity. It is the ability to think and operate in this way that
> separates the physical education teacher from other providers of games
> experiences, e.g. coaches and sports leaders.
>
> (Thorpe and Bunker 1997: 79)

In physical education, activities are the means of achieving its aims. Teachers purposefully select one activity over another in order to achieve a particular aim.

One reason that people may identify physical education as a list of activities is that there has been little consensus as to what physical education is and no single accepted definition. Lack of consensus, and of a clear definition, support views that physical education has been, and remains, contested (e.g. Evans and Davies 1992, Evans, Penney and Davies 1996, Kirk 1992, Kirk and Tinning 1990, Penney 1998, Talbot 1995). Some examples of definitions of physical education are given in Chapters 1 and 8 of this book.

Despite lack of consensus or agreement about a definition, there is a need to identify what physical education is and what lies at the core of the subject. Talbot identified characteristics of physical education as:

- an entitlement within the education system for all children, whatever their personal characteristics, background or level of ability
- focus on the body and its movement in the physical and overall development of young people
- use of the physical beyond the merely mechanical, including demands of, and increases in, physical capacities, including physical skills, speed, stamina, mobility and physical responsiveness
- the centrality of a learning process: not only developmental processes, but activity which demands engagement, effort and attention by the learner
- the passing on of knowledge about, understanding of and respect for the human body and its achievements, both one's own and others'
- the learning of physical skill, critical reflection, refinement and improvement, working towards physical competence and physical literacy.
- an integration of the physical self with the thinking and social person
- a shared language and value system, with capacity for adaptation of practice according to children's needs: a central value would be that children and their successful development are more important than the activities in which they may be engaged
- careful selection of physical activities, to meet developmental and individual learning needs
- working towards an understanding and appreciation of the role of physical development and physical activities in personal development, health maintenance and social lifestyle.

(Talbot 1998: 107)

The Department for Education and Employment and the Qualifications and Curriculum Authority identified the importance of physical education thus:

Physical education develops pupils' physical competence and confidence, and their ability to use these to perform in a range of activities. It promotes physical skillfulness, physical development and a knowledge of the body in action. Physical education provides opportunities for pupils to be creative, competitive and to face up to different challenges as individuals and in groups and teams. It promotes positive attitudes towards active and healthy lifestyles. Pupils learn how to think in different ways to suit a wide variety of creative, competitive and challenging activities. They learn how to plan, perform and evaluate actions, ideas and performances to improve their quality and effectiveness. Through this process pupils discover their aptitudes, abilities and preferences, and make choices about how to get involved in lifelong physical activity.

(DfEE/QCA 1999: 15)

Both of these descriptions of physical education identify physical development as a central feature of the subject. Her Majesty's Inspectors identified three aspects of physical development:

- the development of motor competence of the kind required for successful, controlled and co-ordinated participation in contexts of sport, dance and physical exercise
- the development of fine motor control of the kind demonstrated in the manipulative skills of writing, craftwork, painting etc., and
- a knowledge of the impact of gross muscular exercise on the body, particularly in terms of its consequences for health and for the enjoyable and constructive use of leisure time.

(DES 1985)

Although other subjects in the school curriculum cater for the physical dimension of a child's development, e.g. the development of fine motor control in Art and Music, physical education performs a unique role in catering for those aspects of physical learning identified under the first and third points made by the DES, that is, 'where whole body competence is a potential source of satisfaction for everyone for health and recreation (and an additional source of satisfaction for those capable of elite and/or professional/vocational levels of involvement in sport, dance and exercise contexts)' (Piotrowski and Capel 1996: 187).

Priorities for physical education

Thus physical education has a unique contribution to make to the education of pupils. This unique contribution should be central to physical education teachers' work. If physical education teachers lose sight of that which is unique to the subject and the justification for physical education is made only in terms of what it contributes to general educational and cross-curricular aims, the justification for physical education as a subject in the curriculum is weakened. Other subjects may be equally or better placed to serve the purposes identified. This issue is discussed further in Chapter 1 of this book. However, while recognising the unique contribution of physical education to physical development and physical competence, different priorities for physical education can be identified.

Priorities for physical education influenced by the personal values of teachers

Physical education teachers have their own priorities for the subject; these are based on their own personal values. It is important that teachers are clear about their personal values and reflect on the impact these may have on their priorities for the subject. Personal values are a result of a number of factors, e.g. personality, previous experience and background. For example, many physical education teachers come into the profession because they have had good experiences, and been successful, in physical education and sport (e.g. Evans and Williams 1989, Mawer 1995). However, personal values can also be developed as a result of increased knowledge and understanding, training and support, and reasoned reflection. Readers are invited to reflect on why they have chosen to become physical education teachers, what their personal values are, and therefore what their priorities for physical education are.

Priorities for physical education influence the curriculum content selected and the teaching methods adopted. Two examples of the link between priorities and curriculum content and teaching methods are given below.

Teachers who value the competitive experiences which sport may provide may prioritise the importance of the sports experience for all pupils. One model of teaching that has some support is the *sport education* model (see, for example, Siedentop 1994). The aim of this model was articulated by Siedentop *et al.* as 'to help students become skilled participants and good sports persons [and] . . . to teach them to be players in the fullest sense of that term' (Siedentop *et al.*1986: 186–7). The sport education model was designed to promote a positive sport experience to pupils through stimulating an authentic sport experience, incorporating as many aspects of the sport as possible in the programme, for instance:

1   Sport takes place in seasons. A unit of work on one sport is called a season. The season/unit is often longer than six weeks or half a term. At the beginning of the season/unit more time is spent on practice, but later in the season/unit, more emphasis is placed on competitions.
2   Players are members of teams and remain in a team for a season/unit (pupils are placed in teams that practice and play matches together throughout the season/unit).
3   Seasons/units are defined by formal competitions. A formal competition extends through the season/unit on the particular sport.
4   There is a culminating event to each season/unit. The season/unit concludes with an organised event such as a championship.
5   There is extensive record keeping. Records are kept for teams during the season/unit, e.g. matches won, patterns of play, etc.
6   There is a festive atmosphere in which the season/unit, particularly the culminating event, takes place.

Pupils are therefore players, but also have the opportunity to become coaches, referees, managers, organisers, statisticians, publicity officers. The teacher begins by coaching all the teams but later in the season/unit pupils can become coaches of their own teams.

Proponents of sport education identify reasons for basing a curriculum on this model, e.g. the positive experiences of pupils in units of work; greater knowledge and understanding developed by pupils due to the length of time they participate in one sport and the ability to undertake different roles in the team.

A second example is teachers who value the benefits of physical education for health; such teachers may prioritise the health benefits of participation in physical activity. There is no single model for effective delivery of a *health based physical education curriculum*; debate about the best curriculum and teaching methods is focused around a number of factors, including the emphasis on health versus fitness and a permeation model of delivery versus discrete units of work devoted to a health focus (see Chapter 11 for further discussion about different modes of delivering a health related physical education curriculum). Almond and Harris suggested that 'how teachers deliver HRE [health related exercise] is an empirical and procedural issue which is open to evidence-based practice. In the absence of documented evidence, a range of possible organisational models should be explored in order to substantiate gains of practice' (Almond and Harris 1997: 27, parentheses added). Thus, without evidence-based practice, it is possible that the approach adopted to delivering a health based curriculum is based on personal values and priorities. For example, if the priority is fitness of pupils, the emphasis in the curriculum may be on fitness testing. If the priority is to encourage all pupils to adopt a healthy lifestyle, the emphasis in the curriculum may be on enjoyment of participation in physical activities and/or the development of a knowledge base/theory associated with health and HRE. This may be reflected in providing pupils with a wide range of experiences in physical education to motivate them to participate and to enable them to choose those activities in which they want to participate during extra-curricular, out of school or post-school time. If such an approach is adopted, it is important to reflect on the balance between the range of activities taught and the time necessary for pupils to develop knowledge, skill and understanding necessary as the basis for developing competence for later participation; between breadth and depth of activities. (Further consideration is given to breadth and balance in the curriculum in Chapter 7.) In this approach, a health focus can be taught as an independent unit of work or it can permeate other activities in the curriculum. Also, the approach may be extended beyond HRE into the rest of the school encouraging the development of a health promoting school.

Thus, it is important that physical education teachers reflect on their personal values and how these influence their priorities for physical education. In turn, these priorities can have a significant effect on the physical education curriculum offered. However, physical education teachers are also operating in a societal context. Thus there may be different priorities for physical education in different contexts. The next part of the chapter looks at how priorities for physical education have changed over the last century and how they may change in the twenty-first century.

Changing priorities for physical education over time

The Forster Education Bill of 1870 allowed for physical education to be included in the elementary school curriculum. Following the Forster Bill, the School Board for London adopted a military training approach which Her Majesty's Inspector for the City of London believed would lead to health and physical development as well as to good habits of obeying orders and aptitude for military service (Morrell 1871, cited in McIntosh 1976: 21). Objections to military drill, especially for girls, led, in 1876, to 'non-secular' physical education for girls. This marked the introduction of a form of physical education other than military drill and the beginning of separate curricula for boys and girls. Following this decision, Swedish gymnastics was introduced for girls in all schools in London in 1878. In 1890 swimming was introduced into schools.

A New Code was developed in 1904 in which the purpose of elementary school physical education was identified as forming and strengthening character and providing opportunities for the development of the body. This was achieved by training children in appropriate physical exercises, encouraging them in organised games and instructing them in some of the simpler laws of health. Schools also had a responsibility to develop the instinct for fair play and loyalty to one another as the basis for a wider sense of honour in later life (McIntosh 1976: 30). This Code led to games being added to the elementary school curriculum in 1906, with the objective of providing 'for moral and social education' (ibid.: 29–30).

A report from the Chief Medical Officer of the Board of Education in 1932 stated that

> the ultimate criterion of the success of any scheme or system of physical training is the carriage, mobility and equilibrium of the human body. If there is one test of the strength, tone and balance of the body it is posture, for this depends on the co-ordination of the muscles acting on the skeleton. Good posture indicated health and soundness; bad posture the reverse.
>
> (cited in McIntosh 1976: 32)

This led to an emphasis on good posture in the 1933 physical training syllabus. During the Second World War 'movement' replaced posture as the means by which the curriculum was judged; changing the shape and focus of physical education after the war. The 'movement' approach was influenced by a number of factors, including: modern dance of Laban; orthopaedic and remedial exercises; and obstacle training in the army. Different aspects of physical activity were identified in the curriculum, e.g. games, gymnastics, dance, and swimming. Girls' and boys' departments became further separated, with girls focusing more on movement education than boys.

Changes in the physical education curriculum over the last century were influenced by and linked to the changing context of society over time, such as the importance of military drill in physical education at the end of the nineteenth century was due mainly to the number of recruits who were rejected for military service in the Boer war as they were unfit for duty (see, for example, McIntosh 1976: 27).

This brief look at the history of physical education shows that as society has changed over time, so priorities for physical education have also changed. Likewise, priorities for the current curriculum framework in which physical education teachers are working are not static; they are determined by the particular context in which it is operating. This is the result of a complex inter-action of factors, including social, technological, economic and political factors. In England, the influence of the market economy on education, the importance of sport as part of the political agenda, and the concern for the health of the nation have been particular influences on the physical education curriculum in recent years. Other more general recent changes which influence education and physical education, have included:

- *Social*: an increase in the number of one-parent families; greater conver-gence of roles between men and women in families; an increased number of working women.
- *Technological*: increased use of and sophistication in information technology; growing influence of electronic communication and the Internet.
- *Economic*: the demise of major manufacturing industries; increased unemployment, particularly among young men under the age of twenty-five; the likelihood of redundancy or changes of job during a career; within education, emphasis on value for money; the introduction of the Euro.
- *Political*: greater emphasis on market forces within education which results in increased competition and, hence, marketing in education; greater emphasis on standards.

There are numerous other changes in each of these areas and readers might like to reflect on these.

Priorities for physical education in the twenty-first century

It is clear that change is going to continue; we are living in a world where it has been said that the only constant is change. Three areas which are likely to have an impact on physical education in the twenty-first century are considered briefly below in order to stimulate reflection on the influence of external factors on physical education in the future.

The information revolution is almost certain to continue. Information tech-nology and its various applications, including electronic communications, look set to play a more important role in society in general. Consideration therefore needs to be given to the role of information and communications technology in helping to develop a physically educated population.

Sport is highly likely to remain important and the influence of sport and sporting bodies on physical education is likely to continue. Gifted pupils are likely to be under more pressure to move into the adult world of sport at an early age. Physical education teachers will need to balance the immediate needs of gifted pupils to excel in specific activities alongside the longer term need for such pupils to become physically educated. Physical education teachers will also need to continue to balance the needs of gifted pupils with the individual needs of other pupils, remaining abreast of developments concerning the rights of the individual and the commitment to equality of opportunity. However, continuing concern about the health of the nation and the financial implications of poor health among the population, along with continuing pressure on the National Health Service to increase efficiency, is likely to lead to greater focus on HRE in physical education. Thus, the differing pressures of sport and health need to be considered in developing a physically educated population. (Chapters 8 and 11 provide further discussion about these influences.)

Safety considerations have always been of paramount importance for physical education teachers. However, litigation appears likely to increase in the twenty-first century and the impact of any increase will require physical education teachers to balance carefully requirements for safety with the need for pupils to be able to have a full range of experiences which will enable them to become physically educated. The breadth and depth of the physical education programme could be adversely affected if the threat of litigation results in physical education teachers offering a limited range of activities considered least likely to result in any injury.

As society changes in the future, priorities for physical education are likely to change. What should be the priorities of physical education in the twenty-first century?

The effect of changing priorities on the physical education curriculum

Despite considerable change in society in recent years and changes in priorities for physical education, the physical education curriculum has remained much the same over many years. It remains dominated by major team games such as cricket, football, netball, hockey and rugby. Other activities such as athletics, dance, gymnastics, rounders, swimming and tennis are included in the curricula at certain times or in certain schools (evidence of this dominance is given in Chapter 7).

Teachers need to question why the physical education curriculum has not changed much. Why is it dominated by competitive team games? Is it because of tradition, because games have long been dominant in the physical education curriculum? Is it due to the value which many physical education teachers place on competitive sports and physical activities? Is it because physical education teachers tend to teach those activities in which they have knowledge and/or expertise? Is it because of political influences, e.g. to produce the next generation of international athletes? What other factors are influential?

Activities should not be included in the curriculum because they have traditionally been included. Activities should be selected for inclusion in the curriculum to serve a particular purpose, that is, to enable the aims of the physical education curriculum to be met. Physical education teachers therefore need to question whether a curriculum dominated by team games is appropriate for physical education in the twenty-first century. Does a curriculum which is dominated by competitive games meet the needs of pupils in the twenty-first century? Does the curriculum take account of the wider range of opportunities for participation in physical activities by young people? Is there a conflict or compatibility between the activities offered in school and those popular in the community? Are the fairly traditional activities included in the curriculum in many schools the most appropriate to enable priorities identified for physical education for the twenty-first century to be met? How can the needs of youngsters in the twenty-first century best be catered for within the physical education curriculum? How should the priorities for physical education in the twenty-first century be translated into the physical education curriculum? What should the curriculum look like? What factors need to be taken into account in determining the physical education curriculum in the twenty-first century?

The influence of physical education teachers on changing priorities for, and curriculum of, physical education in the twenty-first century

While it is likely that change will be needed to the physical education curriculum to ensure that the subject continues to meet the needs of youngsters in the twenty-first century, change should not be made for its own sake, to follow the latest trends or to respond to the latest pressures from various interest groups. Talbot considered the impact of various interest groups on physical education, concluding that 'one common feature between all of these interest groups had been their apparent purpose – to appropriate both the ideology and content of what children should learn, as physical education, in school curriculum time' (Talbot 1998: 104). She also suggested that 'seeing these lobbies essentially as interest groups also raises awareness of the influence of key drivers, leaders, stakeholders and gatekeepers, each with their own agendas and reasons for seeking to influence the theory and/or practice of physical education' (ibid.: 105).

Physical education teachers must not sway with the wind. It is dangerous to be reactive; to continually respond to different trends or interest groups. Curriculum change is difficult, particularly when many people have a vested interest in the curriculum. Physical education teachers can have an important influence on change and changing priorities for physical education in the twenty-first century only if they are clear about what they are trying to achieve, i.e. the aims of and priorities for physical education. They need to recognise the values on which their priorities are based. Physical education teachers then need to plan change in order to meet the identified priorities for physical education.

In order to plan change physical education teachers need to consider the external environment. Therefore, they must remain abreast of current and anticipated external changes, including changes in society which impact on education in general and physical education in particular, and more specifically in the context in which they are working, as well as of developing government educational policy which will help to shape policy and practice within the school and department. They should reflect on changes, trends and pressures and their potential impact on physical education in general and on practice in schools.

Physical education teachers should then try to influence the external factors which impact on what is prioritised at a specific time for physical education. Otherwise, priorities for physical education will be determined by others. For example, priorities to produce future champions to achieve more medals in international competitions may take precedence over the need to physically educate all pupils. Physical education teachers must articulate priorities and determine the direction of the subject in the twenty-first century rather than let others determine priorities and the curriculum for them.

Conclusion

In this chapter consideration has been given to re-reflecting on what physical education is and what lies at its core. It touched on the influence of personal values shaping the priorities of individual teachers. Two examples of how priorities are translated into the curriculum were given. The chapter looked at how priorities for physical education change over time. It provided a brief historical background and identified some recent influence on physical education. It highlighted some likely influences on physical education in the twenty-first century, encouraging readers to reflect on priorities for, and curriculum content of, physical education in the twenty-first century. The discussion of priorities was placed within the context of the unique contribution that physical education makes to the curriculum. The unique contribution will remain to produce a physically educated population, even though priorities are likely to change.

It is important that physical education professionals articulate priorities for physical education to other teachers, the headteacher, governors and others. By being involved in identifying priorities physical education teachers can help to ensure that the subject makes as full a contribution as possible to the education of all pupils and that it remains relevant to the needs of pupils in the twenty-first century. Also, and perhaps most importantly, if physical educationists do not identify priorities, the physical education curriculum is likely to be based on the values and priorities of various interest groups which have an input into shaping the physical education curriculum.

Reflection on changes in society identified in this chapter and other changes which readers consider to be influential, as well as reflection on issues in Chapters 1 to 12 of this book and other issues which arise in day-to-day teaching and beyond, may result in identification of the need for change (beyond change to the teaching of any one activity as a result of ongoing lesson evaluation). In the next chapter consideration is given to making change. The chapter recognises that making change is not easy, but provides some structure to help teachers make complex changes, such as those requiring larger scale change, e.g. in the department and/or school more widely.

Questions for reflection

1   How can you articulate to parents, other teachers, the headteacher or governors what is unique about physical education, and hence the importance of its contribution to the education of all pupils, in order to justify more time for physical education in the school curriculum?
2   What do you identify as social, technological, economic and political changes most likely to impact on education in general and physical education in particular now in the early years of the twenty-first century, and what is their impact likely to be?
3   What are the most important priorities which you identify for physical education? Why? Are they appropriate for all pupils?
4   What should be the priorities for physical education in the twenty-first century?
5   How do these priorities influence your selection of curriculum content and teaching methods?
6   Are any changes needed in your curriculum and/or teaching methods to enable these priorities to be promoted? If so, what; if not, why?
7   How can you contribute to making sure that the voice of physical education is influential in debates about priorities for the subject in the twenty-first century?

Further reading

Almond, L. (ed.) (1997) *Physical Education in Schools*, London: Kogan Page, particularly Chapter 1, 'Generating a new vision for physical education', and Chapter 2 ,'The context of physical education'.

As this chapter is based on reflection on priorities for physical education, the implications for the physical education curriculum and teaching methods, and changes in priorities for physical education over time and in the twenty-first century, it is important that physical education teachers remain abreast of what is happening in society, in education and in physical education. To this end, it is therefore recommended that readers refer regularly to a variety of publications which will enable them to remain abreast of what is happening, for example:

* national newspapers
* the *Times Educational Supplement*
* the *British Journal of Teaching Physical Education* (formerly the *British Journal of Physical Education*) (a quarterly publication sent to all members of the Physical Education Association of the United Kingdom (PEAUK))

- The *Bulletin of Physical Education* (the journal of the British Association of Advisers and Lecturers in Physical Education (BAALPE))
- other professional and academic journals.

For further information about joining PEAUK, please contact:
The Physical Education Association of the United Kingdom
Ling House
Building 25
London Road
Reading, RG1 5AQ
Telephone: 0118 931 6240
Fax: 0118 931 6242
e-mail: enquiries@pea.uk.com
website: pea.uk.com

14 Making change in physical education

Susan Capel

Introduction

Making change is an everyday part of a teacher's job. Teachers have an established routine shown in Figure 14.1.

This cycle provides the basis for making change within a lesson, planning the next lesson and planning future units of work, in order to make continual improvement in, and enhance the effectiveness of, teaching and learning within the lesson, in future lessons in a unit of work and in future units of work. Evaluation of lessons and units of work is an important aspect of critical reflection, enabling teachers to continue to learn from and improve their work.

Making change to teaching and learning as a result of evaluation is important in providing the foundations for making more complex or larger scale change; in planning and managing more complex or larger scale change, teachers already have a basis of knowledge and skills from which to work.

Previous chapters have considered various issues in physical education and encouraged readers to reflect on and to identify their own stance in relation to each issue. In addition, reflection is needed on government policy e.g. the National Curriculum for Physical Education (NCPE), a whole curriculum initiative; and other initiatives/ideas/innovations (hereafter called initiatives), often relating to one part of the curriculum, which are identified or introduced by practitioners and researchers in physical education and sport, for example the

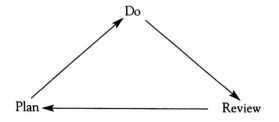

Figure 14.1 Making change

introduction of teaching games for understanding (TGFU), health related exercise (HRE) or the Youth Sports Trust's TOPs programme. Reflection on issues, policies and initiatives may result in identification of a need to change practice.

Change may be required in teachers' own practice in lessons (e.g. changing content or teaching strategy to better enable objectives to be met). It may also require a change in practice by others in the department (e.g. to introduce mixed-sex teaching in physical education), or it may require liaison and co-ordination with, and change by, others in the school (e.g. to introduce a coherent approach to teaching health related aspects of the curriculum). Having identified the need for change from whatever source, actually making that change needs to be considered carefully. Making change may not be easy.

Change which requires involvement by the whole physical education department and/or the school is harder to make than changes to teaching and learning in lessons that do not impact on other people. There could be several reasons why more complex and larger scale change is harder, including different views of change by teachers, for example:

- Teachers have different perspectives on an issue, policy or initiative as a result of, for example, their values, attitudes and beliefs, their personality, individual traits, background, previous experiences, stage of career and current role.
- Some teachers are reluctant to accept the need for change.
- Some teachers see the need to change but cannot see a clear solution therefore, are reluctant to initiate change.
- Some teachers do not share the initiators' enthusiasm for a change.
- Some teachers see change generally or a specific change as a threat.
- Further, over the last decade or so, teachers have been required to make many changes as a result of, for example, the introduction of the NCPE and various government policies/documents, e.g. *Sport: Raising the Game* (Department of National Heritage (DNH) 1995). Some teachers therefore want a period of stability without any further change.

Change that requires other departments or the whole school to participate can be more difficult than change within the department; it involves more people, is more time-consuming and has the potential to be more complex. Thus, attempting to make change within the department and/or school needs to be handled very carefully if it has any chance of being implemented.

Readers should refer to other sources for help with making relatively simple change, such as changes in lessons as a result of evaluation. This chapter is designed to encourage reflection on how to make more complex change in physical education, change involving other people in the department, other departments or the whole school and/or people/agencies outside school (referred to only as 'change' in this chapter).

In this chapter 'real' change is defined as that which fundamentally changes the values, attitudes and beliefs of the teacher, therefore resulting in deep, structural and lasting change rather than change of a more superficial nature.

The chapter begins by considering whether government policies or initiatives introduced in physical education have any deep, structural, lasting impact on pupils' learning experiences in physical education. Some reasons why such policies and initiatives do or do not have an impact are considered. The chapter continues by considering how to make real change, before identifying two different approaches to making change. The model by Fullan (1991) for making change is then explained. An example from physical education is used to illustrate the approach in practice. The example is developed in shaded sections at specific points in the explanation of Fullan's model. The chapter concludes by emphasising that school development planning can be used to encourage agreement to and implementation of a change.

The impact of change

The general perception is that change made to respond to policies and initiatives results in 'transformations in the ways that people think and feel about the world' (Sparkes 1991a: 3), and therefore makes a difference to teaching and learning in physical education. Otherwise, why would change be made?

However, does the implementation of policies and initiatives result in real change? It has been argued that policies and initiatives do not always result in any real change; change may be superficial rather than deep (real). Evans argued that 'stratification, social division, regulation of educational opportunity stand largely unscathed, despite the hustle and bustle of curricular activity which suggests that substantial educational innovation is afoot' (Evans 1985: 147). Likewise, Kirk argued that 'it is possible to present an innovation that embodies some new idea without this ever bringing about any genuine change in what people think or do' (Kirk 1988: 82). Sparkes suggested that 'it is possible for teachers to adopt a curriculum package and experiment with a range of teaching styles without changing the fundamental ideologies that inform their practices' (Sparkes 1989: 60).

For example, as the health related fitness (HRF) movement (now generally called HRE) became more important in the 1980s Sparkes argued that 'whilst many aspects of HRF are innovatory, the HRF movement as a whole is characterised by "innovation without change"' (ibid.: 60). He continued by identifying three levels of change. These are shown in Figure 14.2.

For more complex changes in physical education, such as the promotion of gender equality discussed in Chapter 2, the aim, therefore, is change at level 3: real change in which teachers' values, attitudes and beliefs change fundamentally and change is deep, structural and lasting.

While developments since the late 1980s may have resulted in change in practice as a result of focus on HRE, real change may not be made consistently as a result of policies and initiatives. For example, research by Evans and Penney

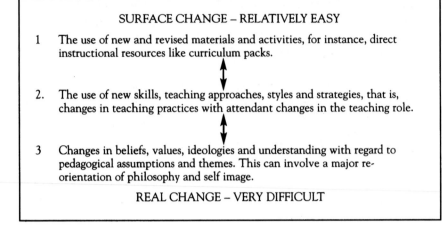

SURFACE CHANGE – RELATIVELY EASY

1   The use of new and revised materials and activities, for instance, direct instructional resources like curriculum packs.

2.   The use of new skills, teaching approaches, styles and strategies, that is, changes in teaching practices with attendant changes in the teaching role.

3   Changes in beliefs, values, ideologies and understanding with regard to pedagogical assumptions and themes. This can involve a major re-orientation of philosophy and self image.

REAL CHANGE – VERY DIFFICULT

Figure 14.2 Levels of change
Source: Sparkes 1989: 60

(see, for example, Evans and Penney 1995, Penney 1998, Penney and Evans 1997) has suggested that the introduction of the NCPE has failed to initiate widespread or comprehensive critical review of school physical education curricula. Rather than innovation and development of practice, they have identified a tendency for consolidation and assimilation. The requirements of the NCPE have been accommodated largely within existing practice. Thus there has been little or no change of practice.

Making real change

There are many reasons why making real change, or successfully implementing complex change, is difficult. For example, teachers may pay lip service to change, especially change imposed from outside in which they feel that they do not have a stake. Often in the past, rational, technical approaches have been adopted, for example, in introducing large scale initiatives. The assumption has been that the initiative is a good one, therefore is going to produce change or a positive result. For example, House described the introduction of large scale curriculum initiatives of the 1960s as 'deliberate systematic attempts to change the schools through introducing new ideas and techniques' (House 1979: 1). However, as a result of emerging evidence of the failure in implementing such initiatives, Fullan (1991) suggested that the introduction of many large scale curriculum initiatives has not succeeded in making any real change.

Perhaps most significantly, making real change requires teachers to consider their values, attitudes and beliefs; little real change will occur if teachers' values, attitudes and beliefs do not change. Sparkes argued that this was the case with HRF as the HRF movement has tended to challenge teachers in terms of their curriculum content and teaching styles . . . but failed to probe deeper to the ideological roots of the curriculum process and the manner in which this prevents children gaining a more coherent understanding of health in our society.

(Sparkes 1989: 61)

At best, change remains superficial, not improving the quality of pupils' learning experiences. One example of such change may be applied to the introduction of mixed-sex teaching, but still adopting a meritocratic approach to teaching (in which qualifications and, hence, recognition and rewards are achieved on merit). Theoretically, in mixed-sex teaching contexts, all pupils have equal opportunity to realise their talents, with those who achieve the best (i.e. are most physically competent) receiving the highest qualifications (i.e. highest performance) and hence the highest recognition and rewards. However, all pupils may not have equal opportunity to realise their talents and receive recognition and rewards, e.g. girls may have less opportunity than boys to participate in ball games outside school, therefore may have less competence. Consequently, they are less able to participate on equal terms with boys in a games lesson. The reverse may be true of boys in gymnastics or dance. Equality of opportunity is

impossible because even if the starting line is uniform (if all pupils have access to the same physical education curriculum) the arrival of the competitors in various states of fitness (social attributes, physical abilities, competence etc. . .) points to a prior race which has already been run in quite unequal circumstances.

(Daunt, cited in Fielding 1987: 54–5; in Evans 1988: 185)

See Chapter 2 of this book for further discussion of this example.

Adopting meritocratic principles may be unquestioned by many physical education teachers, especially if they have entered the physical education profession partly as a result of their own successful sporting experiences. Therefore, in order to make any real change in the quality of pupils' learning experiences by introducing mixed-sex teaching a change in values, attitudes and beliefs is needed. Such change is discussed further by Evans (1988), Fielding (1987) and Laws (1990) and identified in practice in terms of change in one school by Shearsmith (1993). Shearsmith talked of the perceived failure of the adoption of mixed-sex teaching and TGFU in one school within a meritocratic approach to teaching because

children are expected to strive for its limited rewards, but in an unequal contest, the qualification of good performance needed to obtain the rewards being won, not solely on merit, but being greatly influenced by the children's previous experiences, which are, in turn, partly determined by such factors as gender, race and social class.

(Shearsmith 1993: 38)

He continued by describing the resulting attempt by the school to base the physical education curriculum on what they identified should be the guiding principle of what children have in common and is equally available to all pupils: pupils' desire for their learning experiences in physical education to be enjoyable and satisfying. Such a change required a change in the values, attitudes and beliefs of physical education teachers about the subject and, in particular, about games. Existing aims and content were appropriate, but review of curriculum organisation, particularly the dominance of competitive games in which less able performers may suffer greatest discrimination, and a review of pedagogy were required. (See Chapter 7 for further discussion about the dominance of games in the physical education curriculum.)

Various researchers (e.g. Deci and Ryan 1991, Duda *et al.* 1991, Papaioannou 1995, Vallerand and Losier 1994) have emphasised the importance of adopting a mastery orientation and intrinsic reasons for participation in physical activity in promoting, among other things, equality. Papaioannou (1998) found that mastery orientation was a critical indicator of equal treatment towards boys and girls, i.e. that gender equality in physical education was more likely to be evident when emphasis was placed on the development of all pupils' abilities. In classes which emphasised mastery teachers were more likely to be perceived by pupils to focus on the learning of both boys and girls, encourage both boys and girls and motivate both boys and girls. On the other hand teachers who emphasised a performance-orientated climate in physical education lessons were more likely to be associated by pupils with negative treatment of boys and girls (e.g. were more likely to control pupils), which did not increase pupils' motivation. Further, an emphasis on performance-orientated climate may have a negative impact on the motivation of girls to continue their participation in physical activity when they see themselves outperformed by boys in many sports.

Teachers need to bear in mind that the values, attitudes and beliefs they bring with them influence the priority that they give to certain aims of physical education as well as how they view issues, policies or initiatives. It is necessary for teachers to be clear about, able to articulate and justify their aims, their priorities and their stance on specific issues, policies and initiatives. A well argued and justified position is essential if change is to be effective, but this is not enough in itself to persuade other people that change is required, and to get them to agree to and implement change. It is also important that a structured approach to change is adopted.

A structured approach to change

Fullan identified the need to consider 'the nature and extent of actual change, as well as the factors and processes that influence how and what changes are achieved' (Fullan 1992: 21) if any real change is to occur. Thus, in making real change more than the initiative itself needs to be looked at: the context of a specific setting, e.g. the department and/or school, also needs to be considered if any real change is to be achieved. From this perspective, implementation of the initiative is seen as important. Fullan indicated that 'the implementation perspective captures both the content and process of contending new ideas, programmes, activities . . . new to the people involved . . . (and) concerns itself with whether any change has actually occurred in practice' (ibid.: 21). Thus, successful change involves consideration of many factors and is therefore very complex. A structured approach is needed in order to succeed.

One structured approach or model for making change is known as the Systems Intervention Strategy (SIS) (Open University 1986). SIS contains three overlapping phases, as shown in Figure 14.3. The three overlapping phases of SIS are summarised as:

Diagnosis:
• describe the issue
• gather various points of view about the issue
• identify objectives for the change and constraints to making change
• determine ways of measuring if the objectives have been achieved.

Design of a strategy for making the change:
• generate a wide range of options for making the change
• select the most promising options and describe these in detail
• determine for each option: who is involved, what is involved and how it will work.

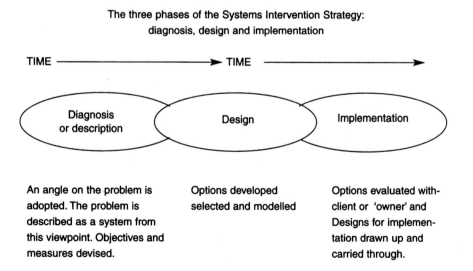

The three phases of the Systems Intervention Strategy:
diagnosis, design and implementation

TIME ⟶ TIME ⟶

| Diagnosis or description | Design | Implementation |

| An angle on the problem is adopted. The problem is described as a system from this viewpoint. Objectives and measures devised. | Options developed selected and modelled | Options evaluated with-client or 'owner' and Designs for implementation drawn up and carried through. |

Figure 14.3 The Systems Intervention Strategy
Source: adapted from Open University 1986

Implementation of the change:
- select criteria against which to measure the options, then test the performance of each of the options against the criteria
- select the preferred option and plan how the change process will be put into place
- carry through the planned changes, bringing together the necessary people and resources, managing the process and monitoring progress.

The SIS approach is not specific to education, but can be applied to education and physical education.

A second structured approach specific to education was developed by Fullan (1991). This identifies factors which characterise how successful implementation occurs. It must be recognised that the factors identified by Fullan to characterise how successful implementation occurs are only one set of factors. Other factors may be important in making effective change.

Fullan's (1991) approach is considered in more detail below with the help of a specific example from physical education in the shaded sections. The example focuses on how to bring about a change which results in greater extra-curricular involvement of pupils in physical activity in schools. The same example is developed in relation to each of the critical factors identified by Fullan (shown in Figure 14.4). Issues arising from the key themes in improvement identified by Fullan (see Figure 14.5) are integrated into the example as it develops. The example is explored in a way which illustrates how to bring about change in

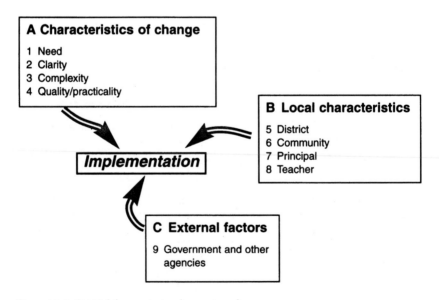

Figure 14.4 Critical factors in implementing change
Source: adapted from Fullan 1991: 68

practice as a result of change in values, attitudes and beliefs of teachers, resulting in real change that is deep, structural and lasting.

Each of these factors are summarised next.

Characteristics of change (see Figure 14.4)

1   In order for real change to be achieved in, for example, departmental practice, teachers should see the *need* for a change; if teachers do not see the need for a change, then change resulting in real change is less likely to be implemented. Change cannot be forced on people; forced change will not result in any change in values, attitudes and beliefs, therefore is unlikely to be successful. To bring about change successfully, time must be spent discussing the need for change, reaching a consensus on the need to change and agreeing to make a change. This process is time-consuming.

2   For a change to be successful there needs to be *clarity* about the objectives of the change and the means of implementation. Lack of clarity (e.g. unclear objectives or unspecified means of implementation) results in teachers not being clear about the meaning of change in practice, which results in many different interpretations of what the change means and, hence, in variety of practice. Unclear objectives and unspecified means of implementation can result in great anxiety. Thus, time is needed to agree the objectives of the changes and how these are going to be implemented.

3   The *complexity* of the change should be considered, i.e. the difficulty and extent of change required by the people responsible for implementation. The amount of change required in values, attitudes and beliefs, as well as in, for example, teaching strategies and use of materials, depends on the extent of the change itself but also on the starting point of each person involved. Fullan suggested that

> simple changes may be easier to carry out but they may not make much of a difference. Complex changes promise to accomplish more . . . but they also demand more effort, and failure takes a greater toll. The answer seems to be to break complex changes into components and implement them in a divisible and/or incremental manner.
>
> (Fullan 1991: 71–2)

The more complex the change, the more time is likely to be needed.

4   Attention should also be directed toward the *quality and practicality* of the change.

> Inadequate quality and even the simple unavailability of materials and other resources can result when adoption decisions are made on grounds of political necessity, or even on grounds of perceived need without time for development. Put differently, when adoption is more important than implementation, decisions are frequently made without

the follow-up or preparation time necessary to generate adequate materials.

(Fullan 1991: 72)

Studies (e.g. Huberman and Miles 1984) have shown that the shorter the time from adoption to implementation of a change, the more problems result. In addition, change must be practical; it must address an identified need, fit into the departmental and school context, and include means of making it work. The steps in the change process need to be identified and agreed. Once a change has been agreed, enough time must be allowed for discussion, agreement of stages of change, development of units of work and lessons and resources to support the implementation.

Example from physical education: characteristics of change

A physical education teacher becomes concerned about the low number of pupils participating in extra-curricular activities. An investigation as to reasons why identifies the major reason to be pupils' lack of interest in physical education and in extra-curricular activities because of the dominance of invasion games. Pupils do not choose to participate in games in extra-curricular time because they want to participate in activities which they enjoy and in which they can participate when their time allows (because other pupils are not relying on them to participate each week), e.g. aerobics.

The teacher raises the issue at a physical education department meeting. Although there is agreement about the low number of pupils participating in extra-curricular activities, there is considerable debate about the role of extra-curricular activities, reflecting, in part, different priorities identified by different members of staff for extra-curricular activities. At the initial department meeting, staff agree to continue discussion. The teacher who raised the issue focused discussion at further meetings on the responsibility of the department to meet the needs of all pupils, not just those who are members of school teams (based on his values and priorities for physical education). He looked again at the department aims for physical education which emphasise a commitment to all pupils. This is a complex change, not only because of the amount of change in curricular and extra-curricular activities, but because of the extent of change needed in values, attitudes and beliefs of some members of staff.

After several meetings, there is agreement among the staff that change is needed in extra-curricular provision. School teams are an important aspect of provision, but greater breadth and balance in the range of extra-curricular activities offered is needed to meet the needs of all pupils. They agree clear objectives and a strategy for change. School teams will be continued in extra-curricular activities from Years 7 to 11; greater links will be made with sports clubs in the community to cater for the needs of elite pupils; and some activities will be offered that cater for a diverse range of needs, identified by the pupils themselves. In order to achieve this, it is recognised that some change is needed to the physical education curriculum. In Years 7 to 9 greater breadth is needed to enable pupils to gain a variety of experiences to better inform choices of participation later. In Years 10 and 11 pupils will be given a limited choice of activities in the curriculum, meeting the requirements of the NCPE, but also trying to meet the needs of individual pupils.

The staff recognise the complexity of the proposed change. They therefore agree that time is needed for discussion and agreement about what is needed. (See *evolutionary planning* in Figure 14.5.) Staff therefore agree that the change should not be implemented until the next but one school year. They identify some proposals for alternative courses of action and implementation and allocate responsibilities for following these up; responsibilities are divided into: the range of extra-curricular provision for Years 7 to 11; the curriculum for Years 7 to 9; the curriculum for Years 10 and 11. Each person works on his or her own area of responsibility. Timescales are set and department meetings are scheduled for each person to report back on work undertaken and developments to date, to seek views from the other members of the department and for discussion. The meetings enable problems, concerns and disagreements to be aired as they arise, with the aim of securing agreement and, hence commitment, to the final proposed change. Discussion identifies practical concerns about implementation of the change, for example, concerns about subject knowledge and confidence to teach different activities, as well as use of a range of teaching strategies, which will affect the effectiveness of the eventual implementation of the change. Therefore, the need for *staff development* (see Figure 14.5) is identified and agreement secured to undertake such development. (This approach allows *vision building* to occur (see Figure 14.5), i.e. time given to discussion of the need for change and seeking clarity enables a vision to be built, shared and to permeate the department. This forms the basis from which to seek support from other people in making the change.)

Local characteristics (see Figure 14.4)

1   Consideration needs to be given to change required outside one teacher's classroom or one school, e.g. across a series of schools in a LEA. A degree of centralisation is necessary in order to make comprehensive change across a series of schools. Practical support is needed to help implement the change, to follow through on decisions and to provide resources to support the change.

Failure is most likely to occur when there is lack of support and follow through to implement an initiative. If implementation is ineffective, teachers are likely to become cynical about change and more apathetic about the next initiative to be introduced. On the other hand, successful implementation can encourage further success. Fullan (1991) suggested that LEAs (and others) can develop a capacity or incapacity for change.

2   *Communities*, including school governors, have a role to play in making change. The role they play is variable, ranging from apathy to active involvement, with the latter varying from co-operative to conflict modes, depending on the conditions. However, community support, including the support of governors, is generally correlated positively with making real change, whereas lack of support or apathy can negate attempts at change of this kind.

3   *The headteacher* has a strong influence on the effectiveness of change. If a headteacher does not play an active role in change, teacher initiated change is less likely to result in real change. On the other hand, if a headteacher actively supports a change, resources are more likely to be made available, increasing the likelihood of success.

4   Some *teachers* are more predisposed to 'considering and acting on improvements' (Fullan 1991: 77) than others (see the different views of change by teachers in the introduction). These views are often shaped by personal issues (identified in the introduction). However, response to change can also be shaped by the culture or climate of the school. One critical factor is relationships with other teachers. Doing something differently or something new, developing new values, attitudes, beliefs, behaviours etc. is more likely if teachers interact with each other, exchange ideas and support each other than if they are acting in isolation. Thus, Fullan suggested that 'the quality of working relationships among teachers is strongly related to implementation' (ibid.: 77).

The amount of involvement and support required depends on the complexity of the change being made.

Example from physical education: local characteristics

The department recognises the need to work with others in changing the breadth and balance of activities in curricular and extra-curricular time. Therefore, suitable people/agencies within and external to the school from whom support is needed are identified (e.g. parents, other teachers, headteacher, governing body, LEA adviser, sports development officer, local sports development committee, representatives of clubs, leisure centre managers).

As the strategy for implementation of the change is formulated, the department discusses the proposed change in relation to the aims of physical education in the school, the requirements of the NCPE, the content of the curriculum and the range of extra-curricular activities to be offered to meet the needs of all pupils. At this stage it is felt that the LEA adviser could make a useful contribution to the discussion in providing a broader perspective on the change; therefore an early meeting is arranged with him or her. Later, the department members recognise their limitations in subject knowledge and their lack of confidence in teaching certain activities if the changes are to be implemented effectively. They therefore seek staff development on subject knowledge, on teaching new activities, adopting different teaching strategies, and resources to support the new activities/strategies. They also identify the need for staff development in managing other members of staff who are involved in delivering extra-curricular activities. Further, the department identifies the need to build up resources in the department to refer to during implementation of the changes. (See also *staff development and resource assistance* in Figure 14.5.)

Active involvement of the community is needed in order to ensure provision of appropriate opportunities to meet the needs of all pupils. A member of staff is given responsibility for identifying and contacting community organisations who can support the change, e.g. clubs to provide opportunities for pupils, and a number of people are identified to initiate/develop contact with these people/agencies.

The department also identifies the need for support from within the school: from governors, the headteacher and other teachers. The headteacher is invited to attend a department meeting in the early stages of the identification of the need to change to seek her support and identify what can be done within the school to encourage support from the governors, other teachers and parents, especially in helping to overcome concerns about mediocrity and the loss of successful school teams. As a result the head of department is invited to a governors' meeting and to address a regular staff meeting to discuss the identified need for change and to seek support. Support is generated from both meetings, along with practical suggestions for influencing the change, e.g. some extra-curricular activities that are open to both staff and pupils, identification of some further contacts in the community to support the change. Further, the meetings serve to reinforce the decisions of the department, supporting those teachers in the department who are more reluctant to change due to the effort involved. Parents are important to the success of the change and it is agreed that the head of department will seek the support of the headteacher to talk to parents at the annual parent-teacher meeting. See also *initiative taking and empowerment* in Figure 14.5.

The third set of factors which Fullan (1991) identified as important in making real change are external factors: that is, those that locate the school in the broader context of society in the United Kingdom, e.g. the Department for Education and Employment (DfEE) and government agencies such as the Office for Standards in Education (OFSTED).

External factors (see Figure 14.4)

Many of the recent changes in education in England and Wales in general, including physical education, have been initiated centrally by government. Perhaps the two most influential have been the introduction of the Education Reform Act (ERA 1988) and with it the NCPE, and the document *Sport: Raising the Game* (DNH 1995), although many other policies/initiatives could also be identified. These policies/initiatives put pressure on LEAs, schools, departments and individual teachers to make changes. For example, the emphasis on league tables by government has resulted in pressure to produce good examination results; emphasis on the market economy in schools has resulted in some schools placing an emphasis on winning sports teams in order to market the school.

Whether or not change as a result of government policy, including curriculum reform, is implemented effectively depends on a number of factors, including how change is introduced and implementation followed through and what support there is for teachers and schools for both its initial and ongoing implementation. Fullan suggested that 'outside assistance or stimulation can influence implementation greatly, provided that it is integrated with the factors at the local level' (Fullan 1991: 180). Government education policy is not likely to be successfully implemented without discussion, understanding by teachers of the objectives and means of achieving the objectives. Time is needed for discussion/agreement of objectives.

Despite many recent changes in education in England and Wales being initiated by central government, support for education is at a local level, e.g. from LEAs. One reason suggested by Penney and Evans (1997) for the implementation of the revision of the NCPE in 1995 not resulting in innovation and development in practice was that the revision was introduced at a time when support, guidance and opportunities for continuing professional development for teachers were being reduced. Further, inspections by OFSTED report on progress by schools in implementing the NCPE but such inspections and reports do not result in ongoing support for change, except in very exceptional circumstances. Thus, it is important that there is support for teachers in implementing change.

Example from physical education: external factors

Although the change to a broader and more balanced range of activities in curricular and extra-curricular time is not directly the result of government policy, the political agenda and initiatives are recognised by the department as being very important and are therefore integral to discussions in department meetings. Early discussions include the importance of providing a range of extra-curricular opportunities to meet the needs of all pupils, but also recognising the role successful school teams have played in marketing the school. These discussions result in the formulation of justifications for the change in order to convince the headteacher of the benefits of a broader curriculum for all pupils.

Key themes in improvement

Fullan (1991) also identified six key themes in the improvement process. Each theme is linked to and by the other themes, i.e. they do not act in isolation. These are identified in Figure 14.5, followed by a brief summary of each of the six themes. (Examples of the themes are included, where appropriate, in the shaded 'examples from physical education' given earlier.)

Vision building

Vision building is related to a shared vision (or view) of, first, what the school should look like; and second, of the change process or the strategy to achieve the shared vision of the school. It is not an easy concept to understand, largely because it is a constant process of forming, implementing, shaping and reshaping within an organisation.

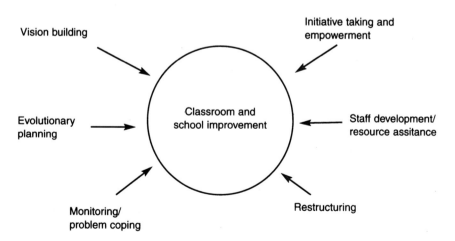

Figure 14.5 Key themes in improvement
Source: adapted from Fullan 1991: 82

Initiative taking and empowerment

Successful change occurs when people who are acting and interacting in purposeful directions are supported. For example, an initiative is more likely to be successful if supported by the headteacher and/or head of department than without such support. A collaborative work culture is also important in successful change. It provides support, allows teachers to share effective/ successful practice and reduces their isolation.

Evolutionary planning

It has been suggested that successful multi-level change uses an evolutionary planning approach which blends top-down initiative and bottom-up participation. Plans for change are not set in stone at the beginning of the implementation but are flexible to cope with changes. Once change has been implemented and is moving in the desired direction, plans are adapted as they proceed 'to improve the fit between the change and the conditions in the school to take advantage of unexpected development and opportunities' (Fullan 1991: 83).

Staff development and resource assistance

Most change involves 'learning new ways of thinking and doing, new skills, knowledge, attitudes, etc.' (Fullan 1991: 84). Thus, for change to be successful, it should be supported by targeted staff development. Training prior to, and ongoing support during, implementation are needed. A one-off training day/workshop prior to implementation is not likely to be successful without ongoing support during implementation. Skill specific training is often mechanical. It does not allow ideas to be assimilated or values, attitudes and beliefs to be changed. It is only when starting to implement a change that problems, concerns and doubts arise. Teachers need support to address these successfully; this can only occur when there is support as problems arise during implementation. Fullan indicated that 'sustained interaction and staff development are crucial. . . . The more complex the change, the more interaction is required during implementation' (ibid.: 86).

Monitoring/problem coping

It is important that there are 'effective ways of getting information on how well or poorly change is going in the classroom and school' (Fullan 1991: 87). Monitoring the process of change as well as measuring the outcome of change is important. Monitoring is more than evaluation in the narrow sense; it includes information systems, resources and acting on results to cope with and solve problems. Information on innovative practice gives access to good ideas and exposes new ideas to scrutiny. Constant attention should be paid in the monitoring process to all aspects of pupils' development, including academic, personal and social. Monitoring should be linked to a process of improvement, i.e. a means to make further changes.

Restructuring

The working environment may need restructuring to provide conditions that support a successful change e.g. 'time for individual and team planning, joint teaching arrangements, staff development policies, new roles such as mentors and coaches' (Fullan 1991: 88).

Continuation of a change

In addition to implementation of a change it is important to consider continuation of a change. Whether or not a change continues depends on whether or not it becomes embedded in the structure and incorporated into policy or guidelines (e.g. accepted as departmental practice). Fullan (1991) reported that reasons why changes are not continued are generally the same as reasons influencing implementation, but with a more sharply focused role, e.g. lack of interest and support from the headteacher, lack of active leadership, lack of ongoing support and staff development for continuing and new teachers. Staff turnover was identified as one of the most important factors threatening the continuation of specific change in a department or school. Support for new members of staff who arrive when the change has been implemented is therefore a key factor in the continuation of a change.

> **Example from physical education: continuation of change**
>
> Ongoing support is planned for each member of the department during implementation to retain staff commitment to the change and enable issues to be addressed. One means of support is the introduction of a system of mentoring; another is peer review of teaching when time is available during Year 10 and 11 examination periods.
>
> In order to share successful aspects of implementation and good practice, to address problems, to consider aspects of change needing further development, as well as discussing and developing other opportunities that arise as a result of the change and identifying further staff development needs, department meetings continue to discuss the change.
>
> Ongoing evaluation is undertaken to determine the effectiveness of the change. The department evaluates pupils' attitudes to physical education and to physical activity and monitors participation rates in extra-curricular activities. It also identifies the need to try to set up a system of monitoring participation of pupils outside and post-school. Updates of evidence-based outcomes of the change are given to the headteacher, governors and other staff at relevant meetings. The factors which caused concern prior to implementation are specifically addressed and feedback is sought to aid future developments. Issues identified from

evaluation and monitoring are included in discussion at department meetings.

Further, in order to start embedding the change in department structures, the department agrees to incorporate its approach, and the rationale behind the approach, into the department handbook. In this way departmental staff will be able to remind themselves and other people of what they are trying to do and why they are doing it. This can form the basis for the induction of new staff into the department as well as any members of staff from other departments or outside school who help with work in the physical education department or with extra-curricular activities.

Fullan (1991) stressed that the critical factors in implementing change (see Figure 14.4) and the six key themes in the improvement process (see Figure 14.5) do not act in isolation; rather they are interacting. The more factors/themes which are working in support of the implementation, the more likely it is that real change to practice occurs.

Although only one approach to implementing change, Fullan's (1991) approach does show the complexity of making real change. One way to encourage a change to be agreed and implemented is to establish it as an integral part of *school development planning* rather than being seen as something separate. A school development plan is:

> a plan of needs for development set in the context of the school's aims and values, its existing achievements and national and LEA policies and initiatives. Detailed objectives are set for one year; the objectives for later years are sketched in outline.

> The purpose of the development planning is to assist the school to introduce change successfully, so that the quality of teaching and standard of learning are improved. It does so by creating the conditions under which innovations, such as the National Curriculum, can be successfully introduced.

> (DES 1991: 2)

Figure 14.6 gives one example of how to write a school development plan.

Conclusion

Teachers who are reflecting critically on their practice and on issues within physical education are likely to identify the need for change. Teachers who are not reflecting on their practice and identifying the need for change at some level are likely to be 'stuck in a rut'. Such teachers are likely to accept policy or initia-

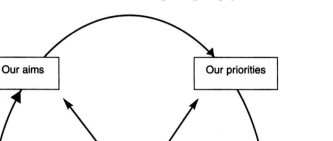

Figure 14.6 How to write a school development plan
Source: Rogers 1994: 13

tives, such as curriculum packages, without question, but are unlikely to make real change. Making complex change successfully may not be easy, as can be seen from the work of Fullan (1991) and others. The aim of this chapter has been to help readers to understand how to approach complex change in order that real change is made, by providing some guidance on initiating, implementing and continuing change. Perhaps most important, successful complex change requires time to discuss and agree with others involved (e.g. other teachers in the department) the need for change, what the change should be, its rationale, aims and objectives and how it should be implemented, i.e. diagnosis, design and implementation. Change which is imposed on others is less likely to be successful (see, for example, Sparkes (1986, 1991b) who looked at the central role of teachers in making successful change, describing different perspectives by members of a department on a change and an attempt by a head of department to impose change on the department).

Making real change is unlikely to be a smooth process. Making real change requires problems to be solved. Reflecting on problems is likely to result in solutions which reinforce the change being made.

To conclude, Fullan stated that 'every person is a change agent' (Fullan 1993: 39). Every teacher has a responsibility to reflect on practice and issues in education in general and in physical education in particular and to help create a department and school capable of real change which enhances pupils' learning experiences in physical education.

Questions for reflection

1 Considering one 'initiative' in physical education, e.g. TGFU, the introduction of the TOPs programmes, what real change has occurred as a result of this initiative? Justify your answer with evidence-based practice.
2 Identify one change which you would wish to make in the physical education department and/or school in which you are working. How would you put this into practice using Fullan's (1991) approach? Use the 'example from physical education' to assist you.
3 Identify one change which you would wish to make in the physical education department and/or school in which you are working. How would you put this into practice using the SIS approach, as outlined in this chapter?
4 How can you incorporate the change(s) identified in questions 2 and 3 above into the school development plan?

Further reading

Almond, L. (1986b) 'Asking teachers to research', in R. Thorpe, D. Bunker and L. Almond (eds), *Rethinking Games Teaching*, Loughborough, Leics.: Loughborough University: 35–44.

Fullan, M. (1991) *The New Meaning of Educational Change*, London: Cassell.

Open University (1986) *P679 Planning and Managing Change: Course Guide*, Milton Keynes: Open University.

Bibliography

Abelgadir, M. H. (1991) 'Community participation in Sudanese villages', *Journal of the Institute of Health Education*.

Alderson, P. (1999) (ed.) *Learning and Inclusion: The Cleves School Experience*, written by staff and pupils of the Cleves School, Newham, London, London: David Fulton.

Allison, S. and Thorpe, R. (1997) 'A comparison of the effectiveness of two approaches to teaching games within physical education. A skills versus a games for understanding approach', *British Journal of Physical Education* 86 (3): 9–13.

Almond, L. (1986a) 'Primary and secondary rules in games', in R. Thorpe, D. Bunker and L. Almond (eds), *Rethinking Games Teaching*, Loughborough, Leics.: Loughborough University: 73–4.

—— (1986b) 'Asking teachers to research', in R. Thorpe, D. Bunker and L. Almond (eds), *Rethinking Games Teaching*, Loughborough, Leics.: Loughborough University: 35–44.

—— (1989) 'Developing personal and social skills within physical education', in L. Almond (ed.), *The Place of Physical Education in Schools*, London: Kogan Page: 139–46.

—— (1996) 'A new vision for physical education', in N. Armstrong (ed.), *New Directions in Physical Education*, London: Cassell: 189–97.

—— (ed.) (1997) *Physical Education in Schools*, London: Kogan Page.

Almond, L. and Harris, J. (1997) 'Does Health Related Exercise deserve a hammering or help?' *British Journal of Physical Education* 28 (2): 25–27.

Aristotle (1946) *Politics*, trans. E. Barker, Oxford, Oxford University Press.

Armour, K. and Jones, R. (1998) *Physical Education Teachers' Lives and Careers: PE, Sport and Educational Status*, London: Falmer.

Armstrong, D. (1998) 'Changing faces, changing places: policy routes to inclusion', in P. Clough (ed.), *Managing Inclusive Education: From Policy to Experience*, London: Paul Chapman: 31–47.

Armstrong, N. (1990) 'Children's physical activity patterns', in N. Armstrong (ed.), *New Directions in Physical Education vol. 1*, Champaign, Ill.: Human Kinetics: 1–15.

Armstrong, N. and Simons-Morton, B. (1994) 'Physical activity and blood lipids in adolescents', *Paediatric Exercise Science* 6: 381–405.

Armstrong, N. and Welsman, J. (1997) *Young People and Physical Activity*, Oxford: Oxford University Press.

Arnold, P. (1968) *Education, Physical Education and Personality Development*, London: Heinemann Educational.

—— (1988) *Education, Movement and the Curriculum*, London: Falmer.

Arts Council (1993) *Education – Dance in Schools*, London: Arts Council.

Asquith, A. (1989) 'Teaching games for understanding', in A. Williams (ed.), *Issues in Physical Education for the Primary Years*, London: Falmer: 76–90.

Association of Swimming Therapy (1981) *Swimming for the Disabled*, Wakefield: EP Publishing.

Atkinson, D., Jackson, M. and Walmsley, J. (1997) *Forgotten Lives: Exploring the History of Learning Disability*, Kidderminster: BILD.

Bailey, L. and Almond, L. (1983) 'Creating change by creating games?', in L. Spackman (ed.), *Teaching Games for Understanding*, Cheltenham: College of St Paul and St Mary: 56–9.

Balshaw, M. (1999) *Help in the Classroom (2nd edn)*, London: David Fulton.

Banton, M. *Racial and Ethnic Competition*, Cambridge: Cambridge University Press.

Bar-Or, O. (1994) 'Childhood and adolescent physical activity and fitness and adult risk profiles', in C. Bouchard, R. Shephard, and T. Stephens (eds), *Physical Activity, Fitness and Health: International Proceedings and Consensus Statement*, Champaign, Ill.: Human Kinetics: 931–42.

Baric, L. (1992) 'Promoting health: new approaches and developments', *Journal of the Institute for Health Education* 30 (1): 6–16.

Barrow, R. and Millburn, G. (1990) *A Critical Dictionary of Educational Concepts (2nd edn)*, Brighton: Harvester Wheatsheaf.

Barton, L. (1993) 'Disability, empowerment and physical education', in J. Evans (ed.), *Equality, Education and Physical Education*, London: Falmer: 43–54.

Bayliss, T. (1989) 'PE and racism: making changes', *Multicultural Teaching* 7 (2): 19–22.

Beer, I. (1988) 'Fasten your seat belts', *Times Educational Supplement* (18 March): 23.

Bell, A. (1992) 'Liaison in physical education between primary and secondary schools: some examples of practice in county Durham', *Primary PE Focus: British Journal of Physical Education* (Winter): 14.

Benn, T. (1996a) 'Female, Muslim and training to be a primary school teacher – experiences of physical education in one college', *British Journal of Physical Education* 27 (1) (Spring): 8–12.

—— (1996b) 'Muslim women and physical education in initial teacher training', *Sport, Education and Society* 1 (1): 5–21.

—— (1998) 'Exploring the experiences of a group of British Muslim women in initial teacher training and their early teaching careers', unpublished Ph.D. thesis, Loughborough University.

Benyon, L. (1981) 'Curriculum continuity', *Education* 9 (1): 3–13.

Berlin, I. (1998) 'The pursuit of the ideal', in *The Proper Study of Mankind: An Anthology of Essays*, ed. H. Hardy and R. Hausheer, London: Pimlico: 1–16.

Best, D. (1976) 'Movement and the intellect', *Journal of Human Movement Studies* 2: 64–9.

Beveridge, S. (1996) *Spotlight on Special Educational Needs: Learning Difficulties*, Stafford: NASEN.

Biddle, S. and Biddle, G. (1989) 'Health related fitness for the primary school', in A. Williams (ed.), *Issues in Physical Education for the Primary Years*, London: Falmer: 54–75.

Bird, S. (1992) *Exercise Physiology for Health Professionals*, London: Chapman and Hall.

Blumenthal, J., Williams, R., and Wallace, A. (1980) 'Effects of exercise on Type A (coronary prone) behaviour pattern', *Psychosomatic Medicine* 42: 289–96.

Board of Education (1905) *Syllabus for Physical Training in Schools*, London: HMSO.

Boniface, M. (1990) 'Primary school PE and the implications for curriculum continuity across the school divide', *British Journal of Physical Education* 20 (2): 301–3.

Boreham, C. A., Twisk, J., Savage, M. J., Cran, G. W. and Strain, J. J. (1997) 'Physical activity, sports participation and risk factors in adolescents', *Medicine and Science in Sports and Exercise* 29: 788–93.

Brackenridge, C. (1979) 'Games: Classification and analysis', cited in L. Almond (1986a) 'Primary and secondary rules in games', in R. Thorpe, D. Bunker and L. Almond (eds) *Rethinking Games Teaching*, Loughborough, Leics.: Loughborough University: 73–4.

Brah, M. and Minas, R. (1985) 'Structural racism or cultural differences: schooling for Asian girls', in G. Weiner (ed.), *Just a Bunch of Girls*, Milton Keynes: Open University Press: 14–52.

Brinson, P. (1991) *Dance as Education: Towards a National Dance Culture*, London: Falmer.

Brisenden, S. (1986) 'Independent living and the medical model of disability', *Disability, Handicap and Society* 1 (2): 173–8.

British Association of Advisers and Lecturers in Physical Education (BAALPE) (1996) *Physical Education for Pupils with Special Educational Needs in Mainstream Education*, Dudley: Dudley LEA Publications.

British Council for Physical Education (BCPE) (1990) *The National Curriculum in Physical Education Report from the Interim Working Group to the BCPE*, July.

British Heart Foundation (1996) *Look After Your Heart and Help Fight Heart Disease with Artie Beat*, London: British Heart Foundation.

Broadfoot, P. (1986) 'Assessment policy and inequality: the United Kingdom experience', *British Journal of Sociology of Education* 7: 205–24.

Brown, A. (1987) *Active Games for Children with Movement Problems*, London: Harper and Row.

Brown, B. (1998) 'Constructive learning in physical education', in M. Littledyke and L. Huxford (eds), *Teaching the Primary Curriculum for Constructivist Learning*, London: David Fulton: 131–49.

Browne, J. (1992) 'Reasons for the selection or non-selection of physical education studies by Year 12 girls', *Journal of Teaching in Physical Education* 11: 402–10.

Bullivant, B. (1981) *The Pluralist Dilemma in Education*, London: Allen and Unwin.

Bunker, D. and Thorpe, R. (1982) 'A model for the teaching of games in secondary schools', *Bulletin of Physical Education* 18 (1): 5–8.

—— (1986a) 'The curriculum model', in R. Thorpe, D. Bunker and L. Almond (eds), *Rethinking Games Teaching*, Loughborough, Leics.: Loughborough University: 7–10.

—— (1986b) 'Is there a need to reflect on our games teaching?', in R. Thorpe, D. Bunker and L. Almond (eds), *Rethinking Games Teaching*, Loughborough, Leics.: Loughborough University: 25–34.

—— (1986c) 'From theory to practice', in R. Thorpe, D. Bunker and L. Almond (eds), *Rethinking Games Teaching*, Loughborough, Leics.: Loughborough University: 11–16.

Burleigh, M. (1994) *Death and Deliverance: Euthanasia in Germany 1900–1945*, Cambridge: Cambridge University Press.

Cale, L. (1996) 'Health related exercise in schools – PE has much to be proud of!' *British Journal of Physical Education* 27 (4): 8–13.

Cale, L. (1997) 'An assessment of the physical activity levels of adolescent girls: implications for physical education', *European Journal of Physical Education* 1 (1): 46–55.

Calfas, K. J. and Taylor, C. (1994) 'Effects of physical activity on psychological variables in adolescents', *Pediatric Exercise Sciences* 6: 406–23.

Campbell, J. and Oliver, M. (1996) *Disability Politics: Understanding Our Past, Changing Our Future*, London: Routledge.

Canterbury Christ Church University College (CCCUC) (1998) *Primary School Experience Booklet*, Canterbury: CCCUC.

Capel, S., Kelly, L. and Whitehead, M. (1997) 'Developing and maintaining an effective learning environment', in S. Capel (ed.), *Learning to Teach Physical Education in the Secondary School: A Companion to School Experience*, London: Routledge: 97–114.

Capel, S. and Whitehead, M. (1997) 'Aims of PE', in S. Capel (ed.), *Learning to Teach Physical Education in the Secondary School: A Companion to School Experience*, London: Routledge: 18–26.

Carlson, T. B. (1995) 'We hate gym: student alienation from physical education', *Journal of Teaching in Physical Education* 14: 467–77.

Carney, C. and Armstrong, N. (1996)'The provision of physical education in primary initial teacher training courses in England and Wales'. *European Physical Education Review*, 2: 64–74.

Carrington, B. and Leaman, O. (1986) 'Equal opportunities and physical education', in J. Evans (ed.), *Physical Education, Sport and Schooling*, London: Falmer: 265–79.

Carrington, B. and Williams, T. (1988) 'Patriarchy and ethnicity: The link between school and physical education and community leisure activities', in J. Evans (ed.), *Teachers, Teaching and Control in Physical Education*, London: Falmer: 83–96.

Carroll, B. (1994) *Assessment in Physical Education*, London: Falmer.

Carroll, B. and Hollinshead, G. (1993) 'Equal opportunities: Race and gender in physical education: a case study', in J. Evans (ed.), *Equality, Education and Physical Education*, London: Falmer: 154–69.

Cashling, D. (1993) 'Cobblers and song-birds: the language and imagery of disability', *Disability, Handicap and Society* 8 (2): 199–206.

Cashmore, E. (1990), (1996, 2nd edn) *Making Sense of Sport*, London: Routledge.

Centre for Studies on Inclusive Education (CSIE) (2000) *Index for Inclusion: Developing Learning and Participation in Schools*, written and ed. T. Booth, M. Ainscow, K. Black-Hawkins, M. Vaughan and L. Shaw, Bristol: CSIE.

Chambers Concise Dictionary (1991), Edinburgh: Chambers.

Chappell, R. (1995) 'Racial stereotyping in schools', *Bulletin of Physical Education* 31 (1): 22–8.

Chaudharay, V. (1999) 'Playing the game could be optional', *Guardian* (12 May).

Child, D. (1997) *Psychology and the Teacher (6th edn)*, London: Cassell.

Clay, G. (1997) 'Standards in primary and secondary physical education: OFSTED 1995–96', *British Journal of Physical Education* 28 (2): 5–9.

Clayton, T. (1993) 'From domestic helper to 'assistant teacher': the changing role of the British classroom assistant', *European Journal of Special Needs Education* 1: 32–44.

Coakley, J. (1994) *Sport in Society: Issues and Controversies (5th edn)*, London: Mosby.

Coakley, J. and White, A. (1992) 'Making decisions: gender and sport participation among British adolescents', *Sociology of Sport Journal* 9: 20–35.

Coe, J. M. (1986) 'Games education', *British Journal of Physical Education* 17 (4): 202–4.

Cole, T. (1989) *Apart or A Part? Integration and the Growth of British Special Education*, Milton Keynes: Open University.

Colquhoun, D. (1990) 'Images of healthism in health-based physical education', in D. Kirk and R. Tinning (eds), *Physical Education, Curriculum and Culture: Critical Issues in the Contemporary Crisis*, London: Falmer: 225–51.

Connell (1989) 'The child in the teaching-learning process', in A. Williams (ed.), *Issues in Physical Education for the Primary Years*, London: Falmer: 104–20.

Cooper, A. (1995) 'Starting games and skills', in C. Raymond (ed.), (1998) *Coordinating*

Physical Education Across the Primary School, London: Falmer: 87.

Cooper, C., Cawley, M., Bhalla, A., Egger, P., Ring, F., Morton, L. and Baker, D. (1995) 'Childhood growth, physical activity and peak bone mass in women', *Journal of Bone and Mineral Research* 10 (6): 940–7.

Corbin, C., Pangrazi, R., and Welk, G. (1994) 'Towards an understanding of appropriate physical activity levels for youth', *Physical Activity and Fitness Research Digest*, Series 1, 8: 1–8, President's Council on Physical Fitness and Sports.

Council of Europe (1992) *European Sports Charter*, Strasbourg, France: Council of Europe.

Craig, S. B., Bandini, L. G., Lichtenstein, A. H., Schaefer, E. J. and Dietz, W. H. (1996) 'The impact of physical activity on lipids, lipoproteins and blood pressure in pre-adolescent girls', *Pediatrics* 98 (3): 389–95.

Dahrendorf, R. (1962) 'On the origin of social inequality', in P. Laslett and W. G. Runciman (eds), *Philosophy, Politics and Society, 2nd Series*, Oxford: Blackwell: 88–109.

Daiman, S. (1995) 'Women in sport in Islam', *Journal of the International Council for Health, Physical Education, Recreation, Sport and Dance* 32 (1): 18–21.

Daniels, H. (1996) 'Back to basics: three 'R's for special needs education', *British Journal of Special Education* 23 (4): 155–61.

Daunt, P. (1975) *Comprehensive Values*, London: Heinemann.

Dearing, R (1994) *The National Curriculum and its Assessment. Final Report (The Dearing Report)*, London: SCAA.

Deci, E. L. and Ryan, R. M. (1991) 'A motivational approach to self: integration in personality', in R. Dientsbier (ed.), *Nebraska Symposium on Motivation – Volume 38: Perspectives on Motivation*, Lincoln: University of Nebraska Press: 237–88.

De Knop, P., Theeboom, M., Wittock, H. and De Martelaer, K. (1996) 'Implications of Islam on Muslim girls' sports participation in Western Europe', *Sport, Education and Society* 1, 2: 147–64.

Department for Culture, Media and Sport (DCMS) (2000) *A Sporting Future for All*, London: DCMS.

Department for Education (DfE) (1993) *Handbook for the Inspection of Schools*, London: HMSO.

—— (1994a) *The Code of Practice on the Identification and Assessment of Special Educational Needs*, London: DfE.

—— (1994b) *Circular 6/94: The Organisation of Special Educational Provision*, London: DfE.

Department for Education and the Welsh Office (DfE/WO) (1995) *Physical Education in the National Curriculum*, London: HMSO.

Department for Education and Employment (DfEE) (1997) *Excellence for All Children: Meeting Special Educational Needs (Green Paper)*, London: Stationery Office.

—— (1998a) 'Blunkett strengthens curriculum focus on the basics', *DfEE News OO6/98* (13 January).

—— (1998b) *Meeting Special Educational Needs: A Programme of Action*, London: DfEE.

Department for Education and Employment and the Qualifications and Curriculum Authority (DfEE/QCA) (1999) *The National Curriculum for Physical Education*, London: HMSO.

Department of Education and Science (DES) (1978) *Special Educational Needs: Report of the Committee of Enquiry into the Education of Handicapped Children and Young People (The Warnock Report)*, London: HMSO.

—— (1985) *The Curriculum from 5 to 16: Curriculum Matters 2. An HMI Series*, London: HMSO.

—— (1989a) *Physical Education from 5 to 16, Curriculum Matters 16. An HMI Series*, London: HMSO.

—— (1989b) *National Curriculum: From Policy to Practice*, London, HMSO.

—— (1989c) *The Education Reform Act 1988: The School Curriculum and Assessment* (Circular 5/89), London: DES.

—— (1991) *Development Planning: A Practice Guide 2: Advice to Governors, Headteachers and Teachers*, London: DES.

Department of Education and Science and the Welsh Office (DES/WO) (1990) *National Curriculum Physical Education Working Group. Interim Report*, London: DES.

—— (1991) *National Curriculum Physical Education for Ages 5–16: Proposals of the Secretary of State for Education and Science and the Secretary of State for Wales*, London: HMSO.

—— (1992) *Physical Education in the National Curriculum*, London: HMSO.

Department of National Heritage (DNH) (1995) *Sport: Raising the Game*, London: DNH.

Dewar, A. (1990) 'Oppression and privilege in physical education: struggles in the negotiation of gender in a university programme', in D. Kirk and R. Tinning (eds), *Physical Education, Curriculum and Culture*, London: Falmer: 67–99.

Doolittle, S. (1995) 'Teaching net games to low skilled students: a teaching for understanding approach', *Journal of Physical Education, Recreation and Dance* 66 (7): 18–23.

Doolittle, S. and Girard, K. (1991) 'A dynamic approach to teaching games in elementary PE', *Journal of Physical Education, Recreation and Dance* 62 (4): 57–62.

Downey, M. and Kelly, A. V. (1986) *Theory and Practice of Education (3rd edn)*, London: Paul Chapman.

Duda, J. (1987) 'Towards a developmental theory of children's motivation in sport', *Journal of Sport and Exercise Psychology* 9: 130–45.

Duda, J. L. and Huston, L. (1995) 'The relationship of goal orientation and degree of competitive sport participation to the endorsement of aggressive acts in American football', in R. Vanfraechem-Raway and Y. Vanden Auweele (eds), *Proceedings of the 9th European Congress on Sport Psychology*, Brussels: Belgian Federation of Sport Psychology: 655–62.

Duda, J. L., Olson, L. K. and Templin, T. J. (1991) 'The relationship of task and ego orientation to sportsmanship attitudes and the perceived legitimacy of injurous acts', *Research Quarterly for Exercise and Sport* 62: 79–87.

Dudley Metropolitan Borough (1989) *Physical Education in the National Curriculum: A development of the BAALPE Framework*, Dudley Metropolitan Borough.

Durham LEA (1996) 'Plotting for progression the primary/secondary link', *Primary PE Focus: British Journal of Physical Education* (Spring): 4.

Eccles, J. S. and Harold, R. D. (1991) 'Gender differences in sport involvement: applying the Eccles' expectancy-value model', *Journal of Applied Sport Psychology* 3: 7–35.

Editorial (1997) *European Journal of Physical Education*, 2 (2): 157–58.

Education Act (1981), London: HMSO.

Education Act (1983), London: HMSO.

Education Act (1993), London: HMSO.

Education Reform Act (ERA) (1988) *Education Reform Act, 29 July 1988*, London: HMSO.

English Sports Council (1997) *England, the Sporting Nation: A Strategy*, London: English Sports Council.

Epstein, L. H., Smith, J. A., Vara, L. S. *et al.* (1991) 'Behavioral economic analysis of activity choice in obese children', *Health Psychology* 10, 5: 311–16.

Evans, J. (1985) *Teaching in Transition: The Challenge of Mixed-Ability Grouping*, Milton

Keynes: Open University Press.

—— (1988) 'Body matters: towards a socialist physical education', in H. Lauder and P. Brown (eds), *Education in Search of a Future*, London: Falmer: 174–91.

—— (1990) 'Ability, position and privilege in school physical education', in D. Kirk and R. Tinning (eds), *Physical Education, Curriculum and Culture*, London: Falmer: 139–67.

—— (ed) (1993) *Equality, Education and Physical Education*, London: Falmer.

Evans, J. and Clarke, G. (1988) 'Changing the face of physical education', in J. Evans (ed.), *Teachers, Teaching and Control in Physical Education*, London: Falmer: 125–43.

Evans, J. and Davies, B. (1988) 'Introduction: teachers, teaching and control', in J. Evans (ed.), *Teachers, Teaching and Control in Physical Education*, London: Falmer: 1–19.

—— (1992) 'Physical education post Education Reform Act, in a postmodern society', in J. Evans and B. Davies (eds), *Equality, Education and Physical Education*, Brighton: Falmer: 233–38.

—— (1993a) 'Introduction', in J. Evans (ed.), *Equality, Education and Physical Education*, London: Falmer: 1–9.

—— (1993b) 'Equality, equity and physical education', in J. Evans (ed.), *Equality, Education and Physical Education*, London: Falmer: 11–27.

Evans, J., Davies, B. and Penney, P. (1997) 'Making progress? Sport policy, women and innovation in physical education', *European Journal of Physical Education* 2 (1): 39–50.

Evans, J. and Penney, D. (1995) 'The politics of pedagogy: making a National Curriculum Physical Education', *Journal of Education Policy* 10 (1): 27–44.

—— (1996) 'The role of the teacher in physical education: towards a pedagogy of riches', *British Journal of Physical Education* 27 (1): 28–35.

Evans, J., Penney, D. and Davies, B. (1996) 'Back to the future: education policy and physical education', in N. Armstrong (ed.), *New Directions in Physical Education: Change and Innovation*, London: Cassell Educational: 1–18.

Evans, J. and Williams, T. (1989) 'Moving up and getting out: the classed and gendered career opportunities of physical education teachers', in T. Templin and P. Schempp (eds), *Socialization in Physical Education: Learning to Teach*, Indianapolis, In.: Benchmark: 235–51.

Fairclough, S. and Stratton, G. (1997) 'PE curriculum and extra curriculum time in schools in the NW of England', *British Journal of Physical Education* 28 (3): 21–4.

Farrar, F. W. (1889) 'In the Days of thy Youth', quoted in B. Simon and I. Bradley (eds), (1975) *The Victorian Public School*, Dublin: Gill and Macmillan: 148.

Faucette, N., McKenzie, T. and Patterson, N. (1990) 'Descriptive analysis of non-specialist elementary teacher's choice in class organisation', *Journal of Teaching in Physical Education* 9: 284–93.

Fielding, M. (1987) ''Liberté', egalité and fraternité – ou la mort. Towards a new programme for the comprehensive school', in C. Chitty (ed.), *Redefining the Comprehensive Experience*, Bedford Way Papers no. 32, London: University of London.

Figueroa, P. (1993) 'Equality, multiculturalism, antiracism and physical education in the National Curriculum', in J. Evans (ed.), *Equality, Education and Physical Education*, London: Falmer: 90–102.

Fisher, R. (1996) 'Gifted children and young people in physical education and sport', in N. Armstrong (ed.), *New Directions in Physical Education: Change and Innovation*, London: Cassell Education: 131–43.

Fisher, S. (1991) 'Inner game teaching for the PE teacher', *Bulletin of Physical Education* 27 (1): 20–3.

Flintoff, A. (1993) 'Gender, physical education and initial teacher education' in J. Evans (ed.), *Equality, Education and Physical Education*, London: Falmer: 184–204.

Folkins, C. and Amsterdam, E. (1977) 'Control and modification of stress emotions through chronic exercise', in E. Amsterdam, J. Wilmore and A. DeMaria (eds), *Exercise, Cardiovascular Health and Disease*, New York, Medical Books: 280–94.

Ford, J., Mongon, D. and Whelan, M. (1982) *Special Education and Social Control: Invisible Disasters*, London: Routledge and Kegan Paul.

Fox, G. (1998) *A Handbook for Learning Support Assistants: Teachers and Assistants Working Together*, London: David Fulton.

Fox, K. (1992a) 'Education for exercise and the National Curriculum proposals: a step forward or backwards?' *British Journal of Physical Education* 23 (1): 8–11.

—— (1992b) 'Physical education and the development of self-esteem in children', in. N. Armstrong (ed.), *New Directions in Physical Education, Volume 2: Towards a National Curriculum*, Leeds: Human Kinetics: 33–54.

—— (1996) 'Physical activity promotion and the active school', in N. Armstrong (ed.), *New Directions in Physical Education: Change and Innovation*, London: Cassell: 94–109.

French, K. E. and Thomas, J. R. (1987) 'The relation of knowledge development to children's basketball performance', *Journal of Sport Psychology* 9: 15–32.

French, K. E., Werner, P. H., Rink, J. E., Taylor, K. and Hussey, K. (1996) 'The effects of a 3-week unit of tactical, skill, or combined tactical and skill instruction on badminton performance of ninth-grade students', *Journal of Teaching in Physical Education* 15 (4): 418–38.

French, K. E., Werner, P. H., Taylor, K., Hussey, K. and Jones, J. (1996) 'The effects of a 6-week unit of tactical, skill, or combined tactical and skill instruction on badminton performance of ninth-grade students', *Journal of Teaching in Physical Education* 15 (4): 439–63.

Fullan, M. (1991) *The New Meaning of Educational Change*, London: Cassell.

—— (1992) *Successful School Improvement*, Buckingham: Open University Press.

—— (1993) *Change Forces: Probing the Depths of Educational Reform*, London: Falmer.

Galton, M. (1999) 'Primary/secondary transfer: left behind in secondary transit', *The Times Educational Supplement*, 3 September: 4.

Gilbert, R. (1998) 'Fellows' Lecture 1997 – Physical education – the key partner', *British Journal of Physical Education* 29 (1): 18–21.

Gill, D. (1993) 'Competitiveness and competition orientation in sport', in R. Singer, M. Murphy and L. Tennant (eds), *Handbook of Research on Sport Psychology*, New York: Macmillan.

Gilroy, S. and Clarke, G. (1997) 'Raising the game: deconstructing the sporting text: from Major to Blair', *Pedagogy in Practice* 3 (2): 19–37.

Goacher, B., Evans, J., Welton, J. and Wedell, K. (1988) *Policy and Provision for Special Educational Needs: Implementing the 1981 Education Act*, London: Cassell.

Graham, J. (1994) 'Funding and logistics in managing the "reform" of initial teacher training', unpublished paper, University of East London (February): 1–13.

Grehaigne, J-F. and Godbout, P. (1995) 'Tactical knowledge in team sports from a constructvist and cognitive perspective', *Quest* 47: 490–505.

Grimston, S. K., Willows, N. D. and Handley, D. A. (1993) 'Mechanical loading regime and its relationship to bone mineral density in children', *Medicine and Science in Sports and Exercise* 25 (11): 1203–10.

Gruber, J. J. (1986) 'Physical activity and self esteem development in children: a meta-analysis', in G. Stull and H. Eckert (eds), *Effects of Physical Activity on Children*,

Champaign, Ill.: Human Kinetics: 330–48.

Gutin, B, Basch, C., Shea, S., Contento, I., DeLorozier, M., Rips, J., Irogoyen, M. and Zybert, P. (1990) 'Blood pressure, fitness and fatness in 5 and 6 year old children', *Journal of the American Medical Association* 264: 1123–7.

Hall, S. (1992) 'Our mongrel selves', *New Statesman and Society* 19 June: 6–8.

Hardakre, N. (1998) 'Delivering vocational qualifications in sport through partnerships', *Bulletin of Physical Education* 34 (3): 171–76.

Hargreaves, D. (1984) *Improving Secondary Schools*, London: ILEA.

Hargreaves, J. (1986) *Sport, Power and Culture*, Oxford: Polity Press.

—— (1994) *Sporting Females*, London: Routledge.

Haring, N., Lovitt, C., Eaton, M. and Hansen, C. (1978) *The Fourth R: Research in the Classroom*, Columbus: Charles Merrill.

Harris, J. (1993) 'Challenging sexism and gender bias in Physical Education', *Bulletin of Physical Education* 29 (1) (Spring): 29–36.

—— (1995) 'Physical education: a picture of health?' *British Journal of Physical Education* 26 (4): 25–32.

—— (1997a) 'A health focus in physical education', in L. Almond (ed.), *Physical Education in Schools*, London: Kogan Page: 104–20.

—— (1997b) 'Good practice guidelines for HRE', *British Journal of Physical Education* 28 (4): 9–11.

—— (1998) 'Monitoring achievement in health-related exercise', *British Journal of Physical Education* 29 (2): 31–2.

Harris, J. and Cale, L. (1997) 'Activity promotion and physical education', *European Physical Education Review* 3 (1): 58–67.

Harrison, J. M., Blakemore, C. L., Richards, R. P., Oliver, J., Wilkinson, C. and Fellingham, G. W. (1998) 'The effects of two instructional models – tactical and skill teaching – on skill development, knowledge, self-efficacy, game play, and student perceptions in volleyball', *Research Quarterly for Exercise and Sport*, March 1998 Supplement, A93–A94.

Harrison, P. (1998) 'Editorial: why physical education teachers should reject the new proposals for primary education', *British Journal of Physical Education* 29 (1): 4–6.

Hastie, P. (1998) 'The participation and perceptions of girls within a unit of sport education', *Journal of Teaching in Physical Education* 17: 157–71.

Haw, K. (1998) *Educating Muslim Girls – Shifting Discourses*, Buckingham: Open University Press.

Head, J. (1996) 'Gender identity and cognitive style', in P. F. Murphy and C. V. Gipps (eds), *Equity in the Classroom*, London: Falmer/UNESCO Publishing: 59–69.

Health Education Authority (HEA) (1998a) *Young and Active: A Policy Framework for Young People and Health-Enhancing Physical Activity*, London: HEA.

—— (1998b) *New Recommendations for Promoting Health-enhancing Physical Activity with Young People (5–18 yrs)*, London: HEA.

Hellison, D. and Templin, T. (1991) *A Reflective Approach to Teaching Physical Education*, Champaign, Ill.: Human Kinetics.

Henderson, S. and Sugden, D. (1992) *Movement Assessment Battery for Children*, Sidcup: The Psychological Corporation.

Hepworth, N. (1999) 'Continuity and progression: Key Stages 2 and 3', *Bulletin of Physical Education* 35 (1): 23–35.

Her Majesty's Inspectorate (HMI) (1989) *Curriculum Continuity at 11-plus*, London: DES.

Higher Education Funding Council for England (HEFCE) (1993) *Circular 9/93 Special*

Initiatives to Encourage Widening Participation, Bristol: HEFCE Publications.

—— (1995) *Special Initiative to Encourage Widening Participation of Students from Ethnic Minorities in Teacher Training*, Bristol: HEFCE Publications.

Hill, C. (1984) 'An analysis of the physical education curriculum in a local education authority', unpublished M.Phil. thesis, Loughborough University.

Hoberman, J. (1984) *Sport and Political Ideology*, London: Heinemann.

Hodkinson, P. and Sparkes, A. (1993) 'Pre-vocationalism and empowerment: Some questions for PE', in J. Evans (ed.), *Equality, Education and Physical Education*, London: Falmer: 170–83.

Holland, J. (1995) 'An evaluation of a local health promoting school award scheme', unpublished M.A. dissertation, Canterbury Christ Church University College.

Hooper, M. (1998) 'Monitoring TOP Play and BT TOP Sport within Dudley LEA', *Bulletin of Physical Education* 34 (1): 49–55.

House, E. (1979) 'Technology versus craft: a ten year perspective on innovation', *Journal of Curriculum Studies* 11: 1–15.

Howarth, K. and Bull, C. R. (1982) 'The teaching of games', *Bulletin of Physical Education* 18 (3): 36–7.

Howarth, K. and Head, R. (1988) 'Curriculum continuity in physical education: a small scale study', *British Journal of Physical Education* 19 (6): 241–3.

Huberman, M. and Miles, M. (1984) *Innovation up Close*, New York: Plenum.

Humberstone, B. (1990) 'Warriors or wimps? Creating alternative forms of physical education', in M. Messner and D. Sabo (eds), *Sport, Men and the Gender Order*, Champaign, Ill.: Human Kinetics: 201–10.

Humphries, S. and Gordon, P. (1992) *Out of Sight: The Experience of Disability 1900–1950*, Plymouth: Northcote House.

Hunt, M. (1998) 'TOP Play BT TOP Sport: an effective influence on teaching?', *Bulletin of Physical Education* 34 (3): 194–206.

Hurt, J. (1988) *Outside the Mainstream: A History of Special Education*, London: Batsford.

Husband, C. (ed.) (1982) (1987) *'Race' in Britain: Continuity and Change*, London: Hutchinson.

Hutchinson, F. P. (1996) *Educating Beyond Violent Futures*, London: Routledge.

Inner London Education Authority (ILEA) (1988) *My Favourite Subject*, London: ILEA.

Jawad, H. (1998) *The Rights of Women in Islam: an Authentic Approach*, London: Macmillan.

Jenkins, R. (1997) *Rethinking Ethnicity Arguments and Explorations*, London: Sage.

Johnson, D. W. and Johnson, R. T. (1975) *Learning Together and Alone*, Englewood Cliffs, N.J.: Prentice Hall.

Johnstone, D. (1998) *An Introduction to Disability Studies*, London: David Fulton.

Jones, G. (1996) 'Major's problem' = physical education + 'Major's games', *Bulletin of Physical Education* 32 (2): 17–19.

Jordan (1958) 'Big school', unpublished work.

Kannel, W. and Dawber, T. (1972) 'Atherosclerosis as a paediatric problem', *Journal of Pediatrics* 80: 544–54.

Kay, W. (1998) 'A case for clarifying the physical education rationale', *Bulletin of Physical Education* 34 (3): 177–84.

Kenward, H. (1997) *Integrating Pupils with Physical Disabilities in Mainstream Schools*, London: David Fulton.

Kirk, D. (1988) *Physical Education and Curriculum Study: A Critical Introduction*, London: Croom Helm.

—— (1992) 'Physical education, discourse and ideology: bringing the hidden curriculum into view', *Quest* 44: 35–6.

Kirk, D. and Tinning, R. (1990) *Physical Education, Curriculum and Culture: Critical Issues in Contemporary Crisis*, London: Falmer.

Klint, K. and Weiss, M. (1987) 'Perceived competence and motives for participating in youth sports: a test of Hartner's Competence Motivation Theory', *Journal of Sports and Exercise Psychology* 9: 55–65.

Knight, E. and Chedzoy, S. (1997) *Physical Education in Primary Schools: Access for All*, London: David Fulton.

Labour Party (1996) *Labour's Sporting Nation*, London: Labour Party.

Lacey, P. and Lomas, J. (1993) *Support Services and the Curriculum: A Practical Guide to Collaboration*, London: David Fulton.

Laventure, B. (1992) 'School to community – progress and partnership', in N. Armstrong (ed.), *New Directions in Physical Education, Volume 2: Towards a National Curriculum*, Leeds: Human Kinetics: 169–97.

—— (1997) 'Physical activity and health – recent developments in public policy', *British Journal of Physical Education* 28 (2): 29.

—— (1998) 'Young and Active? The development of a policy framework for young people and physical activity', *British Journal of Physical Education* 29 (1): 31–2.

Lavin, J. (1989) 'Co-operative learning in the primary physical education context', *British Journal of Physical Education* 20 (4): 181–2.

Laws, C. (1990) 'Individualism and teaching games: a contradiction of terms?', *British Journal of Physical Education Research Supplement* no. 8 (Winter): 1–6.

Lawton, J. (1989) 'A comparison of two teaching methods in games', *Bulletin of Physical Education* 25 (1): 35–8.

Leaman, O. (1988) 'Competition, co-operation and control', in J. Evans (ed.), *Physical Education Teachers, Teaching and Control*, London: Falmer: 97–107.

Ledwidge, B. (1980) 'Run for your mind: aerobic exercise as a means of alleviating anxiety and depression', *Canadian Journal of Behavioural Science* 12: 126–39.

Lee, M. (1986) 'Moral and social growth through sport: the coach's role' in G. Gleeson (ed.), *The Growing Child in Competitive Sport*, London: Hodder and Stoughton: 248–55.

Lewis, A. (1992) 'From planning to practice', *British Journal of Special Education* 19 (1): 24–7.

Lewis, D. (1999) 'An assessment of the effectiveness of TOP Play and BT TOP Sport in County Durham with suggestions for the enhancement and development of the programme', unpublished B.A. (hons) dissertation, University of Durham.

Lindsay, G. and Thompson, D. (eds) (1997) *Values into Practice in Special Education*, London: David Fulton.

Loose, S. and Abrahams, M. (1993) 'Peer assessment: some thoughts and proposals', *British Journal of Physical Education* 24 (4): 8–13.

Macpherson Report (The) (1999) *The Stephen Lawrence Inquiry. Report of an Inquiry by Sir William Macpherson of Cluny*, London: Stationery Office.

Madood, T. (1992) 'British Asian Muslims and the Rushdie affair', in J. Donald and A. Rattansi (eds), *Race, Culture and Difference*, Buckingham: Oxford University Press.

Maguire, J. (1991) 'Sport, racism and British society: a sociological study of England's elite male Afro/Caribbean soccer and rugby union players', in G. Jarvie (ed.), *Sport, Racism and Ethnicity*, London: Falmer: 99–123.

Malina, R. M. (1996) 'Tracking of physical activity and physical fitness across the lifespan', *Research Quarterly for Exercise and Sport* 67 (3): Supplement S1–S10.

Martens, R. (ed.) (1978) *Joy and Sadness in Children's Sports*, Champaign, Ill.: Human Kinetics.

Mauldon, E. and Redfern, H. B. (1981) *Games Teaching: An Approach for the Primary School*, London: MacDonald and Evans.

Mawer, M. (1995) *The Effective Teaching of Physical Education*, London: Longmans.

McChonachie-Smith, J. (1991) 'Assessment of progression in National Curriculum Physical Education', *British Journal of Physical Education* 22 (2): 11–15.

—— (1993) 'Assessment in physical education: foundation or fringe', *British Journal of Physical Education* 24 (4): 5–7.

Mcguire, B. and Collins, D. (1998) 'Sport, ethnicity and racism: the experience of Asian heritage boys', *Sport, Education and Society* 3 (1): 79–88.

McIntosh, P. (1976) 'The curriculum of physical education – an historical perspective', in J. Kane (ed.), *Curriculum Development in Physical Education*, London: Crosby Lockwood Staples: 13–45.

McPherson, S.L. (1995) 'Expertise in women's collegiate tennis: development of knowledge and skill', paper presented at the annual conference of the North American Society for the Psychology of Sport and Physical Activity, Monterey, Calif. ,June.

McPherson, S. L. and French, K. E. (1991) 'Changes in cognitive strategies and motor skill in tennis', *Journal of Sport and Exercise Psychology* 13: 26–41.

McPherson, S. L. and Thomas, J. R. (1989) 'Relation of knowledge and performance in boys' tennis: age and expertise', *Journal of Experimental Child Psychology* 48: 190–211.

Merton, R. K. (1968) *Social Theory and Social Structure*, New York: Free Press.

Messner, M. and Sabo, D. (eds) (1990) *Sport, Men and the Gender Order*, Champaign, Ill.: Human Kinetics.

Mitchell, S. A. and Chandler, T. J. L. (1996) 'Motivation in middle school physical education: the role of perceived learning environment', *Pedagogy in Practice* 2 (2): 41–51.

Mitchell, S. A., Griffin, L. L. and Oslin, J. L. (1994) 'Tactical awareness as a developmentally appropriate focus for the teaching of games in elementary and secondary physical education', *The Physical Educator* 51 (1): 21–8.

—— (1997) 'Teaching invasion games: a comparison of two instructional approaches', *Pedagogy in Practice* 3 (2): 56–69.

Morgan, I. (1997) 'The preparation of physical education teachers during initial teacher training', *Bulletin of Physical Education* 33 (2): 29–33.

Morrell, J. D. (1871) 'Reports of Her Majesty's Inspectors' in J. May (1971) 'Curriculum development under the School Board for London', Physical Education M.Ed. thesis, University of Leicester.

Morris, J. (1989) *Able Lives: Women's Experience of Paralysis*, London: Women's Press.

Mosston, M. and Ashworth, S. (1994) *Teaching Physical Education (4th edn)*, Columbus, Oh.: Merrill.

Murdoch, E. (1990) 'Physical education and sport: the interface', in N. Armstrong (ed.), *New Directions in Physical Education, vol. 1*, Champaign, Ill.: Human Kinetics: 63–79.

—— (1996) 'The learning child: progression and development with particular reference to physical education', *Pedagogy In Practice* 2 (2): 21–40.

—— (1997) 'The background to, and developments from, the National Curriculum for PE', in S. Capel (ed.), *Learning to Teach Physical Education in the Secondary School: A Companion to School Experience*, London: Routledge: 252–70.

National Curriculum Council (NCC) (1989) *Curriculum Guidance One: A Framework for the Primary Curriculum*, York: NCC.

—— (1990) *Curriculum Guidance 3: The Whole Curriculum*, London: HMSO.

—— (1992) *Physical Education Non-statutory Guidance*, York: NCC.

National Primary Centre (1994) *Continuity and Progression: Critical Issues Affecting Teaching and Learning with a Particular Emphasis on the Transition Between Primary and Secondary Schools*, Oxford: National Primary Centre.

Needham, J. (1994) 'An approach to personal and social education in the primary school: or how one city schoolteacher tried to make sense of her job', in A. Pollard and J. Bourne (eds), *Teaching and Learning in the Primary School*, London: Routledge: 157–63.

Neurath, O. (1983) *Philosophical Papers 1913-1946*, ed. and trans. R. Cohen and M. Neurath: Dordrecht.

Newham Local Education Authority (1997) *Inclusive Education and Charter*, London: Newham LEA.

Nielsen, J. (1986) 'Islamic law and its significance for the situation of Muslim minorities in Europe', *Research Papers: Muslims in Europe 39*, Birmingham: Selly Oak Colleges, Centre for the Study of Islam and Christian–Muslim Relations.

Nietzsche, F. (1969) '*Thus Spoke Zarathustra*', trans. R. J. Hollingsworth, Harmondsworth: Penguin.

Noakes, T., Opie, L. and Rose, A. (1984) 'Marathon running and immunity to coronary heart disease: fact versus fiction', *Clinics in Sports Medicine* 3 (2): 527–43.

Noddings, N. (1992) *The Challenge to Care in Schools: An Alternative Approach to Education*, New York: Teachers College Press.

Norwich, B. (1994) 'Differentiation: from the perspective of resolving tensions between basic social values and assumptions about individual differences', *Curriculum Studies* 2 (3): 289–308.

—— (1996) 'Special needs education or education for all: connective specialisation or ideological impurity', *British Journal of Special Education* 23 (3): 100–4.

Office for Standards in Education (OFSTED) (1995a) *Physical Education. A Review of Inspection Findings 1993/94*, A Report from The Office of Her Majesty's Chief Inspector of Schools in England, London: HMSO.

—— (1995b) *Physical Education and Sport in Schools – A Survey of Good Practice*, London: HMSO.

—— (1998a) *Secondary Education 1993–97: A Review of Secondary Schools in England*, London: HMSO.

—— (1998b) *Inspecting Subjects 3–11: Guidance for Inspections*, London: OFSTED Publications Centre.

—— (1998c) *Standards in the Primary Curriculum 1996–97*, London: OFSTED Publications Centre.

—— (1998d) *Teaching Physical Education in Primary Schools: The Initial Training of Teachers*, A Report from The Office of Her Majesty's Chief Inspector of Schools in England, London: OFSTED Publications Centre.

—— (1999a) *Raising the Attainment of Minority Ethnic Pupils - School and LEA Responses*, London: OFSTED Publications Centre.

—— (1999b) *Initial Teacher Training Inspected: A Summary Report of Secondary Subject Inspections: Physical Education (1996–98)*, London: OFSTED Publications Centre.

Office of Her Majesty's Chief Inspector of Schools in Wales (OHMCI) (1995) *Report by HM Inspectors. Survey of Physical Education in Key Stages 1, 2 and 3*, Cardiff: OHMCI.

O'Hear, A. (1988) *Who Teaches the Teachers?*, London: Social Affairs Unit.

Oliver, M. (1996) *Understanding Disability: From Theory to Practice*, Basingstoke:

Macmillan.

Oliver, M. and Barnes, C. (1998) *Disabled People and Social Policy: From Exclusion to Inclusion*, London: Longman.

Open University (1986) *P679 Planning and Managing Change: Course Guide*, Milton Keynes: Open University.

Orlick, T. (1979) *The Co-operative Sports and Games Book: Challenge Without Competition*, London: Writers and Readers Publishing Co-operative.

Owen. R. C. (1999) 'The effectiveness of TOP Play and BT TOP Sport in the primary schools of County Durham', unpublished B.A. (hons) Dissertation, University of Durham.

Palmer, C. Redfern, R. and Smith, K. (1994) 'The four 'P's of policy', *British Journal of Special Education* 21 (1): 4–6.

Papaioannou, A. (1995) 'Motivation and goal perspectives in physical activity for children', in S. Biddle (ed.), *European Perspectives on Exercise and Sport Psychology*, Leeds: Human Kinetics: 245–69.

—— (1998) 'Students' perceptions of the physical education class environment for boys and girls and the perceived motivational climate', *Research Quarterly for Exercise and Sport* 69 (3): 267–75.

Parker-Jenkins, M. (1995) *Children of Islam*, Stoke-on-Trent: Trentham.

Parry, J. (1988) Physical education, justification and the National Curriculum', *Physical Education Review* 11 (2): 106–18.

Peach, S. J. and Thomas, S. M. (1998) 'Ego threat and the development of competitive trait anxiety in elite junior British tennis players', *European Journal of Physical Education* 3 (1): 51–64.

Penney, D. (1998) 'Positioning and defining physical education, sport and health in the curriculum, *European Physical Education Review* 4 (2): 117–26.

Penney, D. and Evans, J. (1994) 'It's just not (and not just) cricket', *British Journal of Physical Education* 25 (3): 9–12.

—— (1997) 'Naming the game: discourse and domination in physical education and sport in England and Wales', *European Physical Education Review* 3 (1): 21–32.

Penney, D. and Harris, J. (1998) 'The National Curriculum for physical education – have we got it right?' *British Journal of Physical Education* 29 (1): 7–10.

Physical Education Association of Great Britain and Northern Ireland (PEA) (The) (1987) 'National Curriculum 5–16: a response by the primary and secondary curriculum committees of the Physical Education Association', *British Journal of Physical Education* 18 (6): 242.

Physical Education Association of the United Kingdom (PEAUK) (1994) *Memorandum and Articles of the Physical Education Association*, Reading: PEAUK.

—— (1998) 'Mission Statement', *British Journal of Physical Education* 29 (2): 4–7.

Pickles, P. (1998) *Managing the Curriculum for Children with Severe Motor Difficulties*, London: David Fulton.

Pieron, M., Cloes, M., Delfosse, C. and Ledent, M. (1996) 'An investigation into the effects of daily physical education in kindergarten and elementary schools', *European Physical Education Review* 2: 116–32.

Piotrowski, S. M. (2000) 'Physical education and health promoting primary schools', in A. Williams (ed.), *Primary School Physical Education: Research into Practice*, London: RoutledgeFalmer: 51–66.

Piotrowski, S. M. and Capel, S. (1996) 'Recent influences on the training of physical education teachers in England and Wales', *Sport, Education and Society* 1 (2): 185–99.

Plato (1955) *The Republic*, trans. H. D. P. Lee, Harmondsworth: Penguin.

Pointer, B. (1993) *Movement Activities for Children with Learning Difficulties*, London: Jessica Kingsley.

Pollard, A. (1988) 'Physical education, competition and control in the primary school', in J. Evans (ed.), *Physical Education Teachers, Teaching and Control*, London: Falmer: 109–23.

Pollard, A. and Tann, S. (1993) *Reflective Teaching in the Primary School: A Handbook for the Classroom (2nd edn)*, London: Cassell.

Qualifications and Curriculum Authority (QCA) (1998) *Maintaining Breadth and Balance at Key Stages 1 and 2*, London: QCA.

—— (1999a) *The Review of the National Curriculum in England: The Consultation Materials*, London: QCA.

—— (1999b) *The Review of the National Curriculum in England: The Secretary of State's Proposals*, London: QCA.

—— (1999c) *Terminology in Physical Education*, London: QCA.

Rabinow, P. (ed.) (1984) *The Foucault Reader*, New York: Pantheon.

Race Relations Act (1976) London: HMSO.

Raymond, C. (1998) *Coordinating Physical Education Across the Primary School*, London: Falmer.

Read, B. (1995) 'National Curriculum: the teaching of games', *British Journal of Physical Education* 26 (3): 6–11.

Revell, P. (1999) 'Schools: less teamwork more fun', *Guardian* (18 May).

Rioux, M. (1996) 'Overcoming the social construction of inequality as a prerequisite to quality of life', in R. Renwick, I. Brown and M. Nagler (eds), *Quality of Life in Health Promotion and Rehabilitation*, London: Sage 119–31.

Robertson, C. (1998) 'Quality of life as a consideration in the development of inclusive education for pupils and students with learning difficulties', in C. Tilstone, L. Florian and R. Rose (eds), *Promoting Inclusive Practice*, London: Routledge: 264–75.

—— (1999a) 'Initial teacher education for inclusive schooling', *Support for Learning* 14 (4): 169–73.

—— (1999b) 'Early intervention: the education of young children with developmental co-ordination disorder', in T. David (ed.), *Young Children's Learning*, London: Paul Chapman: 67–89.

Robinson, S. (1996) *Planning the Physical Education Curriculum: Assessment*, Stowmarket: Aspects.

Rogers, R. (ed.) (1994) *How to Write a School Development Plan*, Oxford: Heinemann.

Ross, J. G. and Gilbert, G. G. (1985) 'The National Children and Youth Fitness Study: a summary of findings', *Journal of Physical Education, Recreation and Dance* 56: 45–50.

Rowe, G. and Whitty, G. (1993) 'Five themes remain in the shadows', *Times Educational Supplement* (9 April): 8.

Rowntree, D. (1977) *Assessing Students: How Shall We Know Them?*, London: Harper and Row.

Ruddock, J., Galton, M. and Gray, J. (1998) 'Lost in the maze of the new', *Times Educational Supplement* (20 November): 19.

Runnymede Trust (1997) *Islamophobia – A Challenge for all of us: Report of the Runnymede Trust Commission on British Muslims and Islamophobia (chaired by Professor G. Conway)*, London: Runnymede Trust.

Sahgal, G. and Yuval-Davis, N. (eds) (1992) *Refusing Holy Orders*, London: Virago.

Saifullah Khan, V. (1987) 'The role of the culture of dominance in structuring the experience of ethnic minorities', in C. Husband (ed.), *'Race' in Britain – Continuity and Change*, London: Hutchinson: 213–31.

Salisbury, J. and Jackson, D. (1996) *Challenging Macho Values – Practical Ways of Working with Adolescent Boys*, London: Falmer.

Sallis, J. F. and Patrick, K. (1994a) 'Physical activity guidelines for adolescents: consensus statement', *British Journal of Physical Education Research Supplement* 15: 2–7.

—— (1994b) 'Physical activity guidelines for adolescents: consensus statement' *Pediatric Exercise Science* 6: 302–14.

Sarwar, G. (1994) *British Muslims and Schools*, London: Muslim Education Trust.

Satterly, D. (1981) *Assessment in Schools*, Oxford: Blackwell.

School Curriculum and Assessment Authority (SCAA) (1996a) *Consistency in Teacher Assessment: Exemplification of Standards*, Hayes: SCAA.

—— (1996b) *Promoting Continuity Between Key Stage 2 and Key Stage 3*, Hayes: SCAA.

—— (1997a) *Physical Education at Key Stages 3 and 4. Assessment Recording and Reporting: Guidance for Teachers*, London: SCAA.

—— (1997b) *Physical Education and the Health of the Nation*, London: SCAA.

School Sport Forum (1988) *Sport and Young People: Partnership in Action*, London: Sports Council.

Scraton, S. (1993) 'Equality, coeducation and physical education in secondary schooling' in J. Evans (ed.), *Equality, Education and Physical Education*, London: Falmer: 139–53.

Seals, D. and Hagberg, J. (1984) 'The effects of exercise training on human hypertension: a review', *Medical Science and Sports Exercise* 13: 316–21.

Sebba, J. with Sachdev, D. (1997) *What Works in Inclusive Education?* Ilford: Barnardos.

Semple, M. (1993) 'Physical education and dance', in A. King and M. Reis (eds), *The Multicultural Dimensions of the National Curriculum*, London: Falmer: 160–72.

Sevak, L., Mckeigue, P. and Marmot, M. (1994) 'Relationship of hyperinsulinemia to dietary intake in South Asian and European men', *American Journal of Clinical Nutrition* 59: 1065–74.

Sex Discrimination Act (1975) London: HMSO.

Sfeir, L. (1985) 'The status of Muslim women in sport: conflict between cultural traditions and modernisation', *International Review for Sociology of Sport*, 20, 4: 283–304.

Shearsmith, K. (1993) 'An alternative ideology to underpin PE practice', *British Journal of Physical Education* 24 1: 37–41.

Shepherd, R. J., Jequier, J-C., Lavallee, H., La Barre, R. and Rajic, M. (1980) 'Habitual physical activity: effects of sex, milieu, season and required physical activity at school', *Journal of Sports Medicine* 20: 55–66.

Sherborne, V. (1990) *Developmental Movement for Children: Mainstream, Special Needs and Pre-School*, Cambridge: Cambridge University Press.

Sherif, C. (1973) 'Intergroup conflict and competition', in O. Grupe (ed.), *Sport in the modern world - chances and problems*, Berlin: Springer.

—— (1978) 'The social context of competition', in R. Martens (ed.), *Joy and Sadness in Children's Sports*, Champaign, Ill.: Human Kinetics.

Sherrill, C. (1998) *Adapted Physical Activity, Recreation and Sport: Cross Disciplinary and Lifespan (5th edn)*, Madison, Wis.: Brown and Benchmark.

Siedentop, D. (1994) *Sport Education: Quality Physical Education Through Positive Sport Experiences*, Champaign, Ill.: Human Kinetics.

Siedentop, D., Mand, C. and Taggart, A. (1986) *Physical Education: Curriculum and Instruction Methods for Grades 5–12*, Palo Alto, Calif.: Mayfield.

Simon, B. and Bradley, I. (eds) (1975) *The Victorian Public School*, Dublin: Gill and

Macmillan: 148.

Simons-Morton, B. G., Parcel, G. S. and O'Hara, N. M. (1988) 'Implementing organisa-tional changes to promote healthful diet and physical activity at school', *Health Education Quarterly* 15 (1): 115–30.

Siraj-Blatchford, I. (1993) 'Ethnicity and conflict in physical education – a critique of Carroll and Hollinsheads' case study', *British Educational Research Review* 19 (1): 77–82.

Sleap, M. (1990) 'Promoting health in primary school physical education', in N. Armstrong (ed.), *New Directions in Physical Education. vol. 1*, Champaign, Ill.: Human Kinetics: 17–36.

Sleap, M. and Warburton, P. (1994) 'Physical activity levels of pre-adolescent children in England', *British Journal of Physical Education Research Supplement* 14: 2–6.

Slemenda, C. W., Reister, T. K., Hui, S. L., Miller, J. Z., Christian, J. C. and Johnson, C. C. (1994) 'Influences on the skeletal mineralization in children and adolescents: evidence for varying effects of sexual maturation and physical activity', *Journal of Pediatrics* 125: 201–7.

Smith, C. (1999) 'What role can the arts and sport make in overcoming social exclusion? – a government overview', presentation at a 'QMW Public Policy Seminar' at the University of London, 1 February.

Smith, M. D. (1991) 'Utilizing the games for understanding model at the elementary level', *The Physical Educator* 48 (3): 184–7.

Spackman, L. (1995) 'Assessment in physical education', *British Journal of Physical Education* 26 (3): 32–4.

—— (1998) 'Assessment and recording in physical education', *British Journal of Physical Education* 29 (4): 6–9.

Sparkes, A. (1986) 'Strangers and structures in the process of innovation', in J. Evans (ed.), *Physical Education, Sport and Schooling: Studies in the Sociology of Physical Education*, London: Falmer: 183–93.

—— (1989) 'Health related fitness: an example of innovation without change', *British Journal of Physical Education* 20 (2): 60–3.

—— (1991a) 'Curriculum change: on gaining a sense of perspective', in N. Armstrong and A. Sparkes (eds), *Issues in Physical Education*, London: Cassell: 1–19.

—— (1991b) 'Exploring the subjective dimension of curriculum change', in N. Armstrong and A. Sparkes (eds), *Issues in Physical Education*, London: Cassell: 20–35.

Special Educational Needs Training Consortium (1996) *Professional Development to Meet Special Educational Needs: Report to the Department for Education*, SENTC, Flash Ley Resource Centre, Stafford: Staffordshire County Council.

Spencer, K. (1998) 'Sportsmark: a personal view', *Bulletin of Physical Education* 34 (3): 222–5.

Sport England (1999) *Sport England Factsheet*, London: Sport England.

Sports Council (1995a) *Young People and Sport: National Survey Selected Findings*, London: Sports Council.

—— (1995b) *Young People and Sport in England 1994*, London: Sports Council.

Sports Council for Northern Ireland (1996) *Women in Sport Policy Framework*, Belfast: Sports Council Northern Ireland.

Sports Council for Wales (1995) *Changing the Rules: Women, Girls and Sport*, Cardiff: Sports Council for Wales.

Stein, J. U. (1988) 'Competition – a developmental process', *Journal of Physical Education, Recreation and Dance* 59 (March): 30–2.

Steptoe, A. and Butler, N. (1996) 'Sports participation and emotional well-being in adolescents', *The Lancet* 347: 1789–92.

Stewart, D. (1990) *The Right to Movement: Motor Development in Every School*, Basingstoke: Falmer.

Stoddart, P. (1985) 'Teaching games for understanding – the practicalities of developing new courses in schools', *Bulletin of Physical Education* 21 (2): 29–34.

Stoker, A. (1991) *Liaison and Transition at Key Stages 2/3: A Resource Pack for Teachers in Primary and Secondary Schools*, Lancaster: Framework.

Sugden, D. (1991) 'PE: movement in the right direction', *British Journal of Special Education* 18 (4): 134–6.

Sugden, D. and Henderson, S. (1994) 'Help with movement', *Special Children* 75 (13): 57–61.

Sugden, D. and Talbot, M. (1996) *Physical Education for Children with Special Needs in Mainstream Education*, Leeds: Carnegie National Sports Development Centre.

Sugden, D. and Wright, H. (1996) 'Curricular entitlement and implementation for all children', in N. Armstrong (ed.), *New Directions in Physical Education: Change and Innovation*, London: Cassell: 110–30.

Sumner, G. (1989) 'Physical education in the new era – a primary perspective', *Physical Education in the New Era*, BAALPE Annual Congress Report (1989), Chester: Bemrose.

Sunday Times (1999) 'Having disabled babies will be "sin", says scientist', report by Lois Rogers, London: *Sunday Times* (4 July) (Internet version).

Swain, J. Finkelstein, V., French, S. and Oliver, M. (1993) *Disabling Barriers – Enabling Environments*, London: Sage.

Swan Report (1985) *Education for All*, London: HMSO.

Talbot, M. (1986) 'Gender and PE', *British Journal of Physical Education* 17: 120–2.

—— (1987) 'Physical education and school sport into the 1990s', Physical Education Association Fellows Lecture.

—— (1990) 'Equal opportunities and physical education' in N. Armstrong (ed.), *New Directions in Physical Education*, Champaign, Ill.: Human Kinetics: 101–21.

—— (1995) 'The politics of sport and physical education', in R. Fleming, M. Talbot and A. Tomlinson (eds), *Policy and Politics in Sport, Physical Education and Leisure*, Brighton: Leisure Studies Association: 3–26.

—— (1998) 'Physical education: contested positions, competing discourses – the need for renaissance?', *European Physical Education Review* 4 (2): 104–16.

Tannehill, D., Romar, J., O'Sullivan, M., England, K. and Rosenberg, D. (1994) 'Attitudes toward physical education: their impact on how physical education teachers make sense of their work', in M. O'Sullivan (ed.), 'High school physical education teachers: their world of work' (monograph), *Journal of Teaching in Physical Education* 13: 323–441.

Teacher Training Agency (TTA) (1998) *National Standards for Subject Leaders*, London: TTA.

Thirlaway, K. and Benton, D. (1993) 'Physical activity in primary-and-secondary school children in West Glamorgan', *Health Education Journal* 52: 37–41.

Thomas, G., Walker, D. and Webb, J. (1998) *The Making of the Inclusive School*, London: Routledge.

Thomas, S. (1993) 'Education reform: juggling the concepts of equality and elitism', in J. Evans (ed.), *Equality, Education and Physical Education*, London: Falmer: 105–24.

Thompson, D. (1995) *The Concise Oxford Dictionary of Current English*. Oxford: Clarendon Press.

Thorpe, R. (1986) 'A demonstration of a different focus', in R. Thorpe, D. Bunker and L. Almond (eds), *Rethinking Games Teaching*, Loughborough, Leics.: Loughborough University: 17–24.

—— (1990) 'New directions in games teaching', in N. Armstrong (ed.), *New Directions in Physical Education: Volume 1*, Leeds: Human Kinetics: 79–100.

Thorpe, R. and Bunker, D. (1986) 'Landmarks on our way to "teaching for understanding"', in R. Thorpe, D. Bunker and L. Almond (eds), *Rethinking Games Teaching*, Loughborough, Leics.: Loughborough University: 5–6.

—— (1997) 'A changing focus in games teaching', in L. Almond (ed.), *Physical Education in Schools*, London: Kogan Page: 52–80.

Thorpe, R., Bunker, D. and Almond, L. (1984) 'A change in the focus for the teaching of games', paper presented at the Olympic Scientific Congress, Eugene, Or., July.

—— (1986a) *Rethinking Games Teaching*, Loughborough, Leics.: Loughborough University.

—— (1986b) 'A change of focus for the teaching of games', in M. Pieron and G. Graham (eds), *Sport Pedagogy (Proceedings of the 1984 Olympic Scientific Congress: vol. 6)*, Champaign, Ill.: Human Kinetics: 163–9.

Times Educational Supplement 11 July 1986.

—— 3 July 1998.

Tinning, R. (1995) 'The sport education movement: a phoenix, bandwagon or hearse for physical education?', *ACHPER Healthy Lifestyles Journal* 42 (4): 19–20.

Tomlinson, S. (1982) *A Sociology of Special Education*, London: Routledge and Kegan Paul.

Tozer, M. (1970) 'Opinions on the possible introduction of an advanced level course and examination in physical education', *Bulletin of Physical Education* 8 (3): 35–7.

Treadwell, P. (1987) 'Giftedness and sport in school – a comparative perspective', *British Journal of Physical Education* 18 (2): 63–5.

Troyna, B. and Carrington, B. (1987) 'Anti-sexist/anti-racist education: a false dilemma: Reply to Walkling and Brannigan', *Journal of Moral Education* 16 (1): 60–5.

Turner, A. P. and Martinek, T. J. (1992) 'A comparative analysis of two models for teaching games (technique approach and game-centered (tactical focus) approach)', *International Journal of Physical Education* 29 (4): 15–31.

—— (1995) 'Teaching for understanding: a model for improving decision making during game play', *Quest* 47: 44–63.

United Nations (1989) *The United Nations Convention on the Rights of the Child*, New York/Geneva: United Nations.

—— (1993) *The United Nations Standard Rules on the Equalization of Opportunities for People with Disabilities*, New York/Geneva: United Nations.

United Nations Educational, Scientific and Cultural Organisation (UNESCO) (1994) *The Salamanca Statement and Framework for Action*, Paris: UNESCO.

United Nations Universal Declaration of Human Rights (1948) in O. Harris (1983) *Latin American Women*, London: Minority Rights Group: 2.

Valimaki, M. J., Karkkainen, M., Lamberg-Allardt, C., Laitinen, K., Alharva, E., Heikkinen, J., Impivaara, O., Palmgren, J., Seppanen, R. and Vuori, I. (1994) 'Exercise, smoking and calcium intake during adolescence and early adulthood as determinants of peak bone mass', *British Medical Journal* 309: 203–5.

Vallerand, R. J. and Losier, G. F. (1994) 'Self-determined motivation and sportsmanship orientations: an assessment of their temporal relationship', *Journal of Sport and Exercise Psychology* 16: 229–45.

VandenBergh, M. F., DeMan, S. A., Witteman, J. C., Hofman, A., Trouerbach, W. T. and

Grobbee, D. E. (1995) 'Physical activity, calcium intake and bone mineral content in children in the Netherlands', *Journal of Epidemiology and Community Health* 49 (3): 299–304.

Vickerman, P. (1997) 'Knowing your pupils and planning for different needs', in S. Capel (ed.), *Learning to Teach Physical Education in the Secondary School: A Companion to School Experience*, London: Routledge: 139–57.

Walkling, P. and Brannigan, C. (1986) 'Anti-sexist/anti-racist education: a possible dilemma', *Journal of Moral Education* 15 (1): 16–25.

—— (1987) 'Muslim schools – Troyna and Carrington's dilemma', *Journal of Moral Education* 16 (1): 66–8.

Warburton, P. (1999) 'Our sporting nation – have we got the agenda right for our young people?', *British Journal of Physical Education* 30 (1): 18–24.

Warburton, P. and Woods, J. (1996) 'Observation of children's physical activity levels during primary school physical education lessons', *European Review of Physical Education* 1: 56–65.

Waring, M. and Almond, L. (1995) 'Games-centred teaching – a revolutionary or evolutionary alternative for games teaching', *European Physical Education Review* 1 (1): 55–66.

Watson, G. G. (1984) 'Competition and intrinsic motivation in children's sport and games: a conceptual analysis', *International Journal of Sport Psychology* 15: 205–18.

Wedell, K. (1995) 'Making inclusive education ordinary', *British Journal of Special Education* 22 (3): 100–4.

Weinberg, R. S. and Gould, D. (1995) *Foundations of Sport and Exercise Psychology*, Champaign, Ill.: Human Kinetics.

Welton, D. C., Kemper, H. C. G., Post, G. B., van Mechelen, W., Twisk, J., Lips, P. and Teule, G. J. (1994) 'Weight-bearing activity during youth is a more important factor for peak bone mass than calcium uptake', *Journal of Bone and Mineral Research* 9: 1089–96.

Werner, P. and Almond, L. (1990) 'Models of games education', *Journal of Physical Education, Recreation and Dance* 61 (4): 23–7.

White, A. and Coakley, J. (1986) *Making Decisions: A Report*, London: Greater London/SE Region Sports Council, West Sussex Institute of Higher Education.

Whitehead, M. (1988) 'Dualism, monism and health related exercise in physical education', *Health and Physical Education Project Newsletter no. 19*, November.

—— (1990) 'Meaningful existence, embodiment and physical education', *Journal of Philosophy of Education* 24 (1): 3–13.

—— (1997) 'Teaching styles and teaching strategies', in S. Capel (ed.), *Learning to Teach Physical Education in the Secondary School: A Companion to School Experience*, London: Routledge: 130–8.

Whitson, D. and Macintosh, D. (1990) 'The scientization of physical education: discourses of performance', *Quest* 42 (1): 40–51.

Williams, A. (ed.) (1989a) *Issues in Physical Education for the Primary Years*, London: Falmer.

—— (1989b) 'Girls and boys come out to play (but mainly boys) – gender and physical education', in A. Williams (ed.), *Issues in Physical Education for the Primary Years*, London: Falmer: 145–59.

—— (1989c) 'Physical education in a multicultural context', in A. Williams (ed.), *Issues in Physical Education for the Primary Years*, London: Falmer: 160–72.

—— (1996a) 'Physical education at Key Stage 2', in N. Armstrong (ed.), *New Directions in Physical Education: Change and Innovation*, London: Cassell: 62–72.

—— (1996b) 'Problematising physical education practice: pupil experience as a focus for reflection', *European Journal of Physical Education* 1 (1): 19–35.

—— (1997) 'Continuity and staff development: Key Stage 2 – Key Stage 3: a Mid-Wales approach', *Bulletin of Physical Education* 33 (2): 39–43.

Williams, B. (1962) 'The idea of equality' in P. Laslett and W. G. Runciman (eds), *Philosophy, Politics and Society (2nd Series)*, Oxford: Blackwell: 110–31.

—— (1981) *Moral Luck*, Cambridge: Cambridge University Press.

Winders, P. (1997) *Gross Motor Skills in Children with Down's Syndrome: A Guide for Parents and Professionals*, Bethesda, Md.: Woodbine House.

Wood, D. (1986) 'Aspects of teaching and learning' in M. Richards and P. Light (eds), *Children of Social Worlds*, Cambridge: Polity.

Woodhouse, J. (1998) 'The physical education curriculum: a suggested framework to meet the reality', *Bulletin of Physical Education* 34 (3): 185–93.

World Health Organisation (WHO) (1980) *International Classification of Impairments, Disabilities and Handicaps*, Geneva: WHO.

—— (1985) *Targets for Health for All 2000*, Copenhagen: WHO Regional Office for Europe.

—— (1996) *Ottawa Charter for Health Promotion*, Copenhagen: WHO Regional Office for Europe.

Wright, C. (1992) 'Early education – multi-racial primary school classrooms', in D. Gill, B. Major and M. Blair (eds), *Racism and Education – Structure and Strategies*, London: Sage: 5–41.

Wright, H. and Sugden, D. (1999) *Physical Education for All: Developing Physical Education in the Curriculum for Pupils with Special Educational Needs*, London: David Fulton.

Index

Lightning Source UK Ltd.
Milton Keynes UK
10 February 2011

167296UK00002B/32/A